Magick Without Peers

Ariadne Rainbird & David Rankine

Magick Without Peers

Cover design by Paul Mason

Published by:

Capall Bann Publishing
Freshfields
Chieveley
Berks
RG20 8TF

Dedication

To She Who is all that is and was and ever shall be, and
to He Who is all and nothing in the arms of His love.
May Their sacred flame be enkindled in the hearts
of those who set foot on the Path.

List of Illustrations

Figure

Contents

Introduction

Witchcraft, in one form or another, has existed since the beginning of humanity and across cultures. The word itself comes from the Anglo Saxon Wicca, Wicce (a witch) or Wicce-craeft, meaning something like the art of bending, changing things to one's will, spell-casting, working with natural forces. It may also be related to the Anglo Saxon word Witan, to know, connected with Wotan, and from which we get words like Wisdom, Wit and Wizard. Anthropologists use the word Witchcraft to describe certain shamanic and "black magick" practices common to many tribal societies. Although harmful magick can be practised, we do not cover its use in this book, nor do we recommend it.

Witchcraft is about tuning in to the forces of nature, which includes the law of cause and effect. What we give out we get back, often multiplied - Modern Wicca teaches of the law of threefold return. We do see Witchcraft as containing elements of Shamanism, and we make use of Shamanic techniques such as dance, breathing techniques and the use of sacred herbs to explore other states of consciousness and tune in to the forces of nature. We see Witchcraft as being composed of three main elements - Magick, Mysticism and Religion, each of which has equal importance. Mysticism is about direct experience of the Divine, feelings of oneness with nature and with the universe, the feeling of wonder and awe which we may experience when we perceive a natural wonder such as a beautiful sunset, a vast mountain range, or the night sky, or when we hear the song of a wild bird.

Meditation and trance techniques may open us up to more mystical experience and give us a greater appreciation of life and the natural world, giving us a greater sense of well-being and insight. When we feel a sense of wonder at nature, we may wish to actively celebrate it, and this is where the religious side of Witchcraft comes in. Witchcraft involves natural religion, and the seasonal rituals and myths are based on the cycles of nature and natural forces. Exactly what form you choose to celebrate the seasonal festivals or Sabbats in will depend partly on what part of the

1

world you live in, and partly on your own personal preferences. Part two of this book contains a solitary ritual for each of the eight Sabbats celebrated by most modern western (Northern Hemisphere) pagans. Feel free to adapt these as you need to.

Magick has been defined as "the art and science of causing change in accordance with will" (Aleister Crowley). It is about taking positive control of one's own life, and includes personal development and psychology. Magick is sometimes divided into "high magick", which is about self transformation, and "practical magick" (also sometimes termed "low magick", but we do not consider it so), which involves spell-casting, and may include healing, protection, spells for gaining things you want or need, love magick, etc. We include both types of magick in this book, and believe that they should go together. Concentrating entirely on practical or results magick can make one greedy, power hungry, and lacking in spiritual insight and direction. Concentrating entirely on high magick on the other hand can make one aloof, self-centred and detached from reality. Part one of this book is a course in Magickal and Mystical techniques. Part two is more about the religious elements of Witchcraft.

This is not a book on Wicca, in the Alexandrian and Gardnerian Craft sense, but about Progressive Witchcraft, which we see as more eclectic and universal. Thus you will find in the pages of this book, techniques and teachings from many different countries and cultures - Hindu, Voodoo, Celtic, Egyptian, Saxon, Greek, to name but a few. It is written primarily for the solitary practitioner, although pagan groups may also find it helpful. We should stress though, that it is not intended as a training manual for a self-initiated coven. Coven work is quite different to solitary work, and can only be learned by experience.

Group magickal techniques are learned through doing them in a coven, led by an experienced High Priestess and High Priest. However this book will give you a good grounding in personal magickal work should you ever wish to join a coven. Many covens do not give much training for individual work, and this book will fill that gap. We do include some helpful points for starting your own group in part two, but please note this is for starting a Pagan group as opposed to a coven. We see witchcraft as an initiatory tradition, and whereas self-initiation is valid for solitary practitioners, those who wish to initiate others should have received initiation themselves first,

2

from a properly initiated group or individual. Anyone who wants to find out more about Progressive covens and coven initiation, should contact us via the publishers address, but please note, that working through this book will not guarantee that you will be accepted by a coven.

Most of the material in this book derives from the Fellowship Of Isis and Progressive Witchcraft courses we run. The Fellowship Of Isis is a worldwide Goddess-centred organisation with its headquarters at Clonegal Castle in Ireland. We run a Lyceum (teaching centre) in the Fellowship Of Isis. The Progressive Witchcraft Foundation is our own organisation for disseminating training and information on progressive witchcraft. As has already been stated the material is eclectic in nature, our aim being to provide a solid foundation of magickal techniques which can be incorporated into existing experience and knowledge of technique and that will enable the practitioner to pursue their magickal growth and self-integration well equipped with the necessary magickal vocabulary.

Part one should be worked through chapter by chapter, but part two may be dipped into at any time, as and when appropriate. The Sabbat rituals, obviously are best performed on the actual dates of the Sabbats. Lunar rituals, or esbats can be performed at any time (although obviously it is best at night), and the tides of the moon are discussed. It is best to work through the first six chapters of part one, and do a few Sabbat rituals, before working esbats if you are new to Paganism and Magick, as the esbats require experience and practice of meditation. This book provides a complete course in Progressive Witchcraft for the solitary practitioner, starting with the basics, and working up to enable you to perform effective rituals, attune yourself to nature, gain greater self understanding, and be more in control of your life.

Part One

Mysticism
and
Magick

Chapter One

Preliminaries

The Working Environment

The space where you do any magickal work should be a quiet, comfortable place where you can remain undisturbed for the work`s duration. The ideal is a permanent consecrated Temple space, but for most people this is not possible. By default, the space is usually a bedroom or living room. If this is the case and a room is in general use, an atmosphere can be generated by having sacred items such as statues, candlesticks, pictures, etc, which are set up whenever the room is being used for magickal practise.

Making the space sacred in this manner is probably the next best thing to having a permanent space, and allows for discretion in your activities. You may wish to purify the space before use, common methods are by offering incense (or joss) at the four cardinal points and above and below, or by sprinkling salt water at the same points around the room (the latter has the advantage of not producing noticeable smells which may raise questions).

We do not wish to sound apologist here, but it is a fact that many people live in shared accommodation, and may have to cope with hostile people, so discretion may sometimes be called for, though having sympathetic people around you is obviously preferable. A natural outdoor environment is of course also good, if you are lucky enough to have such a place available, which is quiet and free from disturbance, although you will probably want to work indoors some of the time, depending on the weather. It is good to find a friendly tree to sit by and meditate with.

Body Posture

Posture is strongly connected to relaxation, so you should experiment and find a posture in which you feel comfortable and relaxed, and which you will be able to maintain for the duration of the exercises without distraction. The most common positions used are the Lotus position (for those who do yoga), sitting cross-legged, lying down, kneeling, with your buttocks resting on your legs, or for those who can manage, kneeling with buttocks between legs, resting on the floor (variations of Vajrasana, the pose of the thunderbolt in yoga), and sitting in a chair with an upright back.

Lying down can result in falling asleep, so if you prefer this position, you may find it easier to not use a pillow so your body is straight along the floor/bed. Sitting in an upright chair with your forearms and hands resting lightly along the upper legs is an easy and comfortable position to maintain (this is known as The Hero position). Sitting with the legs underneath you is a very comfortable position, and allows for the placing of a cushion under your buttocks for added comfort. Sitting cross-legged or in the Lotus position are probably the most common positions, and they have the added benefit of giving the feeling of being more in contact with the Earth beneath us. You will find it more comfortable, and that you can maintain a still position longer if you sit on a cushion when you sit cross-legged, so that your buttocks are higher up than your knees, and your knees and lower legs touch the floor.

For all meditation postures it is important that your back is straight, and that you do not slouch, or tense your shoulders. Hands can be rested gently on the knees, or held in a mudra (a Sanskrit term which can be translated loosely as *gesture*). A common Mudra is to touch the forefinger of each hand with the thumb of the same hand (as in the O.K. gesture), and to rest the backs of the hands on the knees. This symbolizes the ego (represented by the forefingers) under the control of the Higher Self or Spirit (symbolized by the thumb).

Clothing and Equipment

You will need loose comfortable clothing for meditation and ritual, or temperature and privacy permitting it is good to work skyclad (naked). When you remove your clothing you are symbolically casting off your social self or persona, and the stresses of the day, and it is part of the process of preparing yourself for the work in hand. It is a good idea to have a loose fitting robe kept specially for your meditation and magickal work. Natural fibres are best, and a cotton kaftan will suffice, or you may wish to make a special robe. Putting this on helps you psychologically to make the transition from ordinary consciousness to the state of mind required for magickal work. You may also have some special items of jewellery which you wear for ritual, but jewellery might be a hindrance for meditation, and simplicity is better. Bathing is also recommended before important magickal work.

You will also require some candles and candleholders, small dishes for salt and water, a chalice or goblet. You will also want to burn incense, and whereas joss sticks are adequate at first, as you progress through the course you will want to experiment with the effects of different herbs, oils and resins, and to blend your own incenses and oils. You will then need a censer and/or an oil burner.

For burning incense in a censer, you will need charcoal blocks, which are available from new age and occult suppliers, but are usually cheaper from church supply shops. A platter will also be useful, for placing ritual food and offerings on, and a cloth, preferably of natural fibre such as cotton or silk, to be used as an altar cloth. It can also be used to wrap your other objects in when not in use. As you progress through the course, you will probably want to obtain, or make, other magickal tools - a magickal knife will be particularly useful, but to begin with the above should suffice.

Relaxation

You need to be relaxed to perform daily exercises and gain the full benefits, so here are a couple of simple practises which can aid relaxation. The exercises are worth doing even if you think you are relaxed, as we tend to hold a lot of tension in our bodies without even realizing it.

A] Starting with your toes, tense the muscles and then relax them.

Proceed to the other areas of the feet, tensing and relaxing, and work up the body repeating this process of tensing and relaxing. By the time you have worked up the legs, body, hands, arms and neck to the face and head, your body should feel a lot more relaxed.

B] Regulate your breathing, breathing in to a count of 5, holding the breath for a count of 5, and breathing out to a count of 5. Do this for a few minutes, and as you do so, you may become aware of areas of tension in your body. Tense these areas more and then relax them. You may also find it beneficial to visualize the air you inhale being a vibrant and pure white, filling you with purifying, cleaning energy, and the air you exhale being dark and smoky, taking with it all the stress and tension you have in you from the day`s events. As you do this, you will notice the air you exhale becomes less and less smoky, until it loses all colour and becomes colourless; at this point you should feel relaxed and comfortable.

C] Ensure that you are in the right frame of mind for the work - deal with any tension by stamping, shouting, or doing yogic body flops. For the latter, stand with your feet a shoulder width apart, breathe in and stretch up, raising your arms above your head, stretching to the sky, and going up onto tip toes. Then, exhale sharply and noisily, at the same time flopping your upper body and arms, bending at the waist, and bending your knees slightly, letting your head hang down, and arms swing, hands nearly touching the floor. Repeat this process twice more.

The Magickal Diary

The magickal diary is a very important item on the path of spiritual development. It serves several functions, namely

1] to encourage discipline, by the writing of entries every day,

2] to indicate progress, functioning as a monitor of the subtle changes one undergoes which may not be registered at the time, but which become clear with hindsight,

3] to check the effectiveness of practical magick performed, by detailing rituals and spells, and writing results which occur and critically relating them to causes, allowing a positive scepticism to develop which helps prevent ego inflation and over-rated self-opinionation (the "I'm a great Magus who can do anything just by thinking about it" complex),

4] to be a private space for examining and questioning the self honestly without the influence of ego-bias, a place where doubts and questions can be freely expressed, and all the psyche's shadows allowed to come into light,

5] to express creative insights as they occur in life, helping one to see the cycles that tend to occur, and thus helping development by using them positively and directing energies appropriately.

One can record one's dreams in a magickal diary, but personally we recommend having a separate dream diary, as it makes it easier to see themes and symbolisms in dream sequences.

Chapter Two

Meditation, Mantra & Pranayama

Meditation

Meditation can be described as Concentration on a single stimulus, rather than the ever-changing stimuli we are surrounded by (there are exceptions to this, but these will be discussed later in the chapter). The stimulus is usually an image or absence of image (such as a blank wall of colour), or a repeated simple action, such as chanting (in Sanskrit *Mantra*) or rhythmic breathing (in Sanskrit *Pranayama*).

Meditation calms and stills the mind and spirit, producing a state of serene being. It enables you to detach yourself from the rush of everyday life, and all its influences, which may often pull you in unwanted directions. It also provides a state for introspection and contemplation. Regular practise of meditation enables you to feel the texture of life more richly and appreciate it more, sharpening the senses and awareness. It can also increase personal identity, creativity and self expression, and the ability to deal with stress.

Meditating requires practise! People often find their initial attempt successful, and are then disappointed that it takes time and practise to repeat this state. When settling down to meditate, you should not let the ego think "I'm going to meditate, this is easy", as this can often lead to failure. Rather, concentrate on concentration, let all the events and actions of daily life slip away as you relax, concentrate and still yourself.

How do you meditate? Make yourself comfortable, for static meditation (which most are), sitting cross-legged on the floor is usually recommended. If you find this position uncomfortable, the "Hero" position mentioned in Chapter One may be used equally well. Concentrate the mind on the focus, (we will start with Breath Meditation) and keep it there. Concentrate on the nostrils, on the breath entering and leaving. Do not try and control your breathing initially, it is good to practise this meditation for a week or so before moving onto breath control, and this is covered in the next section on Pranayama.

Whenever your find your attention has wandered as a result of boredom or fatigue, or thoughts intrude, gently but firmly return your attention to your nostrils. Do not be disturbed by this in any way as it is inevitable, simply return your attention to the nostrils and continue. The frequency with which the attention wanders merely highlights how little we focus our minds, and regular practise of meditation helps us become more aware of ourselves, and able to concentrate without being distracted. Do not be distressed by the frequency with which thoughts may intrude at first, keep returning the concentration to the nostrils, eventually you will find your internal voice shuts off and all is still.

This process of "shutting off the internal dialogue" can take time to master completely, but the time will come when you can shut the dialogue off at will, and focus easily without too much distraction. Another form of distraction which occurs frequently is irritating itches or nagging pains. When these occur, ignore them, they will usually continue to nag and annoy you for a while, and then go away. DO NOT scratch or shift position unless it is absolutely necessary and you are in agony. When these distractions occur it is usually your conscious mind trying to exert its influence and stop you blocking it as you open your awareness beyond its boundaries.

When you start your meditation, you may find images of events that have occurred in the day slipping into your mind. This is to be expected, and you should just return your concentration to the focus (in this case the nostrils). Our minds can be described as being composed of three parts:

1] Conscious Mind - what occupies your awareness at a given time;

2] Preconscious Mind - what you can recall in an instant (such as the days events, or details of your house);

3] Unconscious Mind - the store of your experiences, and knowledge.

Meditation usually connects you fairly immediately to the Preconscious Mind, and then more slowly to the Unconscious Mind. This opening to the unconscious is of tremendous value in coming to know yourself and finding your direction. It enables us to access, learn from and come to understand the ideas and symbols it brings to us. A symbol is a word or image which has meanings beyond the obvious, and which can enable us to grasp ideas and truths we might not otherwise realize. Symbols are the language of the unconscious.

As well as Breath Meditation, there are a number of other forms of meditation, the commonest ones being listed below. Although there are a number of forms of meditation given, do not feel you have to try them all at once, they are being included so you can work through them with time, and to try to provide as thorough information as possible. For the first few months it is probably best to concentrate on Breath, Mantra and Awareness meditations; the other forms will be covered in the relevant chapters. You will also notice that there tends to be a degree of overlap between types of meditation, such as visualization in the purification meditation.

Awareness Meditations may take several forms. They are different to most other forms of meditation in that they can involve multiple stimuli rather than a single focus. An example of this is the Listening Meditation, where you use a simple focus such as concentration on the nostrils to concentrate your awareness, and then open your awareness to focus on the sounds around you. As you listen, you will become more aware of the sounds around you, and the effect they have on you (soothing, irritating, etc). You will also become aware of the peripheral sounds which you do not consciously hear, but which are always there. Try to just listen without analysing. Practise of this meditation helps develop awareness of our environment, and enriches our daily life by greater appreciation of the environment. Another good practise is to sit and relax as described for the previous meditation, and then say "I am aware" followed by what you are aware of (e.g. "that I am cold", "that I am wearing a black shirt", etc), and carry on for about five minutes, without trying to analyse or question, and see what things your awareness does focus on.

Elemental Body Meditation concentrates your focus internally in your own body. Become aware of how the four elements are present in your body and how they affect the operation of your body (e.g. air as oxygen in your lungs and bloodstream, fire as the nerve impulses and fire of digestion, water as the blood and bulk of the tissue, earth as the bones, teeth and hair, etc,). The Four Elements will be covered in detail in chapter six.

Pathworking is a form of guided meditations where you normally explore mental landscapes and go on symbolic journeys to gain insights and wisdom about yourself and your direction. Chapter Five concentrates on the forms of pathworking and their uses.

Visualization Meditation is where you use either a symbol, image or colour as the focus. When using a symbol (such as a Circle, Equal-Armed Cross, Pentagram, YinYang, Spiral, etc), it can produce understanding of the layers of meaning symbols have, and how we relate to them and may use them in our growth. It is important to note the effect particular symbols have on you - you can then concentrate on using them beneficially in your growth (e.g. an equal-armed cross may produce feelings of balance, YinYang of harmony, circle of completion, etc). The importance of exploring symbols and their meanings and truths for you cannot be over-stressed. As was stated above, they are the language of the unconscious, and a great deal of our energy and power is stored there. The more you can access the energies of the unconscious, the more you can harness them and direct them into your life and growth. When visualizing symbols, you will find it takes a lot of practise to hold an image for a period of time without it changing or breaking up, or just general breaks of concentration.

Walking Meditation is a practise best tried after you have practised the other forms of static meditation for a while. It is a common misconception that you have to be motionless to meditate, and indeed, most forms of meditation are static, but meditation whilst in motion is equally valid and useful. Concentrate the mind on the focus of your stride as you walk, maintaining a slow even stride. Each step should be taken slowly and deliberately, feeling the earth beneath you with each step; if you can control your breath at the same time, even better. It takes practise, but after a while you will find your mind focused and the environment clearer and sharper - all your senses will be heightened so sounds are sharper, colours are crisper, etc. This form of meditation requires a lot of concentration at first, and the mind will wander a lot, as there are more stimuli to distract the awareness than in most forms of meditation (not least of which is avoiding walking into people and things!).

To sum up, the stages of meditation are:-

1) Concentration (Focus the Mind)

2) Serenity (Still the Mind)

3) Insight (Explore the Mind)

Pranayama

Pranayama is the collection of breathing techniques for focusing the mind and increasing control over the vital forces of the body to promote health and well-being. The techniques are also used for transforming physical energy into spiritual energy. The Purification Meditation is a form of pranayama, as is the Breathing Meditation. Most of the techniques, however, involve regulating the breath and maintaining an equal rhythm by counting. Some simple techniques are given below.

To start, inhaling to a count of four, holding the breath to a count of four, and then exhaling to a count of four. This technique will accustom you to regulating your breath. With practise it becomes automatic so you do not have to concentrate on your breath when meditating, and you can control your breath automatically whilst meditating using another focus.

For relaxation inhale to a count of four and exhale to a count of eight. This can be increased with practise, but the exhalation should always be longer than the inhalation, preferably double the length.

With experience (say after a few months), retention of the breath for longer periods is a powerful technique. Inhale to a count of four, hold for a count of sixteen, and exhale to a count of eight. With practise this can be increased, but it should be in equal increments, such as to six (inhale), twenty-four (hold), twelve (exhale). This is known as north-south breathing. To become proficient in this technique and gain the maximum effect, close the right nostril with the right thumb whilst inhaling, close both nostrils while holding the breath, then open the right nostril and exhale through it. For the next breath reverse the process and inhale through the right nostril (i.e. the one that is already open), close both nostrils for the hold, and then open the left nostril and exhale through it. Repeat this process, reversing the nostrils each breath for as long as you feel able and build up the time spent doing it.

If at any time you feel light-headed, palpitations or breathless, stop immediately. Relax and take it easier next time. Pranayama is not something to push and should not cause any tension. As a technique it needs to be developed slowly and never rushed.

Mantra

Mantra is chanting a word or phrase repeatedly to focus the concentration and block out distracting influences. It also serves to turn off the internal dialogue by overloading it. Mantras can be tremendously powerful, and are beautiful in the simplicity of the technique. Mantras may be used as the primary focus for a meditation (being a simple repeated action), or in conjunction with other meditations and/or pranayama (if the inhale-hold-exhale counts are equal as in four/four/four or with practise unequal as in four/sixteen/eight) to alter your consciousness quite dramatically. Sudden insights may enter your head, if so try and store them and continue, as more may well follow.

Mantras are usually chanted at a slow and constant speed, sung rather than spoken. If you wish to regulate the time you spend doing a mantra it is a good idea to get a rosary of beads, and count one off each time you chant the mantra. With practise this action becomes automatic and is not at all distracting. You know you have finished when you reach the counter bead, which should be larger than the rest. Traditionally rosaries have one hundred and eight beads. Following are some examples of good mantras to use.

OM (also written AUM) - the Sound of the Universe (Sanskrit)

OM MANI PADME HUM - Sanskrit, the most well known of mantras, translated as *The Jewel in the Lotus* and referring to spiritual union.

A KA DUA
TUF UR BIU
BI AA CHE FU
DUDU NER A
AN NUTERU

This is an ancient Egyptian mantra meaning: *Unity uttermost showed! I adore the might of Thy breath, Supreme and terrible Being, Who makest the Gods and Death to tremble before Thee:- I, I adore Thee!*

OM NAMA SHIVAYA - "*Om! He whose name is Shiva*" (Sanskrit, Shiva is a Hindu God of tranformation and liberation. This mantra is calling to Shiva to remove illusion and impedance to spiritual growth.)

Any phrase or word can be used as a mantra (e.g. "I am happy"). It should be simple and expressive, and the syllables should preferably flow so it can be sung to a simple rhythm.

Practical Work

Try to practice meditation every day. Set aside between ten minutes and half an hour a day, and practice at least one type of meditation each day. If you really cannot practice every day, then practice at least three times a week, but set aside at least half an hour each time. If you have difficulty concentrating on the meditations you may wish to make a tape for yourself to use at first, but dispense with the tape in time. Start with meditation on the breath each day, and choose other types of meditation to follow from the meditations below. When you first start to meditate you should attempt to meditate for ten minutes at a time, having a short break before doing a second ten minutes. With practice you can increase this time.

1 Meditation on the breath

Sit with your eyes closed or half closed, relax, and focus on your nostrils. Feel the breath entering and leaving your nostrils. Begin to count your breaths in cycles of ten. After each tenth in breath you count, start again at one. Keep this going for at least ten minutes. If your attention wanders, gently bring it back, and don't get annoyed with yourself if you find yourself counting to eleven by mistake!

2 Listening Meditation

Relax and clear your mind as much as possible. Listen to the sounds around you without attachment, and without trying to interpret any of the sounds. Be aware of pure sound, rather than thinking "that's a car" or "that's a bird". Keep this up for at least ten minutes.

3 Watching the Mind

Close your eyes, relax, and just watch your thoughts, without getting caught up in them or attached to them. Acknowledge each thought as it appears, and gently let it go. Don't try to force the thoughts away, or to empty your mind completely, just be a passive observer, watching your own mind. If you find yourself getting caught up in thoughts and images, gently remind yourself to observe, and let them go. Keep this up for at least ten minutes.

4 Candle Meditation

Light a candle and focus on the flame, noticing the shape, colours and movement. Close your eyes and try to recreate that image in your mind's eye, and hold it for five to ten minutes. You will probably find this very difficult at first, and have to keep opening your eyes to remind yourself of its exact colours and shape, but it will get easier with time.

5 Purification Meditation

Sit comfortably with your eyes closed. Imagine yourself completely surrounded by a pure white light, stretching out into infinity. Be aware of your breathing, and with each in breath, imagine that you are breathing in this pure white light. Feel it filling your body, cleansing and energizing you, permeating your whole being. With each out breath, breathe out any tension or negativity you have within yourself, in the form of a thick black smoke. Continue breathing in pure white light and breathing out the smoke, with the smoke gradually getting lighter and less dense. Continue until there is no more smoke to come out, and you are breathing in and out pure white light. Rest in the feeling of peace and purity for as long as you will.

6 Body of Light Meditation

Visualize a ball of light below your feet. Feel your feet glowing, relaxed and filling with light. Slowly move this ball of light up the body, feeling each part filled with pure, energizing light, until the whole body is glowing with light. Hold this body of light for about ten minutes, then let the light fade, feeling that the energy is contained within you.

7 Mantra Meditation

Chant the component sounds of the Aum, the sound of the universe. The first sound is "*Aaa*". Take a deep in breath, and then intone this sound for as long as you can. Feel it reverberating in your body, in the first three Chakras (see chapter 4). The second sound is "*Ooo*", take a deep breath and intone this sound, feeling it in your heart and throat centres. The third sound is "*Mmm*", intone this, feeling it in your third eye. Lastly, intone "*Ngng*", feeling it in your crown chakra. Now put all these sounds together, into the "*AUM*", take a deep breath, and chant Aum for as long as you can. Repeat the Aum several times. You may find yourself becoming one with the sound. This is particularly effective if a group of people are chanting the mantra, keeping the sound continuous.

8 Alternate Nostril Breathing

Place your first two fingers of your right hand on your third eye, your thumb over your right nostril, your third finger over your left nostril. Close your right nostril with your thumb, and breathe in slowly to a count of four (approx. four seconds) through your left nostril. Visualize the breath going down your left nadi (see chapter 4) as a silver light. Close both nostrils, and hold breath in to a count of four. Breathe out through your right nostril to a count of four, visualizing the breath coming up your right nadi as gold light. Breathe in through your right nostril to a count of four, breathing in the gold light again, hold for four, and breathe out through your left nostril to a count of four, visualizing the silver light again. This is one complete cycle. Do ten complete cycles.

9 Elemental Meditation

Visualize/be aware of the elements in your body. Start with earth, being aware of your bones, muscle, solidity, then water, being aware of blood, bodily fluids, etc., then fire - energy, digestion, respiration, body heat, nerve impulses, etc., then air - breath, gases, etc., then Space - cavities in the body, spaces between organs, tissues molecules and atoms, the space within the atom. Lastly, the element of Consciousness, which pervades all. Rest in the feeling of oneness of consciousness.

10 Walking Meditation

Stand, being aware of movement, focusing on your feet. Put all your weight onto one leg, then lift the other foot slowly off the ground, heel first, being aware of the feel of the ground on your foot. Move the foot slowly forward, and place it on the ground heel first, slowly placing the rest of the foot on the ground. Now transfer your body weight to that foot. Be aware of the feel of the floor on the souls of the feet, the differences in pressure, texture, etc. Continue very slow conscious walking for about five minutes. It is best to be barefoot for this meditation.

Chapter Three

Visualization

Visualization could be described as the process of creating or realizing a symbol (or series of symbols) to focus and harness the power of the mind. The practise of visualization trains and develops the creative imagination. Visualization is one of the most basic and important foundation techniques of magick, leading on to pathworking, astral work, image magicks and others, so please concentrate hard on this chapter and be disciplined, it is well worth it. Some people are able to visualize quite naturally, and for others it takes much hard work; however everyone usually finds they need to practise to hone and refine their skills.

The Tattvas

The Tattvas are a group of five symbols in the Hindu system which depict the five elements. Simple coloured geometric shapes, they are very powerful images to work with. They are:-

Earth	-	Yellow Square
Water	-	Blue Circle
Fire	-	Red Equilateral Triangle (Apex up)
Air	-	Silver Crescent (Horns up)
Aether	-	Black (or Purple) Egg

Many books written by Westerners have transposed the water and air symbols, probably on the premise that the moon pulls the tides. However we prefer to work with the Tattvas in the way they have been used for centuries and as stated in the Indian Tantric texts, so we present them thus.

Sri Yantra

Kali Yantra

Durga Yantra

The Tattvas can be used very effectively as Astral Doorways to access the Elemental landscapes, this will be discussed further in Chapter 6. The main way we shall use the Tattvas is as a focus for meditation, and to improve concentration and visualization skills. Starting with Earth, use the symbol as a focus for meditation and practise holding the image without it changing shape, size or colour. Remember to gently refocus if it does change or attention wanders, do not chastise yourself, as this simple exercise is actually very hard work. When you can hold the image for at least 15 minutes (or after a week, whichever is longer), move onto the Water symbol and repeat the exercise. Do this working through the symbols of Fire and Air and Spirit. The first time you do the exercise you may find your attention wanders a number of times, but with practise it lessens until it does not wander at all. You may wish to include Pranayama with the visualization, but this is not essential, and if you choose to do so, it is probably best to wait until you have done a couple of the symbols first.

Note, the following material is optional, and probably best worked on after at least one month on the Tattvas.

Yantras

Yantras (another Sanskrit term) are images consisting of geometric shapes (especially triangles, circles and squares) which symbolically depict the body of a deity (e.g. the Durga Yantra, the Sri Yantra, etc), as Mandalas symbolically depict aspects of the cosmos (see chapter 21 for more on this). Yantra could be called a creative representation of the unknowable. Yantras are very powerful meditation diagrams, which can be used as a focus to withdraw from the external world and direct the attention inwards to the source of inspiration and creative intuition, often causing profound effects on the consciousness.

There is a saying   MANTRA + YANTRA = TANTRA

Which can be interpreted as *Force + Form = Expansion*

Emphasising the use of yantra as a focus to give form to creative energy (force), here being expressed as Sound (mantra). By using a multi-level

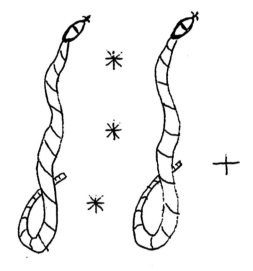

Damballah & Ayida Wedo Vever

focus such as a yantra, you can access deep levels of the unconscious and plumb the depths there through the expression of creative form (yantra). Yantras are much harder to visualize than the Tattvas, so at first you may find it helpful to open your eyes and check the image of the Yantra in front of you is the same as the one you were visualizing.

We have purposefully kept this exposition brief, as Yantras are a subject of immense depth, and to cover any more material would become complex and detract from the basic aim of visualization. (For anyone wanting to learn more, we would recommend "Tools for Tantra" - Haresh Johari).

Vevers

Vevers (or Veves) are in many ways the Voodoo equivalent of Yantras. Almost all Vevers are depictions of the Loa (Deities), and the drawing of a Vever is used as a form of invocation. They are usually drawn in sand, or with chalk or ash (or blood in some cases) to focus the attention on the Loa to be invoked, and to let the Loa know you wish to interact with them. The drawing of a Vever will usually be accompanied by drumming, dancing, chanting, etc, and it forms the centre of the ritual preparation.

The Vevers are used in Voodoo more as a physically realized image, created to channel energy by their construction. Vevers are usually destroyed at the end of a ritual. This is not to say that they cannot be used very effectively as a meditatory focus. The use of Vevers is probably best left until after a lot of practise with other simpler symbol systems (like the Tattvas). Drawing a Vever can have dramatic effects on your state of consciousness, and we would recommend it not be attempted until after work with the Chakras which will be covered in the next chapter.

Some of the most common Vevers are included in this chapter, and we have listed very briefly below the basic concepts associated with the Loa. (For further information on Voodoo and Voodoo techniques, cosmology, etc, we would recommend "*The Divine Horsemen*" - Maya Deren [reprinted as "*The Voodoo Gods*"]).

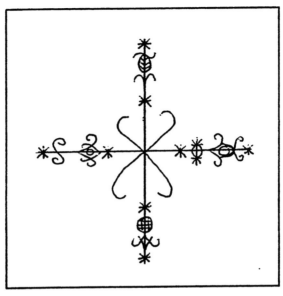

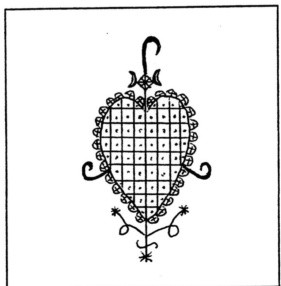

Top: Simbi Vever, Bottom: Erzulie Vever

Loa	Concepts	Planet
Agwe	Sea, Wind, Thunder	Neptune
Ayida Wedo	Sky Serpent, Creatrix	Uranus
Azacca	Agriculture, Fertility	Earth
Damballah	Sky Serpent, Rainbow	Uranus
Erzulie	Love, Fertility, Seduction	Venus
Ghede	Death, Underworld, Trickster	Moon
Legba	Phallic Energy, Fertility, Crossroads	Sun
Ogoun	War, Fire, Blood, Iron, Smithcraft	Mars
Simbi	Magick, Fresh & Salt Water	Mercury

Tantric Meditation

Tantra is an ancient Indian system which employs the use of complex visualizations in order to exhaust the conscious analytic mind and open the way for an experience of expanded consciousness and egolessness. Try the following visualization, which follows the principles of Tantric visualizations, but incorporates more western imagery. This meditation should be done after you have worked on the tattvas and have become proficient in visualisation.

Visualize a calm sea, and a full moon rising from the sea. See the moonlight glistening on the water. A red lotus bud rises from the water and begins to open, petal by petal, eight petals in all. In the centre of the lotus is a solar disc, shining gold. In the centre of the solar disc, is a lunar disc, shining silver. An image of a woman, a Goddess, rises out of the lotus, standing on the lunar disc. The image grows, so that she is a hundred feet tall. She wears a shimmering purple robe which bears Her shoulders.

Her face has the radiance of the full moon, Her hair is long and black, flowing about Her, down to Her waist. She wears a silver crown, with a crescent moon, horns upwards, and a moonstone set in the centre. Her eyes are emerald green. Large opal earrings in the shape of tear drops hang from Her ears. Around Her waist is a golden girdle, studded with nine blue moonstones. Around each ankle are three bangles, one of gold, one of silver and one of copper. Around each wrist are three more bangles, one of ivory, one of horn and one of snakeskin. About Her neck hang seven bead necklaces of semi-precious and precious stones. The first and smallest one is of diamond. It glistens and shines in the moonlight. The second is of sapphire, the third is of turquoise, the middle one is of emerald, the next of yellow topaz, the next of malachite, and the longest necklace is of bloodstone.

In Her right hand She holds a golden sickle, in Her left hand She holds ten ears of corn. Above Her left shoulder hovers an owl, with brown and grey plumage. Above Her right shoulder hovers a golden eagle. To Her right a dolphin rises from the sea. To Her left, a shark rises from the water. About Her, filling the air,is a swarm of bees. They blacken the sky with their numbers. The bees each turn into a Goddess, such that every form and aspect of the Goddess you can possibly think of is there, filling the sky with Their radiance, or with Their darkness. See each one in all Her glory, Ceridwen, Artemis, Kali, Isis, Sekhmet, Arianrhod, Yemanja, Erzulie, Durga, Demeter, Flora, Hecate, Freya, Sulis, Aphrodite, Tara, Ishtar, Lilith, Rhiannon, Kwan Yin, Amaterasu, and thousands more. See them all vividly, filling your vision, expanding to fill the universe.

Creative Visualisation

Creative visualisation is a technique you might like to try when you have become proficient in visualisation. It is a simple technique of practical magick.

First decide what change in your circumstances you want to effect. Then decide how to visualise that change in a manner that will be meaningful to you. This is essential, you must construct a clear image that resonates with the effect that you want. Consider if you are trying to get something you want, or something you need - the ego wants the former, magick gives the latter. Having come up with something you need that will improve your circumstances or personality in some way, reconsider the visualisation, is it concise, is it clear, are the colours, symbols, correspondences, etc, appropriate to what you are trying to achieve? Or are you more likely to dissipate the energy and get crossed wires? Come up with a simple, clear appropriate image for what you want.

When you feel confident you have the image right, build it up, starting with a mental "sketch". Then sharpen the lines and edges, and fill in the colours. As an artist, look critically at your image, are the colours right? Could that bit be larger or smaller? Continue this analysis until it feels right, and seems to glow with energy and purpose.

Now look inside yourself, and draw on the well of your desire to achieve the effect, building up the emotional charge linked with the image, until it is fully charged. See the image becoming a burning blaze, imprinting yourself on your unconscious. Now focus your will, all your drive and determination, and push that into the image as well. By now it should be an incandescent force, fit to burst - so direct all the energy and the visualisation onto the astral, shooting off and up like a rocket, to act as a focus on the subtle planes, to draw the charge to manifestation.

Chapter Four

Chakras, the Aura & Bodywork

The Subtle Body

The Chakras are the energy centres in the subtle body which regulate the energy flows and interaction of the physical and subtle bodies (chakra means "wheel" or "disk" in Sanskrit). There are seven main chakras, from the lowest at the base of the spine to the highest at the crown. Connecting these chakras and flowing through the body there are said to be seventy-two thousand nadis, tiny energy channels woven through the subtle body like "threads in a spider's web".

Coiled three and a half times around the base chakra resides the serpent Goddess Kundalini, an aspect of Shakti, the Great Goddess. "Kundali" means "spiral" or "coil", which is significant in light of the coiling - for the DNA double helix repeats every 3.5 A^0 (angstroms or 10^{-10}m), and of course the double serpents on the caduceus cross three and a half times. These highly suggestive correspondences emphasise the interconnection, both symbolic and actual, of the subtle body with the physical body.

The chakras are depicted as lotuses, which are sacred flowers, as they grow up from the mud symbolizing a path of development from the primitive to the divine. This mirrors the journey from the base chakra which roots us in the earth, to the crown chakra or thousand petalled lotus, which brings us cosmic consciousness. Like lotuses the chakras can be opened and closed. Illness and fatigue can often result from chakras being too open, too closed or out of balance, the physical body reflecting the imbalance in the subtle.

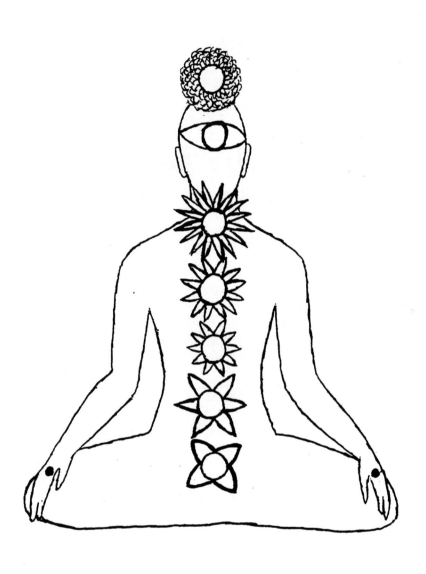

Subtle Body showing the Main Chakras

A balance needs to be reached, where in mundane daily life the chakras are partially open but not too much so, giving us awareness without excessive vulnerability to the inescapable stresses of our existence. During magickal work we may open the chakras more to aid in altering our consciousness and expanding our awareness of the subtle (and subsequently closing them as much as we feel we need to after the magickal work is done).

As the kundalini rises and pierces the chakras, She awakens each chakra. When She reaches the crown and unites with Shiva who resides in the crown chakra a person is said to be fully enlightened. Her journey from the base chakra to the crown reflects the tantric view of the creation of the universe. According to this view, before the beginning Shiva and Shakti were united as one in sexual union and unaware of any division, unaware of themselves. This is the state of bliss and unity of the crown chakra. Slowly Shiva and Shakti began to become aware of each other, they opened their eyes and saw each other (this being the state of the Ajna chakra).

As we move down the chakras Shiva and Shakti separate from each other. Shakti dances the dance of illusion and creates the world of diverse objects. Shiva then perceives himself as many different people and is caught up in this world of illusion. The way to return to this primal state of bliss is to return to worship of the Goddess and awakening the chakras, for according to the tantric view each of us (male and female) has Shiva residing in our crown, and we need to waken the Goddess to unite with Shiva and carry out the creation process in reverse, and return to the state of bliss of the united Shiva and Shakti.

The Chakras

MULADHARA (meaning "root" or "support") is located at the Base of the Spine. It is symbolically depicted as having 4 Red petals, and the seed-sound Lam in a Golden Yellow Square, corresponding to Earth. There is also an Inverse Red Triangle (symbolic of the yoni of the Goddess) corresponding to the Sun, Moon and Fire (the Gold, White & Red Light Rays), where the Goddess Kundalini resides coiled three and a half times. It is the Centre of Instinct, Survival, Pleasure and Base Sexuality. As the chakra of Earth, this element gives us the quality of cohesive resistance and the weight of solidness. In the physical body it represents the sense of Smell, controlling the Gonads and Adrenal Glands, and governs the Excretory System, as well as all that is solid in the body such as bones, teeth, nails and hair. At this level of being, one has the experience of security and satisfaction in one's existing state, being comfortable as one is, hence there is no urge to move on and this may lead to inertia. It has the mantras LAM (Sanskrit) and RA (Tibetan) attributed to it, the energy state of Solid, and responds to Red Light.

As well as being the centre for projecting Prana as Red Light, Muladhara also connects to the chakras in the Feet which connect to the Earth and allow interaction with earth energies, as well as keeping "one's feet on the ground". Without grounding we become unstable, with a tendency to fly off the handle or become deluded and live in a fantasy world. Calling energy down from the Crown chakra to the base is as powerful as sending Kundalini upwards. By grounding we maintain our contact with the Earth, with its boundaries, edges and limitations. Being grounded enables us to hold on to things (to have) and to contain, without this quality we lose our ability to contain and become an empty vessel. Illnesses associated with imbalance in the base chakra are obesity, haemorrhoids, constipation, anorexia, degenerative arthritis and frequent illness.

Animals:	Bull, Elephant, Ox
Colour:	Red
Crystals:	Agate, Bloodstone, Garnet, Lodestone, Onyx, Ruby
Element:	Earth
Energy State:	Solid
Foods:	Proteins, Meat
Force:	Gravity
Goddesses:	Anat, Ceridwen, Dakini, Demeter, Erda, Ereshkigal, Gaia, Lakshmi
Gods:	Ganesha
Incenses:	Cedar, Musk, Patchouli, Sandalwood
Inner State:	Stillness
Metal:	Lead
Planets:	Earth, Saturn
Seed Sound:	LAM
Sense:	Smell
Verb:	I Have

| Yoga: | Hatha |
| Yoga Poses: | All the balancing poses such as The Tree, The Dancer, The Eagle. Also seated meditation postures such as The Lotus and The Thunderbolt. |

Bioenergetic Exercise

Stand straight, arms at your side, feet about a shoulder width apart. Imagine a line drawn from the heavens down through the top of the head to between the feet. Breathing in, rise upon your toes, bringing your hands slowly up to chest height, and keeping your body straight and bottom tucked in. Breathing out, come down on your heels bending your knees as you do, bringing your hands back down again by your sides and sinking down to the floor. Your body should be relaxed as you do this and the movement should flow. Imagine that you are bringing down energies from the heavens into your feet, the earth and your base chakra. Raising and lowering hands with the rise and fall of the body helps to influence the downward flow.

SVADDISTHANA (meaning "sweetness") is located at the level of the Sacrum, below the Navel. It is symbolically depicted with 6 scarlet petals, and the seed-sound Vam in a White (Lunar) Crescent, corresponding to Water. It is the Centre of Change, Creativity (including Procreation), Nurturing, Sexuality and Sensuality. Singleness becomes duality, our point becomes a line, and we develop a degree of freedom and complexity as we become aware of and realise our difference from others.

Polarity manifests itself at this chakra - male/female, night/day, etc. The polarity of opposites by its nature creates movement, without movement there is inertia, entropy. Although in some ways manifest at all levels, socialization, sexuality, sensuality and the desire to reproduce form the kernel of this process, and so this chakra is also concerned with social interaction. In the physical body it represents the sense of Taste, controlling the Ovaries and Testicles, and governs the Spinal Column, the Womb, the Bladder, and the Kidneys. It has the mantras VAM (Sanskrit) and MA (Tibetan) to it, the energy state of Liquid, and responds to Orange Light. Illnesses associated with imbalances in the second chakra are impotence and frigidity (sexual dysfunction), uterine and bladder disorders.

Animals:	Fish, Sea Creatures, Makara
Colour:	Orange
Crystals:	Aquamarine, Coral, Moonstone, Quartz
Element:	Water
Energy State:	Liquid
Foods:	Liquids
Force:	Magnetism, Attraction of Opposites
Goddesses:	Aphrodite, Diana, Mari, Rakini, Tiamat
Gods:	Neptune, Poseidon
Incenses:	Damiana, Gardenia, Orris, Rose
Inner State:	Tears
Metal:	Tin
Planets:	Moon
Seed Sound:	VAM / MA
Sense:	Taste
Verb:	I Feel
Yoga:	Tantra
Yoga Poses:	The Triangle, Forward Bends, The Shoulder Stand, The Plough and The Butterfly.

Bioenergetic Exercises

Lie down on your back on the floor, with your knees together bent and feet flat on the floor in front of your anus. Arms should be next to the body palms flat on the ground. Breathe in and slowly raise your hips off the floor, keeping your shoulders on the floor, going as high as you can get your hips. Breathing out slowly your hips to the floor, moving the back down one vertebrae at a time. Standing up straight, bend knees slightly and drop pelvis forward. Keeping knees bent and flexible, rotate the pelvis in gradually decreasing circles, and then slowly increase the circle rotation size. Then repeat rotating in the other direction. Head and feet should remain totally still. Similar movement to belly dancing.

MANIPURA (meaning "lustrous jewel") is located at the Solar Plexus. It is symbolically depicted with 10 Dark or Black petals, and the seed-sound Ram in an Inverse Red Triangle, corresponding to Fire. It is the Centre of Interaction with the Universe, of the Digestive Process, and of the Emotions. Manipura has the qualities of expansiveness and warmth, of joviality in ourselves. Whilst earth and water in the first two chakras are downward moving, we see upward motion now with the upward expansiveness of fire. This is the chakra of transformation, both through the combustive process of digestion and through transforming the inertia of earth and water into action, energy and power. In magick we must develop our will and power consciously, which we do through increasing our awareness and by disciplined magickal work. Powerlessness often arises through ignorance about how to change our behaviour appropriately to the situations we encounter. Working with this chakra produces feeling of power in ourselves which help our development. In the physical body it represents the sense of Sight, controlling the Pancreas, and governs the Stomach, the Liver, the Gall Bladder and the Nervous System. It has the mantras RAM (Sanskrit) and DA (Tibetan) attributed to it, the energy state of Plasma, and responds to Yellow Light. Illnesses associated with imbalances in this chakra are ulcers, diabetes and hypoglycaemia.

Animals:	Ram
Colour:	Yellow
Crystals:	Amber, Opal, Topaz
Element:	Fire
Energy State:	Plasma
Foods:	Starches
Force:	Will
Goddesses:	Athena, Bride, Lakini
Gods:	Ares, Bel, Dionysus, Mars
Incenses:	Calamus, Cardamon, Carnation, Cinnamon, Coriander, Ginger, Marigold, Orange
Inner State:	Laughter, Joy, Anger
Metal:	Iron
Planets:	Mars, Sun
Seed Sound:	RAM / DA
Sense:	Sight
Verb:	I Can, I Will
Yoga:	Karma
Yoga Poses:	The Cobra, The Bow, The Cat, The Coil and TheTwist.

Bioenergetic Exercises
Sit in an upright position. Taking a deep breath, relax the muscles of your abdomen, then quickly snap in your abdomen ten times causing short quick

exhalations of breath.
Other good exercises for this chakra include sit-ups and running and any exercise which gets energy flowing.

ANAHATA (meaning "unstruck") is located at the Heart. It is symbolically depicted with 12 Red petals, and the seed-sound Yam in a Gold-edged Hexagram on a Smoky Circle, the focus of Air. It is the Centre of Love, Being & Equilibrium, the source of Harmony. Anahata has the airy qualities of mobility, gentleness and lightness. These qualities are expressed through movement towards, thus as relationship or sympathy. In the physical body it represents the sense of Touch - we are "in touch" when we relate positively to something. Too much energy put into relationship with others will produce oversympathy and anxiety. It controls the Thymus Gland, and governs the Heart, Blood, Vagus Nerve, and Circulatory System. It has the mantras YAM (Sanskrit) and SA (Tibetan) attributed to it, the energy state of Gas, and responds to Green Light. Nadis from this chakra run to chakras in the hands which may be used to direct Prana as Gold Light projected from the Anahata. Illnesses associated with imbalances in this chakra are asthma, respiratory problems, high blood pressure, heart conditions.

Animals:	Antelope, Dove, Nightingale
Colour:	Green
Crystals:	Emerald, Rose Quartz, Tourmaline
Element:	Air
Energy State:	Gas
Foods:	Vegetables
Force:	Love
Goddesses:	Aphrodite, Freya, Isis, Lakshmi (as preserver), Maat
Gods:	Avalokita, Vishnu
Incenses:	Jasmine, Lavender, Marjoram, Meadowsweet, Orris Root
Inner State:	Compassion
Metal:	Copper
Planets:	Venus
Seed Sound:	YAM / SA
Sense:	Touch
Verb:	I Love

| Yoga: | Bhakti |
| Yoga Poses: | The Locust, The Camel, The Cobra, The Fish and Pranayama. |

Bioenergetic Exercise

Sit or stand comfortably with hands held out in front of you, shoulder height with elbows straight. Turn one palm downward and the other upward, quickly open and close both hands several times until your hands feel tired. Switch positions of hands and repeat until hands are tired. Continue switching hands until it becomes too uncomfortable. Drop arms, open fists and bring palms together slowly. Move hands closer and further in and out and feel the energy between your hands.

This exercise helps the heart chakra through the hand chakras that connect to it, and is a very good exercise to do before healing work, particularly laying on of hands.

VISHUDDHA (meaning "purification") is located at the Throat. It is symbolically depicted with 16 Smoky petals, and the seed-sound Ham in the centre in a White Circle, the focus of Aether. It is the Centre of Active Magickal Power (through the voice - cf "In the beginning was the Word") and of Dreaming. Vishuddha has the quality of space, it is the place from which the four lower elements are formed and to which they will return, and is the latency behind them. The throat chakra is the bridge between the thought processes of the Ajna chakra and the bodily processes of the lower chakras. In the physical body it represents the sense of Hearing, controlling the Thyroid Gland, and governs the Lungs, Alimentary Canal, and the Hearing, Bronchial and Vocal Apparatus. It has the mantras HAM (Sanskrit) and SE (Tibetan) to it, and the energy state of Vibration. Illnesses associated with imbalances in the throat chakra are thyroid problems, throat and ear conditions.

Animals:	Bull, Elephant, Lion
Colour:	Bright Blue
Crystals:	Amethyst, Lapis Lazuli, Tourmaline (dreamwork), Turquoise
Element:	Aether / Sound
Energy State:	Vibration

Foods:	Fruit
Force:	Creativity
Goddesses:	Bride, Ganga, the Muses, Sarasvati, Seshat
Gods:	Hermes, Mercury, Thoth
Incenses:	Benzoin, Frankincense
Inner State:	Connection
Metal:	Mercury
Planets:	Mercury, Neptune
Seed Sound:	HAM / SE (pronounced "say")
Sense:	Hearing
Verb:	I Speak
Yoga:	Mantra
Yoga Poses:	The Lion, The Shoulder Stand, The Plough, The Headstand, The Camel and The Fish.

Exercises

Singing, such as chanting your own name. Using mantras, shouting, screaming, roaring and generally using the voice.

AJNA (meaning "to perceive") is located at the position of the Third Eye. It is symbolically depicted with 2 Lightning coloured petals, and is the Centre of Spiritual Power, of the redactive (passive) magickal senses (such as Telepathy, Precognition, Clairvoyance, Clairaudience), and is the focus of Light. In the physical body it controls the Pituitary Gland, and represents Intuition, governing the Lower Brain, the Second (least dominant) Eye, Nose, and Nervous System. It has the mantras AUM (Sanskrit) and SO (Tibetan) attributed to it, the energy state of Image, and responds to Indigo Light. Illnesses associated with imbalances in this chakra are blindness, headaches and nightmares.

Animals:	Owl
Colour:	Indigo
Crystals:	Amethyst, Lapis Lazuli, Quartz, Rutile Quartz, Sapphire
Element:	Light
Energy State:	Image
Foods:	Mind-altering substances
Force:	Imagination
Goddesses:	Athena, Hakini, Hekate, Iris, Isis, Tara, Themis

Gods:	Apollo, Belenus, Krishna, Morpheus, Paramashiva
Incenses:	Acacia, Aniseed, Mugwort, Saffron, Star Anise
Inner State:	Intuiting
Metal:	Silver
Planets:	Jupiter
Seed Sound:	AUM / SO
Sense:	Sixth
Verb:	I See
Yoga:	Yantra
Yoga Poses:	The Shoulder Stand, The Headstand, The Corpse and Alternative Nostril Breathing.

Alternative Nostril Breathing, as covered in the first chapter, can be used to keep the nadis clean and energised by visualizing the breath as white light travelling up through the Ida and out through the nostril, then in through the other nostril and down the Pingala. This is reversed as you alternate between the nostrils.

Exercise
Rub palms together vigorously, then close eyes and cup palms over eyes. Let your eyes bathe in warmth and darkness. Open your eyes while your palms are still cupped over them, then slowly move your palms away from your face.

SAHASRARA (meaning "Thousandfold", in reference to the petals) is located at the Crown. It is symbolically depicted with 1000 Brilliant petals and is the Centre of Evolution, the residence of the Divine Spark or Bindu, the focus of Thought. It represents Consciousness, and rules all the processes and actions of the body and mind. In the physical body it controls the Pineal Gland, and governs the Upper Brain and Sorcerer's (First - more dominant) Eye. It has the mantras GN [as in the GN at the end of AUMGN] (Sanskrit) and HUNG (Tibetan) attributed to it, the energy state of Information, and responds to Violet light. Prana may be projected as White Light from this chakra via either the First Eye or the Nadi chakra. Illnesses associated with imbalances in the crown chakra are depression, alienation and confusion.

Animals:	-
Colour:	Violet
Crystals:	Crystals, Diamond
Element:	Thought
Energy State:	Information
Foods:	Fasting
Force:	Enlightenment
Goddesses:	Ama-Kala (upward moving Shakti), Ennoia (Gnostic personification of Thought), Inanna, Nuit
Gods:	Shiva
Incenses:	Lotus, Rose
Inner State:	Bliss
Metal:	Gold
Planets:	Uranus
Seed Sound:	HUNG / GN
Sense:	-
Verb:	I Know
Yoga:	Jnana / Meditation
Yoga Poses:	The Headstand, The Lotus, all Meditation Poses.

Exercise
Head massage.

As well as the seven traditional main chakras there are hundreds of smaller chakras around the body, the other key energy centres being those in the hands and feet, and the Nadi Chakra where the Sushumna, Ida & Pingala channels meet. The two chakras in the hands connect to the Anahata (heart) chakra, and the feet chakras connects to the Muladhara (base) chakra. Directly below the Muladhara is the Kanda, a small egg-shaped bulb from which twelve spokes of the major nadis emanate, as well as all the other minor nadis. The subtle body of energy centres (chakras) and channels (nadis) generates the aura which surrounds the individual. The aura is generally egg-shaped, slightly flattened around the middle, with a dent around the area of the solar plexus under the diaphragm (near the Manipura chakra). It is through this point one absorbs prana (energy) from the environment and interacts with others through emotional energies.

The six chakras from Muladhara to Ajna are contained within the sun-gold

Sushumna nadi, the central channel from the Kanda which rises up the spine to the Sahasrara (Crown Chakra). Inside the Sushumna is the Brahma Nadi, which is used by the Kundalini during her ascent; inside the Brahma Nadi is the vermilion Wajra Nadi, which itself contains the white Chitrini Nadi. More evolved individuals will be "seen" to have a luminescent Chitrini Nadi. On the right and left of the Sushumna run the Pingala and the Ida channels. The Sushumna, Pingala & Ida operate as conduits for prana round the energy-circuits of the subtle body. The prana carried via the sun-red Pingala vitalizes the material body, and the prana carried via the moon-white Ida sustains the mind. Each chakra has a number of nadis connected to it. The Pingala starts from the left ovary or testicle and runs to the right nostril, and the Ida from the right ovary or testicle to the left nostril. These two nadis cross above each chakra as they spiral upwards, producing the criss-cross image of the twin serpents of the caduceus. The Pingala & Ida unite with the Sushumna forming a threefold "knot" at the Nadi Chakra just below the locus of the Ajna Chakra. The twelve major nadis which emanate from the Kanda are the Alambusa (to left ear), Kuhu (to genitals), Waruni (all directions, involved in water generation), Pingala (to right nostril), Pusha (to right ear), Saraswati (to tongue), Shankhini (to throat), Gandhari (to left eye), Ida (to left nostril), Sushumna (to crown), Hastijihwa (to right eye) and Wishwodari (all directions, involved in metabolism of food).

Aura Work

1] A very effective and simple way to keep the aura sealed and energised is the following exercise:-

Visualize the base chakra as a disk (or sphere if you find it easier) of spinning red light (the colour of light it responds to), and when you see it clearly, inscribe a pentagram of gold light on the disk, vibrating (either silently or aloud) the seed sound for the chakra (Ra). Then move to the second chakra and visualize it as a disk (or sphere) of spinning orange light, and when it is clear, inscribe a gold pentagram on it, vibrating the seed sound (Ma). Move up through the chakras repeating this process, moving through the colours of the rainbow up to violet light for the crown chakra, inscribing a gold pentagram on each and vibrating the appropriate mantra. As you do this, you should feel the energy moving up the spine.

After having inscribed the pentagram on the crown chakra, imagine each pentagram was a seed, and visualize that seed bursting forth gold light, surrounding the body and filling the aura. When you can feel the gold light surrounding your body, concentrate the energy on any areas of the body which are in pain or feel weaker. We recommend this exercise be done every day, irrespective of any other magickal work which you may be doing. If it is built in to the daily routine, it will greatly strengthen the aura. Doing the exercise before going to bed at night is strongly recommended.

2] Bathing before ritual work is a time-honoured and often forgotten technique to keep the aura clean. A simple and easy technique which may be employed when ritually bathing is to symbolically remove impurities from the aura by brushing it away. Another equally appropriate and easy technique is to visualize any impurities being washed away into the water, just prior to getting out of the bath. You should also allow yourself to dry naturally rather than using a towel.

3] Prior to rituals, smudging the aura with a suitable incense can help clean the aura. Smudging is widely used amongst shamanic cultures and involves burning incense, and wafting the smoke around the whole body, visualizing the aura being cleansed and purified by the incense smoke. A good purifying mix for smudging is equal parts of Copal, Sage & Pine.

4] A daily course, lasting 15 or more days, of Damiana tea (one tablespoon mixed equally with Saw Palmetto berries for maximum effect) will help keep the aura clean. Smoking Passion Flower, or Damiana, can also help maintain the aura.

Recommended Reading

"*Light on Yoga*" - B K S Iyengar
"*The Serpent Power*" - Arthur Avalon
"*Wheels of Life*" - Anodea Judith
Any good books on Yoga.

Chapter Five

Pathworking

Pathworking (also known as Guided Imagery by Psychologists) is a technique of guided meditation, with the guidance taking various levels depending on the specific instance. It is used for exploration of the self, symbols, and your relationship with nature, divinity, the higher self, other life forms, etc. One of the most useful aspects of Pathworking is the free rein it gives to the imagination, and indeed it is a good tool for helping develop the creative imagination and powers of visualization. It is important to remember that you are not hampered by mundane constraints in Pathworking, interaction with Myths and fantastic creatures and beings often occur and are usually very beneficial.

Pathworking is a very good technique for exploring myths, and it is worth spending time reading different versions of the myth and immersing yourself in the symbols of the pantheon. Doing solo pathworkings where you take the part of an observer, then repeat the pathworking as a character in the myth, such as a deity or hero/ine, allows you to gain different perspectives on the lessons and energies contained within myths. Working with different systems of myths also enables you to find which pantheons you feel the greatest resonance with, and which you can work with most beneficially to access the energies of your unconscious.

Experience has shown that 10-20 minutes is the optimum length for a Pathworking, and 30 minutes the effective maximum. It is very difficult to maintain concentration for longer Pathworkings, with people often falling asleep.

Although Pathworkings can be read from a written copy to a group, it is preferable if the guide experiences the Pathworking as well. This can be achieved by either the guide describing their experience as it occurs, or using a tape recorded beforehand. Using tapes can work very well if appropriate and well-timed sound effects are added, and gentle background music on the tape can also help people.

The usual forms Pathworkings take are detailed below:-

1] **Totally Guided** - the Guide describes the landscape, encounters and everything else in great detail. This tends to be useful for working in a set system of symbolism, such as Qabalah, or for people with little or no experience who may have trouble visualizing. It also keeps the group in a very similar mind-set and often produces strong group rapport.

2] **Guided With Interaction** - the Guide describes the landscape and encounters, but leaves the detail to the vision of the individual, asking how they see the road, person, animal, etc; giving the individual's unconscious a chance to fill out the detail with its own (usually relevant) detail. This technique is useful for people who can visualize fairly well, and for psychological work exploring aspects of the self.

3] **Interactive Group** - starts with one person describing their vision, and other members of the group then describing their vision, building up a group experience. This is good for a group of people who wish to build up group rapport, meshing their symbol systems and helping to build a group egregore.

4] **Astral Doorway** - where one person guides everybody through a symbol, such as a Mandala, Tattva (or other elemental symbol) or Tarot Trump, and then everybody explores the landscape they find themselves in, learning lessons appropriate for them. Good for more advanced work, and self-development. This is covered in more depth in Chapter Six.

Beginning a Pathworking

To start a pathworking you need to change from an ordinary state of consciousness to a more astral and mental state where you can do the pathworking. Close your eyes and relax, adopt a comfortable posture (though preferably not lying down), it is worth spending a few minutes doing pranayama and clearing your mind. Then visualize the room you are in (if you are indoors) in your minds eye, and when you can see it clearly, see the room slowly start to fill with a white mist, which coalesces and obscures everything until you are floating in a sea of white mist. Then see the white mist slowly dispersing and clearing to reveal the landscape of the pathworking you are about to go on. If this technique seems a little quick, visualize the mist changing from white to red, and then changing slowly through the colours of the rainbow, ending at violet, giving you time to alter your perceptions more easily. The same technique should be used at the end of the pathworking to return back to your ordinary state (i.e. seeing the mist returning and obscuring the landscape you are in, and then dispersing and leaving you in the room you are in).

You will notice with the Inner Guide and Underworld pathworking that you retrace your steps. When doing any pathworking as a journey, it is a good idea to retrace your steps and end the pathworking where you started. This helps maintain clarity between the experiences of the pathworking and ordinary consciousness, giving a clear demarcation line for ending the pathworking. We would not recommend doing more than three or four pathworkings a week to begin with. After practise you may wish to do more, but for the first year or so we would not recommend more. Excessive pathworking can lead to escapist tendencies. Pathworking is not escapism, it is for helping you to explore yourself and grow.

Salt Crystal Pathworking

This pathworking is for creating a safe sacred space for contemplation and inner peace and harmony. It is very simple and easy to perform, yet very rewarding.

Start the pathworking as described in the previous section, and as the mists disperse see yourself in a cuboid room. The walls are crystalline and translucent, very solid and pure. You are inside a salt crystal. Nothing can enter the crystal unless you want it to. By concentrating you can change the colour of the walls, to black, or mirrored, or any colour. Scratch the surface of the wall and taste the salt on your finger. Sit in the centre of the crystal and be aware, see how it makes you feel. Take time just to let the universe flow around you while you watch for a while from the untouchable space in the heart of a sacred salt crystal.

If you have problems with visualizing hard edges, and find the crystal becoming more cavelike, persevere with your perception of the crystalline shape, and it will come. There is nothing wrong with a cave/womblike shape, but that is not the purpose of the exercise.

Inner Guide Pathworking

This pathworking is to meet your inner guide, to open your channels of access to your unconscious through the guide, better to tap its energies. This pathworking can be done whenever you wish to try and increase your awareness of a situation or gain insight.

As the mist disperses, you find yourself in a meadow, with birds singing and butterflies and bees flying around. In the undergrowth you can hear animals moving around, you may see them. Look around and enjoy the warm sun and the gentle cooling breeze. Look around the meadow and take stock of your surroundings, noting as you do a path leading away from the meadow and into the hills. Look at the path and note its form. Is it grass, mud, brick, stone, etc? Follow the path towards the hills, looking as you go for something to give your guide, whom you will meet, as a present.

Continue your journey until you come to an obstacle. Is the obstacle a river, boulder, wall, unhappy animal, etc? Go past the obstacle in whatever fashion you can, and follow the path up the hill, until you come to a fork in the path. Ahead the path goes up steeply to the left, and meanders up to the right. The left hand path is obviously a shorter distance, but harder going. Choose one of the forks, noting which, and continue your ascent to the cave of your inner guide. When you have reached the top of the hill, you see a white animal waiting for you at the entrance to a cave. What sort of animal is it? (This is worth taking note of, because it is often an animal you can benefit greatly from working with the energies of, and it is often not what you expect it to be). The animal leads you into the cave, and sitting by a fire in the middle of the cave is a figure. Is the figure male or female, young or old? What does s/he wear? Approach the figure and offer your gift. Your guide will answer questions you ask (though they are occasionally reticent if asked trivial questions) and give you a gift in return. Take time to befriend your guide and be aware how you can help each other. When you have finished conversing, say farewell and leave the cave, returning down the slope to the meadow, and when you reach the meadow, sit down. When you are settled in the meadow, see the white mist forming and filling the air around you, signalling the end of the pathworking and the return to ordinary consciousness.

Underworld Pathworking

This pathworking is exploring the ancient Greek myth of Persephone and her marriage to Hades. It is a good pathworking for exploring different aspects by taking on the roles of the characters (Demeter, Persephone, Hades, even Charon, and seeing how much pathworking can access from your psyche).

Start the pathworking as described in the previous section and as the mist disperses, see yourself in a rocky landscape at the base of a cliff, with a cave in front of you. Standing in the cave mouth is a beautiful woman wearing a robe of green and with grain in her hair. She is tall and noble, but she is crying and her tears scorch the earth beneath her as they fall. Approach the woman and offer your respect, for she is Demeter, Goddess of the Earth, and she has a sad tale to tell. She informs you of how her daughter Persephone was stolen from her whilst picking flowers by dark Hades, Lord of the Underworld in his chariot, bursting from the ground to drag Her to His dark realm.

Demeter asks you to speak to Persephone, see how she is and whether she will return to the upper world, for if she does not Demeter will continue to grieve, and the earth will die. She hands you an ear of corn and two silver coins, obuli, and tells you to give one to the ferryman to take you across the river Styx, and one to return, as is the custom. She bids you find her daughter and give her the corn, and points into the cave. The cave is lit by phosphorescent fungi, growing on the walls and giving you enough light to see by, at the end of the cave ahead you see a tunnel sloping downwards, walls of rough rock and wide enough for you to easily walk down. The tunnel's walls are lit by the same fungi, and the tunnel slopes gently down in a straight path. You walk for a while, noticing the path becoming steeper and steeper. As you walk, you hear the sound of rushing water, and in the distance, the barking of a large dog. As the sound of the water gets louder, the tunnel ends and you find yourself on the bank of a river, with another bank and tunnel at the other end. A mist rises from the river, making the water difficult to see.

As you gaze across the river, you hear the barking emanating from the tunnel on the other side, and you see a robed figure punting a boat across the water to you. The figure is Charon, the ferryman. The boat arrives, and you embark. Charon holds out a hand, and silently takes the first obuli from you. He casts off and starts to push the boat across the river, silently. The barking grows louder as you reach the other shore, and with another silent gesture he points at the tunnel. After disembarking you enter the tunnel, which is lit by torches and much brighter. Ahead the tunnel opens out into a large cave, and at the exit on the other side sits a huge dog with three heads, Cerberus, guardian of the entrance (and exit) to the underworld hall of Hades and Persephone. Cerberus looks curiously at you as you approach the entrance to the hall, but he makes no move to stop you.

Walking through the entranceway, you see a huge cave, with two figures, male and female, clad in black robes and sat on thrones at the other side. As you approach you see the woman is very beautiful, and there is an obvious resemblance to Demeter, you realize she is Persephone. She radiates joy and life illuminating the cave around her. Sat next to her the beautiful yet sombre figure of Hades regards you with penetrating eyes. Hand Persephone the corn, and speak to her and Hades. Learn how, although she was taken by force, she is happy as Queen of the Underworld, ruler in her own right, and how she brings joy and light to the dark realms she inhabits, beloved of all. When Hades hands her the pomegranate to eat, she knows it will bind her to their realm, and perpetuate their love, and she also knows she is the daughter of two worlds, and must live in both of them. Persephone asks you to tell Demeter of her actions, and that she will return to the upper world to bring spring with her.

After talking to Persephone, Hades points to a lead-rimmed circular mirror on the wall and asks you if you would like to scry in it. The mirror can show scenes from past, present and future, in symbolic and real form. It is up to you to learn from what the mirror has to offer, it is a focus to the power of your unconscious mind. After you have scried, Persephone and Hades bid you farewell, and you take your leave of the hall, walking back past the now silent Cerberus to the ever silent Charon on his boat. Handing him the second obuli you embark onto the boat, and are punted back across the Styx. On the other side, you make your way up the steep tunnel, which becomes easier to walk as you get nearer the surface. In the cave you see the figure of Demeter, waiting to speak to you. She already seems to know what you tell her, but she asks you to recall all the details you can remember to her. When you have finished, she has stopped crying and has a look of wisdom and acceptance in her eyes. She bids you farewell for now, and disappears. As she disappears a white mist starts to fill the cave, and you return back from the pathworking in the usual manner.

Chapter Six

The Elemental Worlds & Astral Doorways

The five elements make up everything. They are not merely earth, air, fire, water and spirit - but are concepts, energy states, states of being, philosophical concepts. It is important to realize how fundamental the elements are to our existence. Working with the elements enables us to balance ourselves and remain centred, and promotes growth through realization of imbalances in ourselves (be they qualities, emotions, habits, etc) and the means to change the qualities, through working with them and transmuting them.

The section at the end gives suggested attributions for the elements. These are not hard and fast, and vary from person to person, although many do use the attributions given. The key issue is that the attributions and qualities that feel right to you are the ones to work with. Try copying out the lists, deleting and reattributing any attributions you do not agree with, adding any other details about the element and how you perceive it. As you make your list, note how many of each of the positive and negative qualities of the element apply to you. You will then have a way to check which elements are more or less active in yourself, and be able to concentrate on the weaker elements, and on changing the negative traits of an element in yourself into positive traits of the same element.

When you have your list of negative qualities, ask yourself why you have those qualities. This requires a lot of honest self-exploration, and working through of past events in your life which may have been left unresolved. Whilst you are doing self-exploratory work, remember to meditate on the positive qualities of the element you are working with, and as energy is released from releasing blockages, focus it into meditating on the positive qualities of the element. When doing this work, bear in mind that emotions such as anger and sadness are natural, and often necessary, states, which can produce positive growth as well through their experiences.

A meditation considering the elements within us was presented in Chapter Two. Now meditate on the elements outside yourself as well.

Meditate on each element in turn, facing the direction of the element. Start by considering the element in yourself as you have already done, and then visualize whatever feels right for you (e.g. rivers, rain, waterfalls, the sea, etc for water) and see how it makes you feel. Consider the presence and action of the elements in our lives around us all the time, and add this to your notes. For example, consider when you have bath - you bathe in water, which cleanses you, then you use a towel (earth) to dry, you may use a dryer on your hair (air, powered by electricity - fire), etc. When you use this method of perception you will appreciate the elements and their qualities much more, and develop your relationship with them, and see how you can use them to balance yourself.

Casting the Circle

When performing any magickal work, it is usual to create a sacred space. We create a sacred space to emphasise the stepping out of the mundane involved in magickal work - by changing the nature of the space about us we are demonstrating our willingness to walk between the worlds and transform ourselves. Another consideration with creating a sacred space is that you make a safe space to work within, so you can perform work which may require deep trance states without any nagging doubts to distract you. This is normally done by casting a circle (although it is really a sphere around you). In most traditions the elements are called into the circle after the casting.

Casting the circle can be done in a number of ways. One of the simplest ways is to visualize a sphere of gold (or other preferred colour) light forming around yourself and filling the room (if indoors, or to a reasonable distance, say a couple of yards, giving room for movement, if outdoors). Other ways include walking round in a circle beating a drum, clapping or using bells, visualizing the circle being created as you walk round; representations of the elements may be carried around the circle, such as a censer or joss stick (air), candle (fire), water (water) and salt (earth) [the latter two can of course be combined].

Circles are generally cast clockwise (i.e sunwise) in the northern hemisphere, starting in the east, the place of the sunrise. After the circle has been cast, facing the appropriate direction, call to the element and invite it into the circle, asking it to share its powers and qualities with you to give you balance. This can be done with a statement like "*Powers of Air, of the Eastern Quarter, come into this circle in love and share your qualities of discrimination, clarity and knowledge with me, that I may know you better*", or any phrasing that feels right to you.

If you do cast a circle and invite the elements into it, it is important to remember to thank them and say goodbye after you have finished your meditation, and open the circle again. This is normally done by saying thank you to each element in turn (going either clockwise from east or anti-clockwise from north, depending on your preference) and bidding it farewell as it returns to its own realm (the elemental worlds we intend to explore). After saying farewell to the elements, the circle is opened by reversing the casting, so if you visualized coloured light forming a sphere, you take the light back into yourself; if you walked around playing a musical instrument, you walk round anti-clockwise, playing the instrument again.

To gain more contact with the elemental worlds, it is very beneficial to experience them more personally in their pure states. To this end the use of astral doorways is an ideal way to access and experience the elemental worlds.

Using Astral Doorways

Before using a symbol as an astral doorway, we would strongly recommend performing an aura sealing and empowering exercise. The exercise presented in Chapter Four is ideal. Next visualize a symbol that will depict the doorway to the elemental world. The tattvas are some of the best symbols to use, and you will already be familiar with them. Now, when you have the image steady, instead of just keeping the image there, imagine yourself passing through it, as if is a diaphanous curtain. When you start doing this work, it is a good idea to take your Inner Guide with you (see Chapter Five).

After you have visualized the doorway, call to your Guide and when they have arrived go through the doorway with them. You will find yourself in a landscape which may well be totally alien and strange to you. Take time to explore the landscape and interact with it and anything you may encounter. If you feel uncomfortable at this time, go back through the doorway, which you will see behind you as the symbol where you are standing when you enter the elemental world, and try the other elements first. You may find that you need to work through the elements according to the needs in your life. After a while you may like to experiment with other symbols that feel appropriate. If you find you cannot get through the tattva symbol after you have visualized it, perform some pranayama, the exercise given in chapter one of breathing in gold light and breathing out black until the breath cycle is pure gold is a good exercise to do. When you feel focused and invigorated again, try again. This technique can require a lot of practise, so be patient if it is difficult at first. We would suggest a minimum of one week on each element.

The Elements

AIR - To Know

Direction:	East
Tools:	Dagger / Athame (some say wand), Censer, Flute
Time:	Dawn
Season:	Spring
Colours:	Yellow & White
Sense:	Smell
Concepts:	Intellect, Knowledge, Clarity, Discrimination, Mind, Speed, Sound, Intuition
Qualities (+):	Inspiration, Wisdom, Happiness, Hope, Logic, Joy, Analysis, Discernment, Decisiveness
(-):	Anxiety, Fear, Impulsiveness, Paranoia, Dispersion, Prejudice, Insecurity

FIRE - To Will

Direction:	South
Tools:	Wand (some say athame), Rattle, Sistrum
Time:	Noon
Season:	Summer
Colours:	Reds & Oranges
Sense:	Sight
Concepts:	Energy, Freedom, Success, Drive, Transmutation, Light, Power, Vision
Qualities (+):	Courage, Motivation, Drive, Enthusiasm, Passion, Will, Creativity
(-):	Fickleness, Vengefulness, Violence,Possessiveness, Fear, Hatred - Violent, Cruelty - Physical, Anger, Egotism

WATER - To Dare

Direction:	West
Tool:	Chalice
Time:	Dusk
Season:	Autumn
Colours:	Blues
Sense:	Taste
Concepts:	Emotions, Dreams, Intuition, Death/Rebirth, Taste, Primal Chaos, Underworld, Unconscious, Blood, Womb
Qualities (+):	Compassion, Sympathy, Empathy, Nurture, Sexuality, Trust, Serenity, Tranquillity, Depth
(-):	Sadness, Jealousy, Hatred - Insipid, Treachery, Sorrow, Deceit, Spite, Venom

EARTH - To Keep Silent

Direction:	North
Tools:	Pentacle, Drum
Time:	Midnight
Season:	Winter
Colours:	Greens & Browns
Sense:	Touch
Concepts:	Body, Strength, Stillness, Endurance, Mystery, Power,

		Healing, Skill, Touch, Smell
Qualities	(+):	Strength, Steadfastness, Stability, Sensuality, Humility, Selflessness, Patience, Responsibility, Persistence, Realization, Tolerance
	(-):	Laziness, Stubbornness, Greed, Attention-Seeking, Inertia, Domineering, Depression, Melancholy

SPIRIT - To Go

Direction:	Centre (Within/Without)
Tools:	Cauldron & Sword
Time:	Between the Worlds
Season:	The Turning Wheel
Colours:	Purple, Black, White
Sense:	Hearing
Concepts:	Will, Harmony, Evolution, Life Force, Transcendence, Sixth Sense, Transformation

Chapter Seven

Exploring Symbols

A symbol is an image, picture, sign, term, word or action which we may be familiar with in daily life, but which has more meanings than are immediately obvious. Symbols imply something vague, unknown or hidden from us. They speak to, and emerge from our unconscious minds, and are never precisely defined or fully explained by rational thought. By working with symbols our minds are led to ideas beyond the grasp of reason, and this can lead to transcendent experience. All religions employ symbolic language or images to express that which cannot be fully defined or comprehended. Try to define the meaning of the word "Divine", or "God/dess" and you will probably find that it is not an easy task, yet when you have a direct experience of the Divine, you know it. The use of symbols can help us to attain to experience of the Divine. Symbols are important spiritual and magickal tools, but often there are many ways of symbolizing the same thing, or achieving the same psychological or spiritual state and we should not get too attached to a particular symbol itself.

Ritual gestures are symbols, and in magick we make use of all the senses to achieve an altered state of consciousness. We use symbolic smells in the form of oils and incenses, symbolic images in the form of artwork, God/dess forms, and visualizations, symbolic sounds in the form of mantras, chants, music and intonation, symbolic tastes in the form of ritual food and drink, and symbolic sensation in the feel of power objects, robes, and ritual regalia. Sacred dance employs the kinetic sense of the feel of body movement, and is a symbol. We have already introduced many symbols in this course, the Tattvas, Mantras, Elemental Worlds, to name but a few. In this chapter we will explore more universal symbols, magickal symbols and wiccan symbols. Although some background and explanation is given for these symbols, always bear in mind that a symbol always means more than can be expressed in words. It is up to you to explore these symbols for yourself, and see how they affect you, what experiences they bring you, and how they speak to your unconscious.

Symbols for the Union of Opposites

Many cultures and religions see the universe in terms of polarities, or opposites. In Christianity there is the polarity of God and the Devil, who battle with one another for supremacy. There is little concept of union of these opposites, except that Christianity teaches that both good and evil exist in man. However, most Christian teaching is concerned with trying to rid oneself of the "evil", or the influence of the Devil, and to develop the "good" half, and closeness to God. There is no concept of balancing the forces within, and thus, many Christians are riddled with guilt, because they cannot get rid of the "bad" within them. In some cases, the "evil" may be projected out, onto others, who become scapegoats, and we can see the horrific effects of this process when we look at accounts of the witch hunts of the Middle Ages. We should stress, however, that it is not only Christians who project their "shadow" sides onto others. Pagans can be equally guilty of projecting their shadows on to Christians, when they blame Christianity for the problems of the world.

In Witchcraft, polarity is expressed in terms of the Goddess and the God, male and female, but also as dark and light. These poles do not correspond to the Christian idea of good and evil, but represent two halves of a Unity. It may be compared to the ancient Chinese principle of Yin and Yang, where Yin represents, all that is dark, moist, cold, feminine, pliable, etc., and Yang represents all that is light, hard, hot, dry, masculine, energetic, etc. However, Yin always contains a bit of Yang, and vice versa. The Yin Yang symbol or Tai Chi, depicts the perfect balance of the two great forces of the universe. Each has within it the embryo of the other power, and there is perpetual change and movement. The two forces are contained within a circle, the representation of totality, revolution and dynamism, and the whole represents the perfection of balance and harmony. The two forces are held together in tension, but not in antagonism. They are mutually dependent partners, one in essence, but two in manifestation.

Yin Yang

In Witchcraft, the Goddess and God may be likened to the Yin Yang symbol, although seeing them in human-like form may enable some people to relate to them better than they can to the abstract image of the Yin Yang. But the Goddess and God are not human, and working with more abstract representations of their power can also be beneficial to remind us of this. In the Craft the Union of Goddess and God is often seen as a sexual union, as in Tantra, and sexual magick, when appropriate can also be a powerful symbol, enabling the couple to achieve a state of Oneness with each other and with the Universe. In the Great Rite, the woman represents the Goddess, and the man the God, and their coupling represents the union of these great forces. The power of the emotions, and the energy raised through the physical arousal add power to the ritual, and it can be a profound experience. It should be stressed though, that such a ritual should only be performed by people who are already in a sexual relationship, where there is a sufficient degree of love and trust.

Wiccan rituals generally end with consecration of the wine with an athame, and this is another expression of the union of opposites, the athame representing the phallus of the God, being plunged into the chalice, representing the vulva and womb of the Goddess. The symbolic or token version of the Great Rite employs these symbols rather than the sexual act to represent the union of opposites, but it should be remembered that the "actual" or sexual version of the ritual is symbolic as well. There are many different symbols which can be used to represent this union, and one should not get hung up on one. What is important is the "Inner" Great Rite, the process of balancing the forces within yourself, which is the aim of magick.

Other symbols for the union of opposites include the Sun/Moon symbol used in some schools of Tantra, the Hexagram formed of an upward and a downward pointing triangle, the Yab Yum of Tibetan Tantrism (another sexual image), and the figure of the Andrgogyne or Hermaphrodite.

The circle is often considered to be a female symbol, representing the vulva or womb, containing and soft, with no hard edges. It is cyclic; when we go round in a circle we keep coming back to the same place, we cannot break out of it. It represents the cyclic nature of existence, the Great Round and the cycle of birth, death and rebirth ruled by the Goddess. The arrow, on the other hand may represent the masculine, the phallus, giving direction, looking to the future, the warrior. Its negative side is that because it always points forward, there is no looking back and learning from the past. It represents technology, which, unbalanced by the "feminine" can be destructive.

A symbol which combines the cyclic nature of the circle with the moving forward of the arrow, is the Spiral. When we follow the Spiral path, we come back to similar places, but each time, on a new level. Spirals can be seen in nature, in plant growth, the shells of snails, the horns of goats and rams and in the structure of DNA. It can also be seen in the cosmos, in spiral galaxies. In nature the Spiral represents an ideal solution to the problem of growth, allowing for constructual expansion without requiring a change of form, and the plant or animal can develop harmoniously. When spirals come in pairs, such as in horns, they usually develop symmetrically in relation to each other. The Spiral combines beauty with strength, two more important poles within the Craft. Life doesn't just build spirals, it abandons itself to them. The Spiral Dance is used in Craft rituals as an important ritual symbol which all members of the group can be experientially involved in. The labyrinth may be used in a similar way, and walking the inward path of the labyrinth is a symbol of the inner journey to the Self.

Symbols of Trinity

The concept of trinity is common in many cultures and religions. In the Craft, we have the three-fold Goddess of the Moon, Christianity has the holy trinity, Hinduism has the trinity of Brahma, Vishnu, Shiva, and Sarasvati, Lakshmi, Kali, and there are various examples of threefold Goddesses in Celtic art. The three-fold Goddess represents not only stages of life, but the cyclic nature of the Universe. The Fates in Greek Mythology, the Norns in the Norse, the Wyrd Sisters in Saxon and the Moirai in Roman mythology all represent the Past, Present and Future, and the web of existence.

Tri Yin Yang

The triangle is one of the most obvious symbols of trinity, representing the three-fold nature of the universe; heaven, earth, underworld; father, mother and child; body, mind and spirit; childhood, adulthood and old age, etc. The upward pointing triangle represents life, fire, flame and heat, the masculine principle, and also the trinity of love, truth and wisdom. The down-ward pointing triangle is lunar, the feminine principle, the matrix, the natural world, it symbolizes the Great Mother as genetrix.

Hegel's theory of dialectical idealism is based on a law of threes, with his idea of thesis, antithesis and synthesis. From the bringing together of opposites comes something new. The Tri Yin Yang is a Taoist Sun Symbol which represents energy in its many forms, constantly changing, always balanced, but never still. From the One came the Two, from the Two came the Three, and from the Three grew all the forms of the Universe, according to Taoist philosophy.

Yantras too are often based around the shape of the triangle, the downward pointing triangle representing the Yoni (vagina) of the Goddess, the upward pointing triangle representing the Lingam (phallus) of the God. Hinduism also has the concept of the three Gunas; Sattva, Rajas and Tamas, the active, passive and mediating principles of the Universe.

Triads are distinguished from Trinities in that whereas Trinities are three-in-one, Triads are composed of distinct members, such as the astrological Sun-Moon-Venus, the Zoroastrian Fire-Light-Ether, and the Taoist Great Triad of Heaven-Man-Earth, the Divine, the Human and the Natural, with Man the mediator between the Celestial and the Terrestrial.

The Triad may be symbolized by the Trident, as well as the Triangle. In Taoism, the Tortoise represents the Triad, with the upper shell as the dome of the heavens, the lower shell as the waters and earth, and the central body as man. Many mythological systems have the Triad of Heaven, Earth and Underworld.

Symbols of the Quaternary

From four, the first solid figure is produced, we have solidity and stability, the first three-dimensional shape, the tetrahedron can be produced, which has four corners, and four planes. The square is a symbol of the element of earth, and represents stability and strength. It may be seen as a throne, the foundation on which the other elements may rest. (Compare the Buddhist Stupa, which is composed of a square base for earth, with a circle for the element of water on top of it, a triangle for fire on top of this, a crescent for air on top of this, and finally, a flame shape for spirit.)

Another symbol of quaternary is the equal armed cross, which represents the four elements, and is also a cosmic axis, a point of communication between heaven and earth. The cross may be seen to represent the Tree of Life. It is also a symbol of archetypal man, capable of infinite and harmonious expansion in both planes. The vertical line may represent the

The Structure of the Buddhist Stupa composed of the five elements

The Swastika formed by four women and their hair, from a piece of
Sumerian pottery c. 5000 BCE

celestial, spiritual and intellectual, whereas the horizontal may represent
the earthly, rational and passive. The whole cross can be seen to represent
the primordial androgyne, and as the descent of spirit into matter.

Crosses can also be solar symbols, and this can be seen particularly in the
symbol of the Swastika, and the Circled Cross. This represents the wheel of
the year, the cycles of change and the wheel of fortune. It also represents
the Magick Circle, with the four directions. The Hindu and Buddhist
Mandalas (Symbolic Universes) are based on circles divided into fours by
squares and crosses. The Swastika is a prehistoric, and universal symbol,
found extensively in Asia, pre-Columbian America, in Hittite art, and in
ancient European art. In Celtic art, it was associated with the Goddess
Bride or Brigit. It is a symbol of the Sun, and Dyaus the Vedic Sky God. It
can also be seen as the pole and the revolution of the stars around it. The
Swastika shows more movement than does the Cross, showing the four

directions, the four winds and creative force in motion.

The Pentagram

The Pentagram symbolizes the human microcosm, and upright can be seen to represent the human body standing with outstretched arms and legs. It is endless, drawn from a single line, and thus represents the perfection and infinity of the circle, and thus the whole. It also represents the four cardinal points, plus the fifth point, the centre; it represents the five elements, Earth, Air, Fire and Water, and Spirit. Upright it shows Spirit above matter, and is a symbol of the Goddess and Woman. Inverted it shows Matter above Spirit, or Spirit made manifest in Matter, and is a symbol of the Horned God and the Goat of Mendes. Five is the number of the Sacred Marriage, being composed of the feminine two, and the masculine three (the first two prime numbers, discounting one) and as four and one (the first two square numbers) it is matter (composed of the four elements) and Spirit (the Unity of the Divine). It also symbolizes the five senses. Each point of the Pentagram is assigned to an element. Elemental Pentagrams may be drawn by drawing the first stroke towards the point which represents the element, for invoking, and away from the point, starting at the point for banishing.

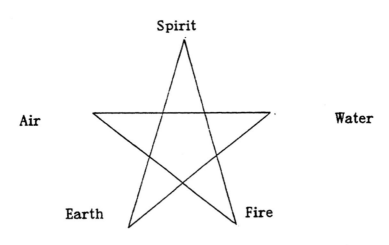

Invoking Pentagrams

Earth   Fire   Water   Air

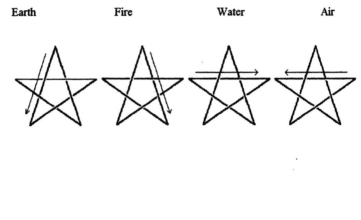

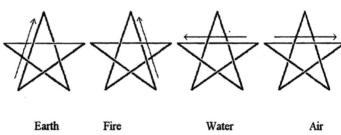

Earth   Fire   Water   Air

Banishing Pentagrams

Planetary Symbols

The symbols for the planets are made from three symbols - the circle, the crescent and the equal armed cross. Hence the planetary energy described by a symbol can be seen as a combination of the forces represented by the symbols which comprise it. The circle represents the self, the will, the spirit. The equal armed cross represents the physical, the material world and body. The crescent symbolises the ebb and flow, waxing (horns to the left) and waning (horns to the right), change, the unconscious and the emotions, the astral. When the crescent is horns upward it symbolises the horns of power and wisdom.

Sun	-	Circle with a dot (which can be considered a small circle) in the centre.	
Moon	-	Crescent.	
Mercury	-	Circle on an equal armed cross, with a crescent, horns up, on the top.	
Venus	-	Circle on an equal armed cross.	
Earth	-	Circle containing an equal armed cross.	
Mars	-	Circle with an equal armed cross (the arrow now used is a modification of this earlier form).	
Jupiter	-	Equal armed cross with a crescent on the left point of the cross.	
Saturn	-	Equal armed cross with a crescent coming off the bottom point of the cross.	
Uranus	-	Equal armed cross surmounting a small circle, with crescents facing outwards on the left and right arms of the cross.	

Neptune   -   Equal armed cross with a crescent horns up bisecting the upper arm of the cross.

Pluto   -   Equal armed cross surmounted by a crescent, horns up, with a circle in the crescent (but not touching).

Animal Symbols

Volumes could be written on the symbolism of animals, and there are a few books available on the subject, so we will not go into it in great depth here. Animals in general may represent Instinctual life, fertility, wildness and freedom. Different animals may represent different aspects of human nature, or reflect to us different aspects of the Divine. There are various animal deities in different cultures, and most deities have their own sacred animals. Friendship with animals, and the ability to communicate with them can symbolize a paradisiacal state, or return to a Golden Age.

In pathworkings or dreams, animals accompanying us can represent aspects of our own natures, which can help us if we tap in to them. Sometimes they can represent our wild and untamed sides which may seek expression, especially if we are the type of person who is usually very self-controlled and image conscious. In myths, animals (including mythical animals such as Dragons) which must be slain or tamed often represent the animal instincts being brought under control by the intellect and reason. However, there needs to be a balance between the intellect and the instinctual and intuitive sides, and our animal natures also need to be expressed, rather than destroyed. In the Craft and in Shamanic ritual, we sometimes use animal masks and body paint in order to "shape change" into our Power Animals, and gain access to instinctual and intuitive wisdom.

Animals such as lions, with prey in their jaws or paws can symbolize all-devouring death. Sometimes animals appear in solar- lunar pairs, such as the Lion and the Unicorn, depicting the two contending powers of the Universe. Some animals can be interchangeable as solar and lunar, such as the boar and bear. In some cultures (such as the Maoris) animals are considered to be the ancestral people.

There follows a list of common associations of some animal symbols:

Ant	Industriousness, orderliness and virtue (e.g. the fable of the ant and the grasshopper).
Antelope	A lunar animal associated with the Great Mother.
Ape/ Monkey	Mischief, Mimicry, cunning, benevolence.
Ass	Humility, patience, peace, stupidity, stubbornness, lewdness, fertility.
Baboon	Hailer of the Dawn in Ancient Egypt, sacred to Thoth and Hapi.
Badger	Supernatural powers, mischief, playfulness.
Bat	Darkness, obscurity, messenger, double nature (bird and mouse), happiness and good luck, longevity, peace, but also hypocrisy, melancholy, revenge and cunning. Wisdom.
Bee	Immortality, rebirth, industry, order, purity, the soul. Chastity, winged messengers between the worlds, secret wisdom from the other worlds, the Mother Goddess and Her Priestesses.
Birds	Transcendence, the soul, spirits of the air, ascent, communication with the Gods, freedom, far sight.
Boar	Solar and Lunar. Lust, gluttony, fertility, prophecy, magick, protection, hospitality.
Bull	Usually solar, generative force sacred to Sun and Sky Gods. Fecundity, male procreative strength, kingship. Can also be ridden by the Moon Goddess, and symbolize the taming of the masculine and animal nature.
Butterfly	The soul, immortality, transformation, rebirth, resurrection.
Cat	Stealth, desire, liberty, pleasure, magick, chthonic powers, lust, pride, vanity, the Moon.
Cock	A Solar bird, attributed to Sun Gods. Herald of the Dawn. Courage, vigilance, supremacy. Carnal passion and pride. Also associated with the underworld.
Cow	The Great Mother, Moon Goddesses in their nourishing aspect. The Cosmic Cow, the Power of the Earth. Plenty, procreation, maternal instinct, gentleness, nurturing.
Crane	Messenger of the Gods, communion, higher states of consciousness, wisdom and knowledge.

Crocodile	Devourer, liberation from the limitations of this world, guardian. Dual nature (land and water), conscious and unconscious. Fertility of the waters. Brutality, viciousness, deceit, treachery, hence "crocodile tears".
Crow	Messengers, death, wisdom, communication, the underworld.
Deer	Swiftness, fleetness of foot, nimbleness, meekness, gentleness, meditation, love, longevity, high rank, kingship, wealth.
Dog	Fidelity, faithfulness, loyalty, watchfulness, protection, guardian of the Underworld, the Wild Hunt.
Dolphin	Saviour and psychopomp, a guide to souls to the Underworld. Saver of the ship-wrecked, sea power, swiftness, intelligence, communication.
Dragon	Power of the Earth, the winged serpent, combining the power of the Serpent and the Bird as matter and Spirit. The life-giving waters, the breath of life. Supernatural power, magick, strength, wisdom, hidden knowledge, guardian of secrets and hidden treasures.
Eagle	Solar, associated with Sun and Sky Gods. Ascension, Inspiration, Victory, Pride, authority, power, royalty, the Spiritual Principle.
Elephant	Strength, fidelity, long memory, patience, wisdom, intelligence, kingly rank, power.
Fish	Symbol of the Great Goddess, the Waters of Life, but also phallic. Fecundity, procreation, life renewed and sustained.
Fox	Cunning, craftiness, guile, trickery, transformation, magick power, messenger, hiding.
Goat	Vitality, fertility, creative energy, abundance, virility, lust.
Goose	Guardian, watchfulness, the wind, the sun, war, inspiration, swiftness, good tidings, conjugal happiness, providence.
Hare	Lunar, rebirth, rejuvenation, resurrection, intuition, fertility, sacrifice, fire, madness, transformation.
Hawk	Solar, heavens, nobility, messenger, far-seeing, clarity, discrimination, inspiration, the soul.
Heron -	Vigilance and quietness. The power of the waters, and the Underworld. Associated with Herne. Tact and delicacy, renewal of life, transformation.

73

Horse	Both a life and a death symbol, lunar and solar. Intellect, wisdom, power, nobility. Raw energy, freedom and wildness. Divination, prophesy, the power of travel, the Sea, fertility, the power of the Land, Kingship and Queenship.
Jackal	Psychopomp, guide of souls between the worlds, associated with cemeteries.
Jaguar	Messenger of the forest spirits, power.
Kingfisher	Beauty, dignity, speed, calmness, serenity.
Leopard	Ferocity, aggression, intrepidity, the Great Watcher. Bravery, activity, swiftness.
Lion	Solar, heat of the Sun, splendour, power and majesty. Strength, courage, kingship, nobility.
Octopus	Related to the dragon, spider, and symbolism of the Spiral. The depths of the waters, the Unconscious.
Owl	Wisdom, darkness and death. Divination, solitude, mourning.
Python	Darkness, feminine, Earth Power, Wisdom.
Ram	Virility, creativity, the Sun. The renewed solar power of the Spring.
Raven	Prophecy, wisdom, war, the trickster, magick.
Serpent	Life, rebirth, resurrection, wisdom, passion, healing, poison, preserver and destroyer. Malice, venom, fertility.
Swan	Beauty, grace, faithfulness, fidelity, solitude, retreat, poetry, sincerity.
Tiger	Creator and destroyer, strength, ferociousness, power, royalty, anger, Earth Power.
Unicorn	Chastity, purity, dreams, virtue, strength, incorruptibility, magick, healing, freedom.
Whale	The power of the Deep Waters, regeneration, and the grave. Death and rebirth.
Wolf	Endurance, wisdom, family, courage, cunning, the wild, the Moon.
Wood - pecker	Prophecy, magick power, guardian of kings and trees. Herald of rain and storms (Rainbird).
Wren	King of the Birds, or "Little King". Represents Spirit, witchcraft, associated with the Oak King.

Practical Work

As stated at the beginning of this lesson, symbols always mean more than can be rationally explained, and thus the best way to understand symbols is to work with them through meditation and ritual. Try slowly walking or dancing the Spiral Dance, spiralling inwards and outwards again.

Meditate on the shapes that make up the planetary sigils, and see what associations come up for you, then put them together into each planetary sigil, and meditate on the different combinations of symbols.

Draw a large pentagram, and label the points with the stages of life; birth, initiation, consummation, repose and death. Contemplate the stages, going round the pentagram in order, starting with birth. Then, contemplate the connections between the different points (e.g. Death - Initiation). Have a note pad by you, and write down any thoughts and insights you may have.

The tools of the Craft may also be considered to be symbols. These will be covered in a later lesson, but for now, try holding each one and meditating with it.

Sit with a cauldron if you have one, or else visualize a large cauldron. Breathe deeply and feel the power of transformation. The cauldron represents the womb of the Goddess, and the Cauldron of Ceridwen, which holds the brew of inspiration, as well as the Cauldron of the Dagda which brings the dead back to life. Imagine yourself sinking into the cauldron, feel yourself going back into the womb of the Goddess. There, nourished by the Earth, absorb the wisdom of the Earth. Feel your power to gestate, to create, to give birth to new things, and to be reborn anew. Emerge from the cauldron with your new wisdom and power.

Chapter Eight

Rite of Dedication

You may feel now that you want to perform some sort of Rite to show your commitment and dedication to the path. This rite makes use of the work you have done so far, and is a Rite of the Four Elements. It is also a good beginning to setting up your own temple, as it involves producing objects for the four quarters, which can subsequently be placed at the four quarters in a temple or magickal working space. Spend some time meditating on each element, and treat this as a quest. You can either find natural objects that represent the elements (such as a feather for air, water from a sacred spring for water, holly for fire and a stone from a sacred site for earth), or you can be creative, and draw, paint, compose music, dance or song. Whichever you choose, it should be based on your meditations with the elements. This might take several weeks or even months, to complete.

When you have completed your task, set up an altar in a quiet space where you can work undisturbed, or go out into the woods or other natural space. Have some anointing oil and some incense. For anointing oil, Olive Oil (sacred to Minerva), Sweet Almond Oil (sacred to Venus) or Grapeseed Oil (sacred to Dionysos) may be used as a base. Avocado Oil, Safflower, Sunflower, wheatgerm, walnut, hazelnut or apricot kernel oil could also be used. Add an essential oil or a combination of essential oils which is pleasing to you, or choose oils corresponding to a specific purpose or God/dess form. Choose incense in the same way. Joss sticks or powdered incense may be used, although the latter is preferable, as it is more pure, and you can choose the ingredients. Have a candle, which may be white or coloured, plain or scented, as you prefer. Beeswax candles are good if you can get them.

The altar may be simple or fancy, depending on personal taste and what you have to hand. An indoor altar should have some natural object or symbol of nature on it, such as a stone (particularly a hag stone, which represents the Earth Goddess), flowers, feathers, corn, etc. An outdoor altar needs very little, as nature is all around you. You may also use water from a holy well, spring or the sea, to sprinkle around and purify the circle. If you use sea water, you do not need to consecrate salt separately. If you have spring water, have a separate bowl of salt. Perform this ritual skyclad if possible, or else wear a plain white robe.

Bless the salt and the water, visualizing them glowing with white light, then mix them together, and sprinkle the area to cleanse and purify it. Light the incense, and offer it to the Goddess and God. Cense the circle, visualizing a sphere of light around yourself. Invoke the elements at the four quarters, visualizing the elemental landscapes. Anoint and light the candle, dedicating it to the Goddess and God. Call upon the Goddess and God. A simple sentence will do, but use poems, flowery invocations, etc. if you prefer. Or chant or intone their names (whichever names you prefer to call them by), or do it silently, and just feel their presence. Perform a simple self-blessing:

> Say "*Bless me Mother, for I am Thy child*"

> Anoint both feet with oil and say "*Blessed be my feet that have brought me in these ways*".

> Anoint both knees and say "*Blessed be my knees which kneel at the sacred altar*".

> Anoint womb area or phallus saying "*Blessed be my womb/phallus without which the world would not be*".

> Anoint breast/s saying "*Blessed be my breast/s formed in strength and beauty*".

> Anoint lips saying "*Blessed be my lips which utter the sacred names. May I speak words of wisdom, and know the virtue of silence*".

Now pick up your offerings, and offer them to the quarters in turn, starting with offering your air object to the East. Tell the elementals that you have created the objects as a sign of your commitment and dedication to the path, and ask for their blessings to help you on your way.

Thank the Goddess, God and Elements, and dismiss the circle.

A couple may perform this rite together, and in this case, they will anoint each other's bodies, and bless each other. The opening sequence, to the end of the self-blessing may also be used from now on at the start of any magickal or mystical work that you do, whether it be simple meditation, visualization, pathworking, devotional practices, spell-casting, healing, inner guide work, or simply asking the Lady and Lord for guidance on the path.

Chapter Nine

Dreamwork - Analysis, Lucid Dreaming & the Dream Diary

From a magickal perspective, sleeping and dreaming are extremely important, taking as they do one third of our lives, and giving us access to our unconscious mind without needing to try. This chapter deals with analysis of dreams, and ways to help promote lucid dreaming. Being able to dream lucidly is very valuable, and some people are fortunate enough to dream lucidly naturally without needing training. Most people require training for consistency, however, and the techniques can take years to really master and use with a degree of regular success. Hence the information in this lesson is for long term work, and a concise background to the main work done on dreaming together with a reading list are included.

1. Analysis & Background

We make the assumption that there is only one reality, the world of wakefulness. Yet we spend a third of our lives asleep. We can survive without food and even water for longer than we can survive without sleep, although sleep is a biologically dangerous condition, as we are immobile and unconscious. The sleeping brain is very active, especially in dreaming. Dreams are the interface between the external world and the unconscious. Some sleep researchers have said that the principal function of sleep is to allow us to dream.

The Dreamer

Dreams may be described as the method by which the unconscious mind sifts and sorts experiences. During sleep, while the conscious mind is inactive, the unconscious processes a vast jumble of material, new facts, situations, past experiences, unsolved worries, fears and desires. It draws up emotions from the deepest recesses of the mind and memory and takes into account all the new information which the conscious mind has received. Then in its own unique style, it presents a visual and emotional image to us - a dream.

Sigmund Freud described the interpretation of dreams as "*the royal road to a knowledge of the unconscious*". Freud also compares dreams to the "*creation of insanity*", but points out that they are also compatible with complete health in waking life. To Freud all dreams represent wish fulfilment, and have a manifest content, i.e. the actual experienced dream, and a latent content, i.e. the deeper motives that the dream disguised.

In Freud's theory of personality, the personality is composed of the id, ego and superego. The id is the basic instinctual unsocialised side of the personality, and contains Eros and Thanatos, the sex and death urges. The superego is the socialised and conditioned part of the personality, often referred to as the "*internalised parent*" or as the conscience. The ego is the thinking and balancing side of the personality, operating with the "*reality principle*" which balances the "*pleasure principle*" of the id with the inhibitions of the superego. Our fundamental urges are suppressed, and only in dreams, when the conscious mind is not on top of the situation, can these suppressed urges have a chance to come out. Because these urges are totally controlled by the conscious mind they can only be let out at night in disguise, using strange combinations of events and a secret symbolism to get past the guard of the superego.

According to Freud most dreams are about sex. Even if dreams do not appear to be about sex at all, Freud maintained that under the surface they invariably are. If a dream merely seems to pick out an event from yesterday, or a recollection from the past, Freud thought that the instant was chosen because it linked up specifically with the urge being expressed in the dream. The unconscious uses a wide variety of normal everyday objects, to stand for sexual things. In his "*Interpretation of Dreams*", Freud says "*all elongated objects such as sticks, tree trunks and umbrellas may stand for the male organ, as well as long, sharp weapons such as knives, daggers and pikes. Boxes, cases, chests, cupboards and ovens represent the uterus, and also hollow objects, ships and vessels of all kinds. Rooms in dreams are usually women."* With this means of disguise, the superego is not alarmed and so allows us to sleep peacefully. The watchful part of the mind does not see through to the basic urge which is being expressed in a wish-fulfilling dream. By allowing these urges to be satisfied in dreams, we avoid the stress we might otherwise have through suppression of the urges.

It must be remembered that Freud lived in Victorian times, when sexuality was more repressed than it is now, and would be more likely to come out in dreams as it was not acceptable in conscious life. A main problem with Freud's theory is that many dreams do not appear to be wish-fulfilling. Later in his life, Freud too began to change his mind about this part of his work. He managed to keep his theory that all dreams are wish-fulfilling by saying that when the sexual (or aggressive) nature of a dream becomes too obvious, the superego steps in and changes it, putting in an ending to the dream that is acceptable to the superego. This explains dreams with bad endings.

According to Freud any one image in a dream can mean a number of things. He called this characteristic condensation. Almost as important as the condensing process in dreams is displacement, when the real concern of the dream is pushed into a small image. The images are skirting round the issue in order to avoid presenting a direct head-on picture of the problem, which may alarm the superego, and turn into a nightmare. Freud argued that this displacing device occurs when you are doing something wrong. for example, if one is attracted to someone who one thinks one should not be, one may have a sexual dream involving a complete stranger.

Many psychologists have disagreed with Freud as to the nature of dreams. Alfred Adler, although agreeing that dreams were wish-fulfilling, rejected Freud's claims as to the sexual nature of dreams. Adler developed *"individual psychology"*, the study of people as goal-oriented individuals seeking personal perfection and wholeness. Adler's most significant theory was that everyone has difficulty in relating their own self-centred satisfaction and happiness to a contentment derived with fitting into a group or society, and his idea of *"will to power"* has led to wide acceptance of the "*superiority*" and "*inferiority*" complexes. Through dreams Adler thought a person could better understand her aggressive impulses and desire for fulfilment. She sees what she really thinks of herself. To Adler, everyone has an equally strong need to dominate, due to some basic inadequacy or lack which is unconsciously recognised at an early age. The rest of life is spent trying to compensate for it. If one dreams of losing or being afraid of something, this may express the inner inferiority complex. However a dream such as this would be a result of the superego stepping in to keep the power urge under control.

Freud and Adler's ideas are based on a sort of unending warfare between basic drives and the need to keep them under control. Letting these drives out in wish-fulfilling dreams is like letting the steam out of a kettle: if they are permanently bottled up a nervous breakdown would result. Dreams, therefore, provide a convenient escape valve.

Carl Jung disagreed quite forcibly with Freud and Adler over this idea of dreams. Jung considered that the basic urge is a spiritual one whereas to Freud dreams were used to get back to the cause of a problem, usually an event in childhood. Jung believed that dreams could be inspirational and can encourage people to do bigger and better things in waking life. Freud's theory seemed to relate all parts of a dream to something inside the dreamer's own make-up. To Jung this did not account for the pictures which appeared to come from a fantasy world outside the dreamer's everyday view of life.

Jung believed that all people have two parts to the unconscious. Freud had looked at the part which hides personal instinctive urges away. Jung now identified a part which is filled with strange primitive imaginings which are common to everyone, everywhere. He called this the collective unconscious. Many civilizations in all parts of the world have created the same pictures and images in dreams, fairy stories and myths, and they are readily understood by people from another country or from another age.

Jung suggests that everyone has a natural tendency to think in these globally familiar ways. These universal ideas were termed archetypes. These are so old and general that we do not need to ask what they mean when they come into the mind's eye: we simply recognise them deep down. These archetypes are the language of dreams. Jung also believed that the archetypes as they appear in dreams are reflections of ourselves. If a dream contains people that we recognise, Jung maintains that they are here because they reflect part of yourself. In this way all Jungian archetypes are simply representations of the human condition. They are made concrete in the world of dreams.

Archetypes occur again and again in the same form. These are termed symbols. People can dream using symbols without being at all clear of the archetypal meaning at the time.

One of Jung's most interesting ideas was perhaps his idea that we all have an opposite side to our personalities. In men this appears as the female figure called the anima, in women as a male the animus. In men the anima is embodied in all the poets ideas of an inspiring muse, who gives them the power to write beautiful things. In religion she may appear as the Christian figure of Mary or the Mother Goddess. Men in women's dreams and women in men's dreams often represent the animus and anima respectively.

Two other parts of the self can appear in dreams in a symbolic form. The first is the persona, which Jung explains as the character or image you project outwardly. This is not the real self. In dreams the persona, rather than the real self, often takes part. The second part of the self is the archetype of the shadow. This is the dark side of the personality which is not seen very often. It is the secret part of us which we feel less able to bring out into real life. Robert Louis Stevenson's "Doctor Jekyll and Mister Hyde" is a story which came to the author during a dream.

Although at first sight the theories of Freud and Jung seem to be poles apart, they are not basically very contradictory. What matters most, is that if a dream points out a problem area, exactly which way you take it will depend on your personal circumstances. Jung advised his students to learn everything they could about symbolism, and then to forget it all before interpreting a dream. This is because the symbolism of dreams is often of a personal nature.

Dreams can be problem solving in that over a period of time dreams may concentrate on a specific area, trying out one possible solution after another, until one dream comes to a realisation of the issue. Friedrick Kekule's was probably the most well known dream discovery. He hit upon the shape of the so-called benzene ring - the atomic structure of the benzene molecule - with the dream image of a snake swallowing its tail. Jung used various methods of getting at the meanings of dreams. One method was free association in which the individual would relax and say all the things that came into the mind when thinking of the dream image. This is a form of trance work, and having a tape recorder with a microphone (particularly voice activated) can be very useful for such work. Another is to "carry on dreaming the dream", in which you take series' of dreams and see how seemingly different dreams make up a complete story, which may get to the root of a problem.

Dreams have then, been variously described as wish-fulfilling, stress relieving, problem solving and inspirational.

According to Gestalt psychotherapy, dreams are:

1] an attempt to "complete a gestalt" (i.e. to complete an unfinished cycle),

2] projections,

3] retroflections,
i.e. dreams are a substitute reality where we do things to avoid doing them in the real world.

However, what are valued most highly in gestalt dreamwork, are the meanings which you discover for yourself through your own phenomenological exploration. Dreams may have multiple meanings and use metaphor. Gestalt uses four main phases in dreamwork:

1] Awareness - telling of content of dream. In general, telling the dream as if it is happening in the present makes it more alive. This raises the feelings of awareness around the dream and gives an overall focus. It is easier to do this type of dreamwork with another person who can help you to become more aware of the process of telling the dream and help you explore your feelings about telling the dream.

2] Finding the focus of energy - when telling the dream which part

85

of it do you feel the most energy for, which parts seem most significant to you? We could also ask what were the most insignificant parts of the dream, i.e. what is glossed over? By concentrating on the part of the dream that feels most important at the time you have established a place to start your dreamwork.

3] Taking the exploration further. You may use experiments such as becoming a part of the dream, e.g. choosing one character from the dream and being them. Working with other people can be very useful as they can act out different characters in the dream. The dream should be acted out as realistically and dramatically as possible using props, getting into the body posture and using the same words used by characters in the dream. You may shift from playing one dream character to another and enact conversations between them, at first saying only what they said in the dream and exploring how it feels to be each character, and then experimenting by developing the dialogue to see where it leads. Getting other people to play the dream characters whilst you step outside the dream and look at it from outside can give you a new perspective. You may walk round the dream and literally examine it from all angles. Bodywork can also be used as an experiment by exaggerating the body language of characters within the dream and seeing what emotions or feelings this brings up.

4] Ending of the work. When one has reached a satisfactory conclusion to one part of the dreamwork, we can rest then come back and recycle working on another part of the dream.

The Gestalt method of acting out dreams is a technique of psychodrama. Videos of psychodrama are more valuable than books, as it is something that needs to be seen to be appreciated.

2. Lucid Dreaming

What is lucid dreaming? When you are dreaming, and become aware that you are dreaming, you are in a very powerful state of consciousness - you are not awake or totally asleep, but have the benefits of both states. Because you are still dreaming, you have access to the unconscious mind and all its power and experience, and because you are lucid and conscious of your activity, you can harness the power and memories and use them to develop yourself beneficially. Also, when you are dreaming, you can do things you cannot do in the waking state, so you can experience flying, transforming into an animal, becoming a galaxy or anything else in a very vivid and "real" way.

The information presented below is all to encourage lucid dreaming and make it an everyday part of life, but as has been stated previously, it can take a long time to do effectively and be consistent.

One simple measure to help lucid dreaming is to drink skullcap tea. Put 2 teaspoons of dried skullcap herb in a cup of boiling hot water, and leave to infuse for at least 30 minutes. Drink warm before retiring to bed. Adding an equal measure of lobelia can also enhance the effect further.

A commonly used method to develop your dreaming from unconscious to lucid is to try and see your hands. Before going to sleep each night concentrate on your hands, and after a while you will see them in a dream. At that point you may become lucid. Sometimes it can take several occurrences of this over a period of time before you do become lucid on seeing your hands. Once you are lucid, you know it, and you can change the events of a dream, or sit and watch the dream go by, and study your dream processes. This technique takes a lot of time and patience, but does eventually pay off.

A technique which can produce results more quickly is to use a telesmatic image (i.e. an image of a figure which embodies the qualities you desire) as a focus. Before going to sleep spend about 10-15 minutes gazing at the image you have drawn (we recommend the Greek God of Dreams, Hypnos). Regular use of this by itself may produce lucid dream states, or you may see the figure in your dreams, in which case if you can go through him like an astral doorway you will become very lucid!

The image of Hypnos given below is the one which arose when working with him. You may find it helpful to concentrate on this image for 15 minutes each night before going to sleep. Hypnos was one of the children of the primal Goddess Nox (Night), who contained all within Herself. She gave birth from Herself to Her son Aether, and joined with Him to give birth to Hypnos (Sleep), Thanatos (Death), Eris (Discord), Lissa (Madness) and Hekate, and various others according to differing versions of the myth. Hypnos guards the twin doorways of ivory and horn, which represent "false" and "true" sleep. "False" sleep could be interpreted as sleep without dreams, or unremembered dreams, and "true" sleep as lucid dreaming, where you experience in a more "true" (conscious) fashion.

Hypnos Image

Hypnos can be seen as a figure robed in black. The only visible parts of him are his hands and his face. His hands are black, with silver stars shining on them, and his face, visible in the cowl of the robe, is a swirl of all the colours, with his golden eyes the only constant in the swirl of colours. From his left hand shoots a ray of brown light, and from his right hand a ray of white light. The rays of light represent false and true sleep respectively. Draw up the image, edged in gold on a black background works well. When you gaze at the image, make sure you have a minimal quantity of light in the room, one candle only.

Obviously, as has already been stated, lucid dreaming is a technique that can take years to perfect. For some it is easier than others, but for everybody, it is a good technique to be able to harness. Magick can be performed as effectively in a lucid dream state as it can in the waking.

3. Dream Diaries

Keeping a diary by your bed and writing down any dreams you remember on waking is a must when doing dream work. You may not remember very many at first, but with time you will probably remember more. Try and be as detailed as possible in your description of your dreams, and after a while you may notice patterns emerging in your dreams. These may not be initially obvious, and sequences may be split in time periods, occurring only every few months say. Analysis of your dreams from the diary will help you feel what your dreams are saying. Listening to your unconscious self is one of the most important things you can do to harness your energies, so do persevere.

Recommended Reading

Freud, Sigmund   - *The Interpretation of Dreams*
Jung, C.G.   - *Man and His Symbols*
                       - *The Archetypes in the Collective Unconscious*
                        (Vol IX Part 1 of The Collected Works)
                       - *The Practice of Psychotherapy*
                        (Vol XVO of The Collected Works)

Dream dictionaries are of limited value, as the symbols may have different meanings to you, and they have a tendency to be simplistic and not very magickal in their approach.

Chapter Ten

Incenses & Oils - Creation and Uses

1. Incense

Incense has been used for many purposes in the long history of religion and spiritual growth. In ancient Egypt, olibanum (frankincense) was burned at sun rise, myrrh at noon and kyphi at sunset to celebrate the passing of the Sun God Ra through the journey of the day. Kyphi is perhaps the most famous incense, and different sources ascribe various ingredients, but the one thing all the sources agree on is that it has sixteen ingredients.

In India, the Dainyal (Sibyl or seeress) would sit over a fire burning pure cedar, with a cloth over her head, and go into trance and prophesy. A similar technique was probably used at Delphi, where the famous Oracle would be surrounded with, and inhale the smoke. It has been suggested that datura leaves were placed in the incense, and this would certainly induce altered states. Other leaves like laurel have also been suggested as being used in the smoke. The Christian church, of course, has long used incense in its rituals (usually very resin based, especially frankincense and myrrh). Most cultures use incense for one reason or another, and in shamanic cultures incense is used for smudging (ritual purification).

The common uses for incense are as follows:

> 1] Devotion - to indicate your love for, and link with, a Deity,
> energy, etc.

2] Focus - to clear the mind and help focus it towards the desired state of consciousness.

3] Stimulant - to give vigour and drive, to encourage you by its olfactory effect on you.

4] Intoxicant - psychoactive plants can help alter the state of consciousness, however they are certainly better in very small doses, where they can aid activities such as divination and skrying. Large amounts can be at least distracting and at most dangerous.

5] Rank - incense has often been burned to indicate the position and status of individuals (e.g. the Roman Catholic Church burns better incense for an archbishop than a priest).

6] Materialisation - in the days of grimoire magick, some plants (especially Dittany of Crete) were placed in incenses to make them produce lots of smoke, the theory being that large amounts of smoke give summoned spirits enough form to manifest in.

7] Healing - many herbs can have a healing effect when burned, a fact shamans around the world have been aware of for a very long time.

8] Relaxation - making incense can be very relaxing and therapeutic, a very good centring and grounding exercise.

Making incense is not just about mixing some ingredients together. Preparation is needed, and there are a few simple techniques which help make incenses smell pleasant and not like bonfires.

Before making an incense, you may wish to check the day and hour you are going to make it in. In the cases of planetary incenses, the days and hours are easily calculable, for deities there may be particular dates sacred to them that can be used. Festival days and moon phases are also obvious times to make incense. You may wish to check lists of correspondences, but these vary, and the ingredients going in need in no way be connected with the end result, as you are trying to achieve a composite smell (or layers of smell). Getting into the feeling of the deity or energy you wish to represent through the incense is also important, and can provide inspiration towards ideas for ingredients. Before actually making the incense, we would recommend doing a grounding exercise, and being well relaxed, and of course casting a circle. Chanting whilst mixing the incense with appropriate chants is also good to help empower the incense. Incense making should be as sacred as possible - the more energy you put into the making, the more you will benefit in the using.

There are a few incense ingredients which come from animals, and should not be used due to the cruel ways in which they are gained - these include ambergris (from the bellies of sperm whales), civet (from the civet cat) and musk (from the musk deer). Synthetic versions of these may be found, some of which are close in smell and far better to use, unless you do not want to use synthetic scents, in which case stick to all the other ingredients available.

There are a variety of ingredients which can be used in making incense, which are:

1] Resins and gums

2] Herbs

3] Barks and roots and woods

4] Flowers

5] Oils and tinctures

6] Wine and alcohol

7] Minerals

8] Drugs

9] Blood, bodily fluids, bones, etc

1]   An incense should be at least half, if not more, resin and gum. Resins and gums need to be well ground up, and form the base to which you add other ingredients.

2]   Herbs are one of the most common ingredients, and should be added in reasonable but not excessive amounts. If you pick the herbs yourself, again, you are adding to the potency of the incense. Herbs should also be very well ground, otherwise they can tend to make the incense very smoky and bonfire-like.

3] Barks and roots and woods should be used in the same manner as herbs, a coffee grinder or blender can be very helpful for working with woods.

4] Flowers may be dried or added fresh, but again in small well crushed quantities.

5] Oils and tinctures should be added dropwise, and are usually added last, or towards the end of the process.

6] Wine and alcohol are used as binding agents, and if the wine is home-made, better still.

7] Minerals in crushed form are rarely used any more, and were added in renaissance incenses for their perceived magickal qualities rather than to produce a smell.

8] Drugs should be added very cautiously, in tiny doses, and can be used well in divination incenses.

9] Blood, bodily fluids and crushed bones have been used in incenses in the past, e.g. in a Kali incense, but are rarely added to incenses.

When mixing an incense remember to grind it very well, and that it may take time. The recipe given for kyphi requires at least six months to prepare. By taking time and adding ingredients over a period you can create layers of smell in an incense, so that as it burns it changes the scent it gives off. Also oils will be bound better in the incense and not burn off too quickly leaving a less pleasant smell.

We usually add one or two oils to the resins and herbs, and leave for a lunar month, then add more over a period of time (powders, such as bay or pine, can also be added later). It is worth getting a nice censer, or if not using a bowl filled with soil or sand, to burn the charcoal blocks for your incense on.

A handy hint to remember when using sticky substances, such as storax, gum elemi, balsams and honey, is to heat them on a teaspoon over a candle, and add when liquid to the ingredients. mixing it in quickly before it becomes more sticky and viscous again.

Correspondences

Note these attributions may differ from those you are familiar with, and are not absolutes. Being from various sources they give what may appear to be contrasting attributions, experience will soon determine what may be used when.

Acacia (Gum Arabic)	Sun, Fire
Agrimony	Jupiter, Water
Almond	Moon, Pluto, Venus, Air, Spirit
Aloes	Jupiter, Mars, Moon, Fire, Water
Amber	Sun, Uranus, Earth, Fire
Ambergris	Sun, Pluto, Air, Water, Spirit
Aniseed	Mercury, Saturn, Sun
Asafoetida	Saturn
Ash	Jupiter, Moon, Saturn, Sun, Venus, Air, Water
Balm	Jupiter
Basil	Mars, Mercury, Fire
Bay	Jupiter, Mars, Sun
Benzoin	Mars, Sun, Venus, Air, Fire, Water
Bergamot	Sun
Camomile	Moon
Camphor	Moon, Saturn, Air, Water
Cassia	Mercury, Sun
Cedar	Jupiter, Moon, Earth, Water
Cinnamon	Mercury, Sun, Fire
Civet	Mars, Saturn, Venus, Fire, Water
Clover	Venus
Cloves	Jupiter, Mercury, Sun
Copal	Jupiter, Water
Cypress	Pluto, Saturn, Earth
Damiana	Moon, Venus, Air

Dammar	Mercury, Air
Dill	Mercury
Dittany of Crete	Earth
Dragons Blood	Mars, Fire
Elemi	Venus, Air, Water
Eucalyptus	Jupiter
Eyebright	Mars, Sun, Mercury, Venus
Frankincense	Sun, Fire
Galangal	Jupiter, Mars, Sun
Galbanum	Jupiter, Air
Geranium	Mars, Venus
Ginger	Mars, Sun, Fire
Hazel	Mercury, Moon, Water
Heliotrope	Sun, Fire
Honeysuckle	Moon
Hyssop	Jupiter
Iris	Moon, Venus
Ivy	Saturn, Earth
Jasmine	Jupiter, Moon, Venus, Air, Water
Juniper	Jupiter, Moon, Sun, Fire
Karaya	Moon, Water
Lavender	Jupiter, Venus
Lemon	Mercury, Water
Lilac	Jupiter, Mercury
Lily	Moon, Water
Lime	Jupiter, Mercury
Lotus	Moon, Water
Marjoram	Jupiter, Mercury, Pluto, Sun, Venus
Mastic	Jupiter, Mercury, Sun, Air, Fire
Melissa	Jupiter, Venus
Mugwort	Venus
Musk	Mars, Neptune, Saturn, Sun, Earth, Fire
Myrrh	Saturn, Sun, Earth, Fire, Water
Myrtle	Moon, Venus
Narcissus	Pluto, Water
Neroli	Sun
Niaouli	Mars, Fire
Nutmeg	Mercury, Venus
Oak	Jupiter, Sun, Saturn, Earth

Opoponax	Mars, Fire
Orange	Sun, Fire
Orris	Sun
Patchouli	Sun, Earth
Pennyroyal	Venus
Peppermint	Mercury, Moon, Venus, Air
Pine	Saturn, Earth
Poppy	Moon, Saturn, Sun, Fire
Primrose	Venus
Rose	Moon, Venus
Rosemary	Moon, Sun
Rue	Mars, Saturn, Sun, Fire
Saffron	Jupiter, Sun, Venus
Sage	Jupiter
Sandalwood	Mercury, Moon, Air
Saunderswood (Red Sandal)	Moon, Venus, Water
Storax	Mercury, Saturn, Sun
Thyme	Venus
Tragacanth	Mercury, Air
Valerian	Venus, Earth
Vervain	Mercury
Vetivert	Saturn, Earth
Violet	Venus, Air
Willow	Moon, Saturn, Water
Wintergreen	Moon, Saturn, Earth
Witchazel	Moon
Ylang Ylang	Moon, Neptune, Venus, Water

Below are a two example incense recipes to demonstrate the principles described:-

Summer Solstice
2 tablespoons Olibanum
2 tablespoons Sandalwood Powder
1 tablespoon dried Rose Petals
$^1/_2$ tablespoon Vervain

4 drops Rose Oil
10 drops Honeysuckle Oil

12 drops Orange Oil

Grind the olibanum to a fine powdery texture, then add in the rose petals (which you have collected and dried previously) and grind these into small pieces mixed in. Add the orange oil and mix again, then add the vervain and mix. Add the rose oil and mix in, then the sandalwood powder, and finally the honeysuckle oil.

This incense is one that you would make in one session, preferably on or around the time of the solstice. The adding of solids and oils in sequence helps to layer the smell and produce a smell that alters through burning. When making sabbat incenses it is worth making a reasonable quantity, it can then be used in future years, and is a good thread of continuity through the work you do through the turnings of the wheel of the year (as is the making of wine with fruits gathered from the wilds). Before making the incense you would cast the circle, and it is good to chant an appropriate chant whilst grinding and mixing to add more energy into the incense.

Greenwood

$^1/_2$ teaspoon dried Bay Leaves

$^1/_2$ teaspoon Benzoin 3 drops Bitter Almond Oil

1 teaspoon dried Crushed Ivy 1 teaspoon Dill Oil

1 teaspoon dried Elder Flowers

1 drop Jasmine Oil

$^1/_4$ teaspoon Lotus Oil

1 teaspoon Mastic 1 teaspoon dried Mistletoe

1 teaspoon Myrrh

1 teaspoon Olibanum

12 drops Patchouli Oil

1 teaspoon Pine Needles

1 teaspoon Pine Resin

1 teaspoon dried Raspberry Leaves

1 teaspoon Red Wine

1 teaspoon White Willow Bark

$^1/_2$ teaspoon Witchazel Oil

Grind together the olibanum and myrrh, then add and grind in the crushed ivy and elder flowers. Add the witchazel oil and the almond oil and mix in.

Add the mastic and grind in. Leave for a lunar month in a cool dark place. Add in and grind the pine needles and mistletoe, followed by the patchouli oil and dill oil. Leave for another lunar month in a cool dark place. Add and grind the raspberry leaves and mastic, followed by the white willow bark. Add the red wine to bind the incense ingredients together. Leave for another lunar month in a cool dark place. Add the pine resin and mix in, then add the jasmine oil. Add and grind the benzoin, bay leaves and the lotus oil. Leave for another lunar month in a cool dark place. The incense is now ready.

As you can see this incense takes four months to make, so it is worth noting when in the lunar cycle you start, and putting on your calender or in your diary the subsequent dates to ensure you don't forget. On burning you should find this incense produces several different smells during the period of time it burns for. Not many incenses have this many ingredients in them, nor do they need to, but it is fun to experiment and see what effects you can produce, sometimes you can really surprise yourself. To this end, it is important you note down your recipes as you concoct, so you are able to duplicate those great incense smells you come up, and modify the ones that don't quite turn out how you wanted or hoped.

2. Oils

Oils may be used in a number of beneficial ways to aid in spiritual growth and to promote happiness and the balanced state of being that promotes growth. They are easily obtainable now from most health food shops, as well as specialist occult shops. Most oils bought in ethnic or hippy shops are not pure essential oils, but are tinctures (brands such as Spiritual Sky for instance). These are diluted and not so effective, although cheaper. We would recommend using pure essential oils for magickal work.

A few drops of oil may be added to a bath to get the benefits of its effect, and they may also be burned in an oil burner to cense a room and generate the desired feelings, and to anoint oneself. Making a personal oil in a base oil (preferably one such as almond or olive) using the oils which represent the energies you wish to attract or work with is also a good way to use them. If you can, they may also be used in a base oil (such as grapeseed) for massage (the basis of aromatherapy). As the oils are absorbed through your skin and into your body, so their energy will start to work and have its effect. It is worth experimenting with oils and seeing which you like and why, and incorporating them into your practices and life.

Remember the oils are absorbed through your skin, and so pure essential oils should not be anointed onto the skin in any quantity as they may burn.

The list given below is not comprehensive, but covers many of the basic oils which are often used and are of benefit.

Aniseed

Pimpinella Anisum

Properties

> Sweet and slightly pungent.
> Warm and dry.
> Works on stomach, intestines and spleen (heart and lungs).

Therapeutic Uses

1. Moves and relaxes vital energy (Chi) and nerves in the stomach and intestines. Good for digestive stagnation, bloating, nausea and colic. Antispasmodic for stomach. Relaxes Chi in the chest, good for palpitations or wheezing when combined with poor digestion. Clears dampness and mucous in the intestines and is especially good for nervous vomiting. Gastric relaxant, good for travel sickness (although ginger is better).

2. Tonifies Chi and can help chronic fatigue due to weak digestion. Used for insufficient breast milk. Strengthens eyesight. Can be used for asthma and lung phlegm due to digestive weakness and stagnation.

Psychological Action

Makes one feel "like a satisfied baby"

Magickal Uses

Works on ajna (third eye) chakra.
Associated with the Moon, Cancer Apollo, Mars (the God rather than the planet) and The Chariot (tarot).

Good for a lack of fulfilment and craving for love. Enchants and warmly reassures. Aphrodisiac - added to wedding cakes and moon cakes. Protects against disturbing dreams. Harmonizes physical and spiritual bodies. Good for Skrying, helps to develop visualization, intuition and psychic skills.

Basil
Ocimum basillicum

Properties

> Sweet, slightly pungent and bitter.
> Cool with warming potential.
> Dry.

Therapeutic Uses

1. Reinforces the yang energy and uplifts the mind. Strengthens the nerves, the brain, the eyes and the adrenal glands. Used for nervous debility, depression caused by deficient yang (lack of confidence etc.). Good for numbness, paralysis, epilepsy and adrenal weakness. Tonifies the Chi. Antispasmodic (first stimulates, then lessens cerebro-spinal activity). Tonic, especially for the nerves and adrenal cortex.

2. Regulates Chi and disperses stagnant cold, especially in the stomach. Good for gastric spasms, nausea and vomiting, intestinal putrefaction, flatulence and colic. Good for migraine and headaches and for tight muscles. Strengthens and calms nerves - harmonizing and regulating. Restorative and stimulant.

Calming, stomachic, intestinal antiseptic, emmenagogue (promotes menstruation). Use when menstruation is scanty due to stagnant cold in the uterus. (The tongue will be slightly blue when there is stagnant cold). Good for lower backache, gout and impotence. Helps one to wake up in the morning. Avoid during pregnancy.

Psychological Action

Aids clear thinking and decision-making. Good for people who constantly wonder whether or not they have done the right thing, especially those who punish themselves with indigestion and stress. It gives a feeling of "what the hell" and helps you to let go of your worries.

Magickal Uses

Associated with Mars, Scorpio, Fire, Krishna, Vishnu and Death (tarot), as well as salamanders and dragons.

Gives spiritual courage and determination; sharpness. Steadies one for Initiation and against fears associated with spiritual growth and the unknown.

Used to attract money.

A funeral herb - planted upon graves and used in Rituals of the Dead as an incense.

A fertility herb. Lightens the atmosphere in the sick room and rids the heavy feeling left by negative or controlling people.

Benzoin
Styrax benzoin

Properties

> Sweet and pungent.
> Warm.
> Dry.

Therapeutic Uses

1. Tonifies the yang energy and Chi especially of the spleen and lungs. Dries cold phlegm-damp and restrains infection. Strengthens the nerves.

Good for lethargy, pallor, feelings of cold, loose stools, lack of appetite, borborygmous, flatulence, and generalized retention of dampness and phlegm. Good for lack of vitality and confidence, pallor, shortness of breath, wheezing, catarrhal conditions and productive coughs. Good for lung infections of a cold nature, sore throats and voice loss. Helps stomach cold with griping pain in the epigastrium, and for nervous debility and worry in deficient conditions/constitutions.

2. Disperses stagnant cold and arrests discharges. Used for genito-urinary infections involving cold and/or dampness; cystitis, gonorrhoea. Antiseptic, vulnerary (heals wounds), carminative, expectorant, diuretic and stimulant. Good for leucorrhea involving a whitish or clear mucous discharge. Promotes urination when there is an obstruction due to cold. Good for skin conditions of a cold-damp nature. Helps chilblains.

Psychological Action

Assists concentration and calms the mind. Stimulates the conscious mind. "Cures" selfishness and teaches give and take.

Magickal Uses

Associated with Mars, Venus (the planet and the Goddess), Mercury, Air, Scorpio, Mut, and the Seven of Cups (illusionary success).

Relates to throat chakra. Communication, creativity, synthesis of ideas with symbols. Dreamwork, work with the unconscious mind. Used for spiritual journeys and transitions. Removes blockages to growth. Assists concentration and meditation, instilling calm. Grounding - brings one down to reality.

Inhaled to revitalize the physical body, and this can be used to aid in building a greater reserve of magickal power. Can be used in heavy magickal operations, such as rituals of protection of property.

Camphor

Cinnamomium camphora

Properties

Cold and hot, depending on the person it is applied to.
Bitter, aromatic.

Therapeutic Uses

1. Strong heart stimulant, may be used in cases of heart failure due to extreme shock, heart disease or resulting from infectious fevers (eg. typhoid, pneumonia). It is effective against the pneumococcus bacteria, and is a stimulant of the circulation. Used when there is coldness of the whole body (excessive yin/deficient yang), and will produce a strong yang reaction. Any cold conditions - colds and flu, cold stomach etc. can be helped by camphor. Because of its dual action, it can also be used in cases of excess yang/deficient yin, such as burning fevers, inflammation, burns etc. Good for dressing wounds and ulcers. Good for oily acne. Numbs the peripheral nerve ends when applied externally. Antispasmodic for digestive system, carminative and laxative, stimulating the flow of digestive juices. Good for both constipation and diarrhoea, vomiting, colic, flatulence and cholera. Best used only for more serious complaints.

2. Stimulating to heart and respiration, raises low blood pressure. Good for when these functions are weakened due to serious depression, serious illnesses, or after an operation. Inhibits mycobacterium tuberculosis. Good inhalant for coughs and colds, and where there are breathing difficulties. Relieves irritation of the sexual organs, and is a powerful diuretic. Balancing effect on yin and yang, and so is good for conditions where the balance of yin and yang is upset, such as heart failure, shock, hysteria, excesses of heat or cold, infection. Stimulates languid depression and sedates hysteria. Good for psychosomatic and nervous diseases. Camphor will often work where milder remedies have not been effective, or when a gentle shock is required to stimulate recovery.

Avoid yellow camphor on the skin. Use only white camphor.

Psychological Action

Balances yin and yang, and so good for mental/emotional agitation as well as debility and depression. Purifies negative emotions.

Magickal Uses

Associated with the Moon, Saturn, Cancer, Water and The Chariot (Tarot). Sacred to Shiva and Vishnu.

Affects svadhistana and ajna chakras. When sniffed with proper visualization, camphor is good for self purification.

Cedarwood

Cedrus atlantica

Properties

> Sweet and pungent.
> Warm and dry.

Therapeutic Uses

1. Tonifies Chi and yang of spleen and kidneys. Clears dampness and promotes urination. Fortifies and soothes the nerves, uplifts the mind. Used for lethargy, nervous debility, anxiety and depression due to spleen and/or kidney deficiency, lack of confidence and worry. Good for chronic dampness, oedema and congestion due to spleen and kidney deficiency. Cellulitis, arteriosclerosis, hyperaemia (blood congestion) of the kidneys due to kidney deficiency.

2. Creates astriction, clears dampness, restrains infection and putrefaction, reduces inflammation. Used for genito-urinary discharges and infections, cystitis, chronic urethritis, pyelitis (inflammation of the renal pelvis), vaginitis, gonorrhoea. Respiratory infections involving lung phlegm-damp: bronchitis. Diarrhoea. Neuritis. Helps to heal wounds and promote tissue repair. Creates astriction. Cell regeneration. Astringent, diuretic,

expectorant, sedative. May help peptic ulcers, ulcerative colitis, circulatory ulcers, and the degeneration of cartilage and ligaments. Benefits and clears the skin, relieves itching. Used for oily skin conditions, acne and dry eczema. Can help seborrhoea of the scalp causing oily hair and dandruff.

Avoid during pregnancy.

Psychological Action

Good for children (and adults) who lack affirmation and approval. Preserver of one's identity. Useful for people in foreign environments, to help prevent feelings of isolation.

Magickal Uses

Associated with Mercury, Earth, Jupiter (God and planet), Sun, Wotan, Ishtar, Zeus, Fire and the four of cups (luxury, dissatisfaction with material success - boredom and estrangement). Used in the Fire of Azrael.

Works on the base chakra, helps us to earth, to develop our root.

A religious herb - used in incense since ancient times. Recommended for the consecration of magickal wands. Related to Wotan, "the fury of the night", who acts as a spiritual guide, initiating us into the realm of the unconscious. Also relates to journeys into unknown countries and territories, meeting with strangers, instability and being at war with current opinion.

Chamomile
Anthemis Nobilis

Properties

> Bitter, slightly sweet.
> Cool, neutral.

Therapeutic Uses

1. Smooths the flow of Chi and calms the nerves and mind. Eases pain and promotes rest. Very good for emotional tension and Chi stagnation affecting intestines, leading to colic and flatulence. Also good for gastric and intestinal ulcers. Useful in menopause/dysmenorrhoea (menstrual pain) and PMT. Very good for insomnia. Good for migraine. Good for gastric nerves and indigestion, particularly of the type which is worse when a person becomes tense or angry.

2. Good for low leucocyte count (white blood cells). Reduces inflammation and clears toxins. Benefits the skin, good for inflammation of eyes, mouth, throat and gums. Good for dermatitis and eczema, especially when itching. Helps burns and stings and neuritis.

Psychological Action

Calms the mind. Good for insomnia. Good for alleviating anger, especially when it is through feeling unsupported and not respected. Gives a feeling of support and nurturing.

Magickal Uses

Associated with the Sun and Cernunnos. Used to invoke Sun Gods.

A herb of protection, guaranteeing success of particular endeavours.

Stimulates the physical body. Purifies negative energies and encourages dreams of prophecy and divination.

Helps in maintaining celibacy and to make use of the sexual energy in other directions. Good for periods of purification.

A visionary herb.

Cinnamon

Cinnamomum zeylandicum

Properties

Pungent, sweet and astringent.
Hot.
Dry.

Therapeutic Uses

1. Tonifies the Yang energy and dispels cold, strengthens the heart and lungs. Used for general debility, heart Chi deficiency and poor circulation. Good for fatigue, palpitations, cold extremities and lack of joy. Stimulant (circulatory and cardiac) and antiseptic. Good for lung Chi deficiency, lack of vitality, shortness of breath and melancholy. Kills Eberth's bacillus (typhoid) at a dose of 1 part in 300. Antispasmodic and vermifuge.

2. Disperses wind-cold. Used for external wind cold with chilliness, aching and exhaustion (colds and flu due to exposure to cold, wet, windy weather). Good for rheumatic pain and neuralgia due to wind-damp. Tonifies and invigorates spleen and kidney yang, warms and moves Chi. Promotes menstruation. Good for lethargy caused by spleen or kidney Yang deficiency. Good for lack of appetite, nausea, abdominal pain and swelling, diarrhoea and impotence. Used for stagnation of Cold in the uterus causing amenorrheoa or delayed menstruation and cramping. Creates astriction, dries dampness and stops bleeding. Used for haemorrhage arising from deficiency, bleeding from the lungs or sinuses, intestinal bleeding, urinary or uterine bleeding, menorrhagia (excessive periods) and metrorrhagia (uterine haemorrhage occurring outside menstrual periods. Leucorrhea due to spleen Yang deficiency, chronic diarrhoea and dysentery. Restrains infections and kills parasites. Used for chronic infectious diseases, intestinal parasites and lice.

Avoid during pregnancy, and in cases of high blood pressure.

Psychological Action

Increases concentration and aids communication.
Magickal Uses

Associated with Uranus, the Sun, Fire and The Lovers (Tarot).

Works on manipura chakra. Gives energy and feelings of power and will.

A visionary herb, used in prophecy. A herb of immortality - brings an understanding of eternity.

Used in China to purify temples. Mixed with other herbs to make love potions. Protects from the jealousy and envy of others.

Inhalation with appropriate visualization can strengthen the physical body. It energizes, and provides us with extra energy which can be used in magickal rituals.

It increases our ability to tap into our psychic minds.

A herb of riches - use it with appropriate visualization to attract wealth.

Eucalyptus
Eucalyptus globulus

Properties

> Pungent and bitter.
> Warm with strong cooling potential.
> Dry with moistening potential.

Therapeutic Uses

1. Disperses wind, reduces fever, clears phlegm and breaks up painful obstruction. Used for colds and flu involving aches and pains, fever, headache, sore throat, and for nasal and head congestion, mucous discharge, sinusitis, congestive headache, ear infections, intermittent fevers, malaria, cholera, typhus, eruptive fevers, measles, chickenpox, scarlet fever, acute rheumatism and neuralgia due to wind-damp

obstruction.

General antiseptic in particular of the respiratory and urinary tracts. Balsamic, soothes coughs, expectorant.

2. Circulates lung Chi, clears phlegm, used for lung Phlegm Heat or cold, coughs, acute or chronic bronchitis, emphysema, asthma, sore throats. Lung Phlegm-Dryness (combined with other oils), such as harsh cough, scanty and viscous sputum, wheezing. Lung Yin deficiency, pulmonary TB, allergic asthma. Tonifies the Defensive Chi, fights infection and eliminates toxins. Used for lung and throat infections, pneumonia, diphtheria, lung abscess, genito-urinary infections, purulent discharges, cloudy urination, cervicitis, cystitis, colibacillosis, pyelitis, nephritis, parasitic skin infections, gangrene. Used for Fire-Poison conditions, such as septicaemia. Used for cancer - made into a pessary it has been used for cancer of the uterus and rectum. Useful for painful obstructions due to Wind-Damp-Cold, muscular pain, neuralgia, rheumatoid arthritis. Good for lethargy, heavy limbs, Dampness and Phlegm causing poor concentration. Diabetes, hyperglycaemia. Stimulates tissue repair and benefits the skin. Used for cervical erosion, skin eruptions, herpes, wounds, ulcers, abscesses. Clears parasites and repels insects. Used for roundworm, pinworm, lice.

Psychological Action

Tonic effect. Aids clear thinking.

Magickal Uses

Associated with Mercury and the Moon, Air and Water.

Used for healing, purification and protection. Eucalyptus leaves can be used to stuff healing poppets, or can be carried to maintain good health. Use to clear a place of negative energy, particularly that which is a result of fighting or arguments. Use in protective rituals, to protect from negative influences and ill health.

Frankincense (Olibanum)

Boswellia Carterii

Properties

Sweet and Pungent.
Slightly warm with cooling potential.
Dry.

Therapeutic Uses

1. Circulates the Chi of the lungs and loosens constraint. Relaxes and strengthens the nerves, eases tension. Used for nervous tension, nervous exhaustion, irritability, restlessness and insomnia. Good for tightness in the chest and constricted breathing. Used for stagnation of Chi in the stomach, dyspepsia with sour belching, stagnation of Chi in the uterus, pre-menstrual tension, dysmenorrhoea and excessive menstruation.

2. Dries Dampness and Phlegm, promotes expectoration, arrests discharges and restrains infection. Used for Lung Phlegm-Damp with cough, wheezing and shortness of breath, lung infections such as bronchitis, Phlegm-Damp in the sinuses, laryngitis, scrofula, leucorrhea, genito-urinary infections, cystitis, nephritis, gonorrhoea. Creates astriction and stops bleeding, helps to heal wounds. Used for pulmonary and uterine haemorrhage, menorrhagia, indolent wounds, ulcers and carbuncles. Benefits and tonifies the skin. Used for mature skin conditions. Helps prevent wrinkles.

Psychological Action

Good for when one is feeling overwhelmed by mental impressions (Compare with lavender which is good for when overwhelmed by emotional impressions). Good for agitation in a mental sense, due to overthinking. Good for people who worry a lot. Calms the mind and brings mental and spiritual wholeness. Good for indecisiveness, as it calms the mind enough so that you can concentrate on one thing. Helps create a meditative state.

Magickal Uses

Associated with the Sun, Fire, Leo, Adonis, Apollo, Bael, Janus, Ra and the Sixes in the Tarot (definite accomplishment and carrying out of a matter).

Frankincense has a long history as a religious herb. Used by the Babylonians to honour Bael. Has been used to invoke both the male aspect of the universe (Apollo, Adonis) and the female aspect (Demeter and various moon Goddesses), calling upon Her heart and bringing Her compassion.

Heightens awareness of spiritual realms, expands consciousness and focuses the mind for meditation.

Works on the throat chakra, but may also be useful for the third eye and heart chakras.

A herb of protection, purifying the soul and spirit and keeping one safe in the astral realm. Restrains excessive pride and self-indulgence (good for Leos). Teaches the value of discipline. Used to consecrate magickal wands and tools of control.

Geranium
Pelaronium odorantissimum

Properties

> Sweet.
> Astringent.
> Slightly pungent and slightly bitter.
> Cool with warming potential.
> Dry with moistening potential.

Therapeutic Uses

1. Tonifies Spleen Chi, creates astriction, clears Dampness, Phlegm and

excessive secretions, stops bleeding and promotes tissue repair. Used for lethargy, abdominal pain and swelling, lack of appetite, loose stools, chronic diarrhoea caused by Spleen Chi deficiency. Good for Damp-Cold and Damp- Heat conditions in the genitourinary system, such as leucorrhea and cystitis. Good for excessive milk production, engorged breasts. Use when there is excessive sweating. Good for haemorrhage, epistaxis (nose bleeds), haemoptysis (bleeding from lungs), menorrhagia (excessive menstrual bleeding), metrorrhagia (irregular periods), internal injury or rupture. Good for wounds, ulcers, abscesses. Astringent and antidiabetic.

2. Clears heat and restrains infection. Used for inflammatory and infectious conditions of the digestive tract, such as gastro-enteritis, typhoid and cholera. Good for Phlegm-Fire and Empty Heat in the stomach, acid reflux, constant hunger, burning pain in the epigastrium, gastralgia, stomach ulcers. Good for Empty Heat in the Lungs, malar flush, low grade fever, night sweats, thirst, haemoptysis, TB. Antiseptic (intestinal), analgesic, and good for cystitis and thrush. Good for lethargy, facial neuralgia, tonsillitis, glossitis, thrush. Tonifies Kidney Chi and Yin, promotes urination, supports the reproductive system, uplifts and relaxes the mind. Used for Kidney Chi deficiency causing fatigue, oedema, adrenal weakness and depression. Yin deficiency causing night sweats, anxiety, nervous tension, menopausal symptoms. Good for blood deficiency in the uterus, involving Liver-Blood deficiency, causing hyposecretion of oestrogen, amenorrhoea, sterility. Hyposecretion of androgens, good for when there is a lack of male hormones. Helps to dissipate stones and tumours. Used for urinary stones and gall stones. May help cancerous tumours, especially those of the stomach and uterus. Good for the skin, especially dry skin conditions, such as eczema, dermatitis, itching, psoriasis, burns, boils, herpes and shingles. Good for parasitic skin conditions such as ringworm and periculosis.

Psychological Action

Very good to help one dream ones dreams. Good for people bogged down with responsibilities and commitments, who don't allow themselves time to relax and be imaginative. Helps one to find ones sexuality. Calms and refreshes the mind and body.

112

Magickal Uses

Associated with Venus, Aries and Libra and the element of Water. Sacred to Ganesha.

The oil may be worn by those who seek sexual fulfilment and the joy of Eros. Represents sexual maturity.

Happiness and protection. Helps us get in control of our lives. Use with appropriate visualization and ritual to guard the home, to spread peace, and to dissolve depression.

Ginger
Zingiber officinale

Properties

> Pungent, slightly sweet.
> Hot, dry.

Therapeutic Uses

1. Disperses Wind-Cold, circulates Lung Chi, expels Phlegm and eases pain. Used for External Wind-Cold, Lung Phlegm-Cold, painful obstructions caused by Wind- Damp, acute intermittent neuralgia. Good for headaches due to sinus congestion.

2. Tonifies Yang energy, warms and invigorates the stomach, spleen and intestines. Moves Chi and blood. Good for stagnation, Yang deficiency, cold limbs, lack of appetite, abdominal swelling, diarrhoea, gastro-enteritis. Good for Stomach-Cold, (dull epigastric pain which feels better with hot food and drink). Good for dyspepsia, flatulence, nausea, vomiting, travel sickness, angina pectoris, cold hands and feet, and for bruises. Moves Chi and blood in the uterus, good for Cold Stagnation, amenorrhoea, cramping pain, dull red clots, pain during ovulation. Good for a feeling of cold and pain in the lower back, and for impotence. May be used with caution in early pregnancy for morning sickness, mixed with

chamomile and peppermint. Strengthens the immune system, tonifies Defensive Chi and fights infection. Antidotes poisons - good for food poisoning. May help with bacterial infections such as tonsillitis and laryngitis.

Psychological Action

Promotes courage, confidence and aggression. Can heighten sexual arousal.

Magickal Uses

Associated with Mars, Sun, Fire and the Moon.

Works on solar plexus chakra, gives energy, vitality, confidence, courage, will and bioelectric energy.

Magickal energy, physical energy, sex, love, money, courage.

Hyssop
Hyssopus Officinalis

Properties

> Pungent and bitter.
> Hot and dry.

Therapeutic Uses

1. Primary action is on the lungs, it warms and tonifies the lungs, and clears Lung Phlegm Cold, relieves wheezing. Indicated for chronic bronchitis or bronchial asthma. It is the best oil to move lung Chi indicated in spasmodic asthma, whooping cough and hayfever.

2. Dispels Wind Cold and Wind Damp obstruction causing acute neuralgia. Raises blood pressure. Restores the nerves and alleviates melancholy. Warms the spleen and the intestines. Promotes menstruation especially when there is Damp Cold.

Cleanses the kidneys and clears urinary stones. It can be used for ear, nose and throat infections. Also good for bruises and toothache. Opens up the chest.

Because it contains very small quantities of ketones it is toxic in high doses and contra-indicated in epilepsy.

Psychological Action

Clears the head and strengthens mental processes.

Magickal Uses

Associated with Jupiter, Mars, Fire, Cancer and the Kings (in the Tarot).

A herb of protection, it keeps negative energies out of the home. Used to purify temples and to cleanse the aura.

Heightens spirituality prior to religious rituals of all kinds.

Jasmine
Jasminum Officinali

Properties

> Sweet and slightly pungent.
> Warm/cool.
> Moist.

Therapeutic Uses

1. Restores, warms and relaxes uro-genital organs. Clears Dampness, stops discharge. Regulates menstruation. Good gentle oil for kidney Yang deficiency, causing lack of sexual desire. Very good for impotence and frigidity, leucorrhea and painful labour. Promotes breast milk (galactogogue). Restoring, relaxing and astringent.

2. Uplifting and warming as well as having a calming and cooling aspect. Uplifting to the heart, raises Yang to the heart, good for lack of joy. Calming and cooling to the heart, good for anxiety. Balancing action, harmonising between sex and emotion. Restoring to the nerves. Soothing to the lungs, especially when they are dry. Especially good for cough and hoarseness of the throat. Astringent action makes it good for diarrhoea. Moistens the skin, good for most dry skin diseases.

Psychological Action

Good for playfulness, brings inner feeling of relaxed playfulness. Good for when someone's chest has become tightened because the were always told they wrong when they were a child. Stimulates the creative mind and original thought. Dispels depression, quiets nerves and stifles worries about tomorrow.

Magickal Uses

Associated with the Moon, Water, Diana and Hekate.

Works on the heart chakra, love, peace, spirituality. Often associated with Goddesses of compassion such as Kwan-Yin, Tara. Enhances feelings of love and uplifts the heart, good for use in love rituals and sex magick. A fertility herb, relates to the manifesting ability of the Great Mother.

Gives psychic protection, aids in sleep and psychic dreams.

Juniper
Juniperus Communis

Properties

> Pungent, bitter, slightly sweet.
> Hot and dry.

Therapeutic Uses

1. Tonifies the Yang. Warms and moves the blood. Very good for feelings of weakness and cold limbs. Very strengthening and moving, like Rosemary. Very good to break through obstruction from Wind and Damp (rheumatism). Very good for menstrual cramps due to cold (when there is a slightly bluish tongue) and for painful labour. Use in moderation.

2. Strengthens the kidneys and clears dampness. Very good for the uro-genitary organs, especially uro-genitary problems due to Yang deficiency, such as leucorrhea, oedema, cold cystitis and lower back ache. Warms the stomach and spleen, good for poor appetite, abdominal swelling and hypo-acidity. Supportive for diabetes and intestinal fermentation. Good to clear toxins, cleanse the kidneys and promote urination. Very good for things such as rheumatism and gout as well as hard deposits such as urinary stones and arterial sclerosis. Sometimes used for skin problems, especially for oily skin and rashes due to toxicity in the blood (for someone with a pale tongue rather than a red tongue). Antiseptic, tonic, stomachic, diuretic and uricolitic (clears out uric acid). Emmenagogue, depurative and invigorating.

Avoid during pregnancy and in cases of high blood pressure.

Psychological Action

Gives the necessary energy to give up unhealthy habits and start good ones. Good for those who tend to retreat (loners).

Magickal Uses

Associated with Mars, Sun, Fire and Aries. Sacred to Inanna/Ishtar, Hermes and Mercury. Used in the Fire of Azrael.

In Europe branches of juniper were smouldered and carried around fields and farms to guard animals and crops.

Protection, purification and healing. Wards off negativity and purges negative energies from a personal place. Protects against theft, attack by wild animals, ghosts and sickness. Added to love potions and the berries are carried to increase male potency. Juniper helps the psychic powers and breaks hexes and curses and is said to drive off snakes.

Lavender
Lavendula officinalis

Properties

Bitter, slightly pungent, slightly sweet.
Cool and dry.

Therapeutic Uses

1. Clears Heat and excessive Yang. Very good for Liver Fire and Heart Fire (agitation), as it is quite calming to the heart, and the best anti-inflammatory. Good for eye inflammation, conjunctivitis, infections, respiratory infections, ear, nose and throat infections, urogenital infections with discharge, intestinal infections and all skin conditions, such as eczema. Antiseptic. Good for wounds and ulcers, and especially good for burns (soak cotton wool in water, add a few drops of lavender and apply to burn). Also indicated for high blood pressure.

2. Moves liver Chi and calms the mind. Anti-spasmodic, calmative, sedative. Very cleansing for the liver. Good for nausea, constipation, irritability, migraine. Cholagogue, analgesic. Good for pain, smoothes the flow of Chi. Calming for the nerves, good for anxiety and spasms. Good for colic, whooping cough and insomnia. Clears Damp Heat, anti-rheumatic. Has a particularly gynaecological action. Good for pre-menstrual tension and menstrual pain. Quite good to use in childbirth during labour. Clears Wind Heat, especially with fever, headache and restlessness. Clears External Wind Damp, good for acute neuralgia.

Psychological Action

Calms the mind. Good for feeling overwhelmed emotionally and emotional oversensitivity. Good for retroflective headaches. Steadies and strengthens the conscious mind, calms stormy emotions by bringing them under control. Promotes inner calm and peace of mind. Dispels depression.

Magickal Uses

Associated with Mercury, Moon, Saturn, Venus, Air, Virgo and Hekate.

Works on the heart chakra, long associated with spiritual love, helps to change our attitudes towards love. Purifying, used in Solomon's Sprinkler. Used to bless homes and attract wealth. For health, love, peace and can be used to maintain celibacy.

The scent is said to calm untamed lions and tigers. Used in love spells. Protects against cruel treatment from your spouse. Carried to see ghosts and worn to protect against the evil eye. Used to promote longevity.

Myrrh
Commiphora Myrra

Properties

> Bitter, pungent and slightly sweet.
> Warm.
> Dry.

Therapeutic Uses

1. Fights infection and putrefaction, clears inflammation and heals wounds. Used for bacterial and fungal infections of the mouth, the gums, the throat and the genital system. Good for stomatitis, gingivitis, vaginitis and candidiasis. Used for putrefying conditions such as gangrene, chronic wounds and ulcers. Expels intestinal worms.

2. Tonifies the Yang, strengthens the Spleen, clears Dampness and creates astriction. Moves the blood. Used for spleen Yang deficiency, lethargy, cold limbs, diarrhoea, Damp Cold causing abdominal swelling or leucorrhea. Used for uterine and pulmonary haemorrhage. Good for poor circulation due to Yang deficiency, and for congealed blood. Tonifies and soothes the lungs and clears Phlegm. Good for hoarseness and loss of voice, and for TB. Disperses Wind-Cold and dispels eruptions, used for

remittent and eruptive fevers. Moves blood in the uterus and promotes childbirth. Used for amenorrhoea involving obstruction due to Damp-Cold, difficult, exhausting labour, and expelling the placenta. Antiseptic, antiphlogistic, tonic, astringent, vulnerary, stomachic, carminative, expectorant and uterine.

Avoid during pregnancy.

Psychological Action

Expands awareness, calms fears and halts questions regarding the future.

Magickal Uses

Associated with Jupiter, Saturn, the Moon, Cybele, Demeter, Hekate, Ra, Rhea, Water, the Queens (the Mother, bringer forth of material force) and Threes (realization of action) in the Tarot. Adonis, born from the myrrh tree.

Protection, healing, exorcism, spirituality, meditation.

Promotes understanding of the currents of energy that flow through a ritual. Brings communion with higher consciousness and greater awareness of any spiritual experience. Brings peace to the situation intended by the practitioner.

A funeral herb, used in the embalming process by the Egyptians, and burned at funeral ceremonies. Eases personal sorrow, has an aspect of peace and solitude about it.

Burned as an incense, Myrrh purifies the area, lifts the vibrations and creates peace. However, it is rarely burned alone, usually in conjunction with frankincense or other resins. Myrrh increases the power of any other incense to which it is added.

Myrrh is used in healing incenses and sachets, for divination, and for consecrating amulets and talismans.

Pine

Pinus sylvestrus

Properties

Pungent and bitter.
Warm.
Dry.

Therapeutic Uses

1. Tonifies Lung Chi and Yang, clears Phlegm and opens the chest. Used for Yang deficiency of the lungs and kidneys, (asthma), lung phlegm damp, (sinus congestion), and stuck phlegm. Pine has a moving quality good for phlegm in the chest.

2. Tonifies Kidney Yang and stimulates the adrenal glands. Used for Kidney Yang deficiency, lethargy, lack of appetite, impotence, adrenal weakness. Good for Damp Cold, painful obstructions due to Kidney Yang deficiency, rheumatism and gout. Tonifies the Defensive Chi, restrains infection and kills parasites. Reduced inflammation and heals wounds.

Used for respiratory infections, bronchitis, pneumonia, urogenital infections, cystitis, prostatitis, scabies and lice, cholecystitis and wounds. Moves Liver and Stomach Chi, warms the abdomen. Used for epigastric bloating, nausea and intestinal pains in those with weak Lung and Kidney Yang.

Psychological Action

Good for guilt. Helps to open you up and throw off responsibility.

Magickal Uses

Associated with Mars, Air, Cybele, Pan, Venus, Attis, Dionysus, Astarte, Silvanus and Poseidon.

A herb of immortality. Protection, physical and magickal energy, money, healing, purification. A counter-magick herb for repelling negative energy and returning it to its source, used in exorcism. Gives magickal protection on the waters.

Rosemary
Rosemarinus officinalis

Properties

> Pungent, slightly bitter.
> Hot and dry.

Therapeutic Uses

1. Excellent for weakness, promotes blood circulation, good for cold extremities, and for low blood pressure. General Yang tonic, works especially on Heart Yang, Kidney Yang and Spleen Yang. Strengthens the blood, strengthens nerves and brain. Very good for memory loss, paralysis and certain kinds of headache, particularly "brain fag". Strengthens the adrenal glands. Good for anaemia.

2. Clears dampness and phlegm, especially in the lungs and intestines. Also clears the head and sinuses, including when there is a sinus headache. Good for Lung Phlegm Cold and for Lung and Kidney Yang deficiency with wheezing. Good for chronic asthma, whooping cough, as well as Damp Cold in the intestines with swelling and gurgling. Helps coldness in the back, causing backache, poor sexual energy and Damp Cold in the uterus casing cramping. Dispels Wind Cold, especially with aching as well as Damp Cold rheumatism. Moves Liver Chi, clears stagnation and promotes urination. Very cleansing, good for Liver Chi stagnation in a cold person. Good for alternating constipation and diarrhoea. The cleansing action makes it good for rheumatism and for poor eyesight. Very good also for high blood cholesterol and chronic migraine. Tonifies Defensive Chi and immune system. Can also be used for wounds and for body lice.

Psychological Action

Good for people who are depressed through lack of confidence and authority. Good for emotions trapped in the chest which make a person's energy all go up to the chest so that they become over-emotional, lacking any physical grounding. Allows the person to be focused and concentrate on action, giving confidence and strength. Good for people who have recoiled from the physical when they have become very emotional and oversensitive. Good for people who never really get their careers off the ground due to being too wrapped up in relationships. Fortifies courage.

Magickal Uses

Associated with the Sun, Fire, Vesta and Magna Pales (Goddess of shepherds).

Remembrance and also used as a funeral herb mixed into the incense for the ceremony and cast upon the coffin. Enhances loving remembrance and reminds us of our mortality. Brings to mind loved ones who have passed beyond, but also connected with longevity and youth.

Enhances the sacredness of any occasion and is used to purify the magick circle. A herb of protection against negative energy, placed beneath the bed to protect from bad dreams, used for exorcism. Mixed with juniper to make in incense for places of illness, to purify the air. Worn before battles to fortify courage. Used for love and lust.

Sandalwood
Santalum album

Properties

Cool and dry.

Therapeutic Uses

1. Anti-infectious, especially good to clear Heat and Dampness, particularly from the intestines. Very good for chronic diarrhoea (astringent), dysentery and cholitis.

2. Works on the uro-genital system, good for genital discharges and

infections such as cystitis and gonorrhoea, as well as lung conditions, such as bronchitis and laryngitis. Also good for Damp Heat in the skin. Good for acne and boils. Mildly tonifies the spleen, calms the heart, cools and refreshes the mind.

Psychological Action

Good for meditation as it calms the mind and allows space for the spiritual aspects of the self to work. Good for restlessness and irritability due to Damp Heat. Good for overthinking, depression and worry.

Magickal Uses

Associates with Mercury, Jupiter, Moon, Water, Hermes and Venus, The Empress in the Tarot (the universal womb in which all manifestation is gestated, the Great Mother of ideas, Mother Nature).

Used in all types of meditation and divination (one of the three ingredients in the Fire of Azrael). Induces spirituality and the peace of religious union. Aphrodisiac, stimulates sexual activity, used in sex magick and Tantra. Works on base chakra.

A funeral herb in the Orient, used in embalming the body and carrying the soul to the next life.

Sandalwood is said to bring success, fulfilment of wishes.

Ylang Ylang
Canaga Odorata

Properties

> Cool/neutral.
> Sweet.

Therapeutic Uses

1. Calms the heart and soothes the liver, good for palpitations, irregular

heartbeat and high blood pressure. Very good for nervous tension and insomnia. Also a euphoric and aphrodisiac. Good for depression, impotence and frigidity.

2. Calms breathing, good for hyperhoea. Good for intestinal infections, especially with fever, and is used in skin care to soothe the skin as well as being indicated for oily skin.

Psychological Action

Helps us to get in touch with our physical/sensual side. Calms the nerves and calms anger and all negative emotional states.

Magickal Uses

Associated with Venus, Moon and Water.

Works on second chakra. Aphrodisiac, used in sex magick and love spells. Brings peace.

Base Oils

Sweet Almond

Softens and nourishes the skin. Associated with Mercury, Air, Attis, Venus and Aphrodite. Symbolic of female beauty. Used for money, prosperity and wisdom magick.

Grapeseed

Light base oil for general massage. Associated with Moon, Water, Dionysus, Pan. Used for fertility magick.

For incense ingredients and essential oils, we would recommend

Baldwins The Medical Herbalists, 179 Walworth Road, London

Chapter Eleven -

Crystals and Power Objects

1. Crystals

Crystals are undoubtedly one of, if not the most, effective energy-matrix for manipulating and storing currents of energy efficiently. Below are listed some of the magickal uses crystals may be put to.

1. As a Magickal Tool: is one of the most obvious uses of a crystal. These days there is a plethora of crystal suppliers eager to sell crystals carved into wands and disks (and increasingly, small chalices) which make excellent magickal weapons, although crystal daggers are not available for the obvious financial and practical reasons of production (though they could be commissioned it you feel rich!). Disks of 'potato slice" cut with a diamond saw are extremely common and very cheap, particularly Agates, and make excellent Pentacles. One should check with these to make sure they have not been stained and are their original colours (and often with necklaces, a sure check is if a coloured crystal necklace, e.g. Rose Quartz, has every crystal the same colour, you know it is stained, as there is always discrepancy among the colour shades of a type of crystal). The crystal the weapon is made from should preferably be relevant to what the weapon symbolizes, e.g. Orange Calcite for a Fire Wand, Obsidian for a Saturn Wand, etc.

2. As a Talisman: is another obvious use dating back to antiquity (e.g. Orpheus carrying a piece of Agate as a protective talisman when he descended into the underworld). Crystals can be found to suit any attribution you may require for a talisman, and are easy to charge and carry - indeed simply carrying a crystal and playing with it while you are doing things will help it build up charge and also focus your unconscious mind on the energy of the talisman and help move you accordingly. Amber is a very good general storer of charge as a non-specific talisman, and Jet is hard to beat as a protective absorption talisman (though it needs regular cleaning, of course), which may explain the witches` traditional love affair with these particular crystals.

3. Skrying: can be practised with any natural crystal (not synthetic crystals such as Zircon), although Obsidian is by far the best, followed by the Quartz family and the Beryls (especially Aquamarine and Emerald). Obsidian is the traditional skrying stone and the name of the Mayan God, Tezcatlipoca, translates as "mirror that smokes", indicating the smoking or misting of the Obsidian Mirror used by the magicians (whose patron he is as God of Magicians) before the images start to form. It was the Elizabethan astrologer and mathematician John Dee who made famous the use of crystals for skrying with his work using an Obsidian ball and mirror, which developed into the Enochian system of magick, a system based on the Angelic language received through his seer Edward Kelly.

4. As an Astral Doorway: is a very rewarding way to use crystals if the right stones are used. By "right" we mean stones that feel right rather than a specific type, although we would recommend Rose Quartz as a starter, as it has one of the most harmonic vibrations (and produces interesting results). One should project through the crystal in the same way you would with a tarot card or mandala. Carrying the crystal around bodily for a period of time prior to using it as a doorway makes projection a lot easier for many people.

5. For Dream Work: produces interesting results. We recommend Quartz as the basic crystal for dreamwork, although others such as Moonstone, Opal, Tourmaline and the Beryls produce stunning results when one has more experience. The Quartz should be held in your dominant hand during sleep, and stored in silk under your pillow during your absence. If the Quartz is used for a period of time, and kept well charged, you will soon find it aids lucid dreaming greatly (seeing your Quartz in the dreamstate shows you are on the right track). Any experiences should be written down immediately upon waking in a dream diary or suchlike.

6. Healing: is one of the most effective ways to use crystals, and by far the most-hyped. There are various ways to use crystals for healing, including placing crystals on the chakras, using a crystal wand as a focus, placing crystals around the body, etc, or a combination of these techniques. A technique we use is working up the chakras in turn, vibrating a mantra which resonates at the correct frequency for each as we focus the energies (through a Quartz wand) and balance the chakra energies, e.g. IAO for the Manipura (Solar Plexus) Chakra (experience teaches which mantras are appropriate for a particular pitch of voice, they should be short with no more than three syllables - a willing guinea pig will soon enable you to find suitable personal mantras). We find Gold light is the best medium for healing, as it is projected from the Anahata (Heart) Chakra which is the centre of balance via the nadis (energy channels) to the healing chakras in the hands. The Quartz family are generally used as healing foci - Quartz, Rose Quartz, Citrine, Amethyst and Smoky Quartz. Jet is a very good absorber of negative charge, but it must be cleaned regularly otherwise it will end up having a negative effect on the recipient/bearer.

7. As a Spirit Trap: is a traditional use ignored by the New Agers. "Demons" or whatever one calls negative energies (well, negative to humans anyway) may be compelled or tricked into crystals, or if the entity is physically detectable, a crystal should be plunged into its form to contain it (not using your hand as you do not want physical contact with the entity). We consider Amethyst and Quartz are the best stones for this purpose, and shapewise, spherical stones are the best to use as spirit traps, not having any corners or edges for an entity to manifest in.

8. As a Personal Focus: to disperse or focus energies in times of extreme emotional duress or for concentration is a very important use of crystals - a sort of crystal "worry-bead" which becomes charged with your energy. We must stress here that we use the term "disperse" to describe translating the energy from you to the crystal for storage in a form useable later, when required, and do not mean waste. The type of crystal used depends entirely on the individual preference.

9. As an Energy Web: is a much-abused but effective use. Crystals may be located in a pattern of some form - mandala, yantra or whatever form is desired - at the corners or vertices of a space, and then charged to act as a web to enhance the energy of that space. As a protection for a Temple or living space this is a fine technique. We have found the Energy Web technique works especially well with the Quartzes, particularly Amethyst, but people might like to experiment with appropriate Elemental crystals in the corners of a room or such like.

Note: Precious Gemstones (such as Diamonds, Rubies, Sapphires, Emeralds, etc) are excellent for using as well, but we have made more reference to commoner, cheaper stones as they are more accessible.

Finally - caring for your crystals. Obviously they should be wrapped in silk, that great insulator of magickal charge, when not being used. Crystals should be washed under flowing water after usage to keep them clean. We would not recommend using tap water, we use water from sacred wells poured over the crystal (so it flows) to cleanse ours. It hopefully goes without saying that personal crystals should not be touched by anybody other than yourself (except in the case of healing). Crystals worn as necklaces, anklets, etc, should be cleaned regularly. If not, you may well find they develop the annoying habit of breaking and scattering crystals everywhere.

The following list of attributions is based on work we have done with crystals over the last 10-11 years, and you will find some of the attributions disagree with various books on the subject. All we can say is do what feels right. For any pedants, we know certain materials like Amber and Jet are not actually crystals, it is convenient to include them as they are used in the same way. This list is not exhaustive, but we have tried to give all the common stones we could think of and have experience of using, noting family relationships, and giving their alternative names.

Agate: trigonal crystal, member of Quartz family.
Colours: green, blue, white, red, brown, yellow, orange.
Attribution: Mercury, Earth.
Notes: protection whilst travelling, massage, healing of the body.

Alexandrite: rhombic crystal.
Colours: emerald green (red in artificial light).
Attribution: Air.
Notes: used for eye problems, helps with clarity and insight.

129

Almandine: isomorphous cubic crystal, Garnet family.
Colours: deep red, violet red, black.
Attribution: Mars.
Notes: used for blood problems, and to produce resolve and determination to attain goals and complete cycles. May have four-rayed asterisms (stars).

Amber: natural resin hydrocarbon, amorphous.
Colours: yellow, reddish-brown, bluish, white, black.
Attribution: Sun, Earth.
Notes: a wonderful storer of charge and talisman. Good for general well being, a sort of psychic worry bead. Amber jewellery has become very popular in recent years, and so good amber is easy to find, though also costly.

Amethyst: trigonal crystal, Quartz.
Colours: violet.
Attribution: Uranus, Neptune.
Notes: used for spiritual growth and protection, purification, mental healing. One of the prime magickal stones.

Aquamarine: hexagonal crystal, Beryl family.
Colours: sea green, sea blue.
Attribution: Neptune, Water.
Notes: good for relieving stress and emotional problems. Helps with psychism and clairvoyance.

Aventurine: trigonal crystal, Quartz.
Colours: green, brown, red or yellow with scales of mica.
Attribution: Venus, Earth.
Notes: used for skin complaints. Good for storing energy.

Bloodstone: trigonal crystal, crystalline member of Quartz family.
Colours: dark green with red spots.
Attribution: Mars, Earth.
Notes: strengthens the will and used with blood problems and protection from poison. Also known as Heliotrope.

Blue Calcite: trigonal crystal, Calcite family.
Colours: blue.
Attribution: Air.
Notes: used for lung and voice problems, helps develop communication.

Carnelian: trigonal crystal, crystalline member of Quartz family.
Colours: translucent with white, blue or green colour.
Attribution: Fire.
Notes: helps with spinal problems, particularly lower spine. Good for clearing blocked sexual energy (works with the kundalini).

Chalcedony: trigonal crystal, crystalline member of Quartz family.
Colours: translucent with white, blue or green colour.
Attribution: Air.
Notes: increases benevolence and reduces irritability.

Citrine: trigonal crystal, Quartz.
Colours: yellow.
Attribution: Mercury.
Notes: helps maintain emotional stability in troubled times.

Coral: axial skeleton of the coral polyp, made largely of calcium carbonate.
Colours: red, pink, white, black.
Attribution: Water.
Notes: for work with the bones, and to provide form to ideas. Coral has become more popular in recent times, and unfortunately is often obtained by using explosives to obtain the coral in quantity, thus destroying underwater ecosystems.

Crysocolla: hydrous copper silicate.
Colours: green, or greenish-blue with black.
Attribution: Venus, Earth.
Notes: good for storing energy, and for working with earth energies.

Crysoprase: trigonal crystal, crystalline member of Quartz family.
Colours: translucent apple green.
Attribution: Water.

Notes: produces insight and hope.

Diamond: cubic crystal.
Colours: colourless, pale tints of yellow, red, pink, green, blue, brown.
Attribution: Spirit, Pluto.
Notes: amplifies any energies, purifies. Diamonds will amplify negative energies as easily as positive ones, so if using diamonds, keep them and any other stones clean and well stored.

Emerald: hexagonal crystal, Beryl family.
Colours: grass green.
Attribution: Venus.
Notes: good for healing, and for determining purity (including magickal purity). A good stone for magickal charge and seeing things clearly.

Fluorspar: cubic crystal.
Colours: violet, green, yellow, orange, blue, red, pink, brown, colourless.
Attribution: Varies.
Notes: concerned with love, both physical and spiritual, and strongly connected with the heart chakra.

Haematite: trigonal crystal.
Colours: black
Attribution: Mars, Earth.
Notes: gives courage and endurance, used with blood problems and ulcers.

Iceland Spar: trigonal crystal, Calcite family.
Colours: colourless.
Attribution: Air.
Notes: good for vision, both physical and astral, may be used with Ajna chakra.

Jadeite: monoclinic crystal.
Colours: green, pink, lilac, white, mauve, brown.
Attribution: Venus, Earth.
Notes: used for earthing and protection, good for kidney problems and "keeping your feet on the ground".

Jasper: trigonal crystal, impure micro-crystalline variety of Quartz.
Colours: reds, browns, greens, greyish-blue.

Attribution: Fire, Earth.
Notes: helps with liver and kidney problems, used to strengthen the physical senses.

Jet: fossilised wood.
Colours: black.
Attribution: Saturn.
Notes: absorbs negative energies like a sponge! Clean regularly or you will pick up the negativity from it. A truly lovely and magickal stone to use. Jet, like amber, has become more popular and increasingly expensive; beware of French Jet, which looks similar but is in fact coloured glass.

Labradorite: triclinic crystal, Feldspar family.
Colours: blue and grey, with play of colour.
Attribution: Spirit, Uranus.
Notes: a stone for magickal growth and strengthening the subtle body and mind.

Lapis Lazuli: mixture of minerals, mainly Lazurite and Calcite.
Colours: deep blue, often with golden specks of pyrites.
Attribution: Jupiter.
Notes: for heart and spleen problems, symbolic of the cosmic Goddess, and a good stone for magickal power, particularly with the throat chakra and voicework.

Malachite: monoclinic crystal.
Colours: green.
Attribution: Venus.
Notes: helps emotional problems and menstruation difficulties.

Marble: trigonal crystal, Calcite family.
Colours: colourless, white, grey with yellow, blue, red, brown or black tints.
Attribution: Earth.
Notes: general earthing stone, helps maintain stability.

Moonstone: triclinic crystal, Feldspar family.
Colours: yellow or colourless with opalescence.
Attribution: Moon.

Notes: good for psychic problems, and for developing the psychic senses.

Nephrite: monoclinic crystal.

Colours: pale to dark green, white, black, brown.

Attribution: Venus, Earth.

Notes: with Jadeite, these two stones are commonly known as "Jade". Use as Jadeite.

Obsidian: volcanic glass.

Colours: black, red and brown.

Attribution: Saturn, Earth.

Notes: perhaps the most efficient director of energy. Good for skrying and developing psychic powers. Also known as Apache Tears.

Onyx: trigonal crystal, crystalline member of Quartz family.

Colours: green, blue, white, red, brown, yellow, orange.

Attribution: Earth.

Notes: general healing, also circulatory problems and hearing difficulties. Used as a protection and grounding stone.

Orange Calcite: trigonal crystal, Calcite family.

Colours: orange, yellow.

Attribution: Sun, Fire.

Notes: used for digestive problems, and to strengthen the emotions.

Opal: silica gel.

Colours: white (cacholong), semi-transparent orange to red (fire), transparent blue-white with red colour (girasol), colourless (hyalite), grey or brown (menilite or liver), yellowish or colourless with a play of colour (Mexican water), yellowish or bluish-white or white (milk), green (prase), yellow (resin). The other forms are harlequin (regular size patches of colour), hydrophane (dehydrated, becomes opalescent in water), lechosos (shows green colour), moss (dendritic inclusions), matrix (showing some ironstone matrix), precious (showing good colour), white (pale ground), black (very dark ground).

Attribution: Mercury.

Notes: used to help lung problems, promotes communication and mental growth.

Pearl: concretion of concentric layers of conchiolin (organic) and calcium

carbonate around a small nucleus.
Colours: white, pink, black, bronze, gunmetal.
Attribution: Moon.
Notes: helps with patience and resolution of outdated ideas and beliefs which need restructuring.

Peridot: rhombic crystal.
Colours: oil green, brown.
Attribution: Venus, Earth.
Notes: good for the digestive system. Helps with powers of analysis. A form of Olivine.

Prase: trigonal crystal, Quartz.
Colours: green.
Attribution: Water.
Notes: used for problems with water retention and urine problems.

Rhodochrosite: trigonal crystal.
Colours: rose red, may have shades of yellow or brown.
Attribution: Venus.
Notes: directs energy, and is good for integrating different types of energy, such as physical, emotional and mental.

Rhodolite: isomorphous cubic crystal, Garnet family.
Colours: violet.
Attribution: Uranus.
Notes: used for lymph problems, and to strengthen the subtle body.

Rose Quartz: trigonal crystal, Quartz.
Colours: pink and white.
Attribution: Venus.
Notes: used for promoting tranquillity and serenity, protection from negative emotions, emotional healing.

Ruby: trigonal corundum crystal.
Colours: red.
Attribution: Mars, Fire.
Notes: good for problems with blood and circulation, and for magickal strength. Both ruby and sapphire can have asterisms (six-rayed stars) and

are hence known as Star ruby and Star sapphire.

Rutile Quartz: trigonal crystal, Quartz.
Colours: colourless with inclusions of rutile.
Attribution: Neptune.
Notes: used for the endocrine glands and bronchitis, also good for work with the ajna chakra. Also known as Needle Stone.

Sapphire: trigonal corundum crystal.
Colours: blue, colourless (white), yellow (golden), pink, green, purple, violet.
Attribution: Jupiter.
Notes: good for mental problems, and developing mental discipline and willpower.

Smoky Quartz: trigonal crystal, Quartz.
Colours: transparent amber-brown.
*Attri*bution: Saturn.
Notes: used for problems with kidneys, pancreas and sexual organs. Good protector and transformer of energies.

Sodalite: cubic complex silicate.
Colours: deep blue.
Attribution: Jupiter.
Notes: general health and well being.

Sunstone: triclinic crystal, Feldspar family.
Colours: spangled bronze, spangled black (Black Sunstone).
Attribution: Sun
Notes: good for general health and well being. Black Sunstone is a very magickal stone and good for spiritual development and will. Also known as orthoclase.

Tigers Eye: trigonal crystal, Quartz.
Colours: yellow or amber-brown chatoyant (cat's eye effect from refraction of light from fibres in the crystal), green chatoyant (Cat's Eye), blue chatoyant (Hawk's Eye).
Attribution: Saturn, Sun, Earth.
Notes: promotes clear self-perception and insight.

Topaz: rhombic crystal.
Colour: yellow, green, blue, pink (usually heat treated).
Attribution: Sun, Fire.
Notes: promotes selflessness and purity of will, benevolence. A good stone for spiritual growth.

Tourmaline: trigonal complex boro-silicate.
Colours: colourless (achroite), red and pink (rubelite), green, blue, yellow-green, honey yellow, pale coloured (elbaite), violet (siberite), dark blue (indicolite), brown (dravite), black (schorl).
Attribution: Uranus, Venus.
Notes: good for dreamwork and spiritual growth. Promotes growth of the throat chakra.

Turquoise: triclinic phosphate of aluminium, copper and iron.
Colour: blue, green.
Attribution: Jupiter.
Notes: used as a protection and charm, to absorb general negative energies.

Zircon: tetragonal crystal (high) or amorphous silicon dioxide and zirconium dioxide (low).
Colour: colourless, gold yellow, blue (all heat treated), honey yellow, light green, blue, red (high); leaf green to brown green (low).
Attribution: Air.
Notes: used for liver problems, and gaining knowledge. Also known as jacinth.

Zoisite: rhombic crystal.
Colours: blue, green,yellow, pink, brown.
Attribution: Venus.
Notes: for emotional problems and emotional growth.

2. Power Objects

A power object can be virtually anything. The definition proposed here is any natural object which possesses inherent mana (magickal energy). Examples of power objects would be crystals, rocks (especially hag stones

- holed stones), jewellery, feathers, tree wands, herbs, bones, etc. The purpose of using power objects is to access a particular type of energy at a particular time, so that it can concentrate and aid the purpose of the ritual. Power objects are often found in magickal circumstances, giving evidence to their inherent magickal nature, often by "chance".

A power object does not have to be worn at all times, indeed this is likely to diminish potency. Power objects are the working tools of natural magick - many sites and parts of the land are not keen on iron, so daggers and swords can be very unpopular with local entities. Far more appropriate is to use an appropriate power object, e.g. if you were planning on working by the sea, a shell you had found at some time and felt embodied those energies would be more useful than a chalice (although of course you can drink from the chalice afterwards and offer libations!).

Having a pouch of power objects which accumulate through experience and working with nature is a boon. With one, you will be able to do spontaneous and improvised rituals with appropriate tools pleasing to the energies you are working with whenever you are out and about.

Chapter Twelve

Earth Energies & Nature Spirits

1. The Sacred Land

Many people have come across the idea of "Ley Lines", yet details and experiences of Leys tend to be rather nebulous. The idea of these mysterious lines of energy connecting sacred sites making a network of energy (sometimes considered to be) connected with the consciousness of the planet is very appealing to many. The reality is probably not as appealing to those with their heads in the clouds, but of more value to those wishing to be connected with their environments and creatures in it.

Alfred Watkins' book *The Old Straight Track*, first published in 1925, has been considered the bible for those wishing to believe (and then dowse where the Leys go and meet, all of which seem to vary from person to person) rather than question and then experience. Watkins idea of the alignment of prehistoric burial mounds, earthworks, standing stones and other sites along straight criss-cross lines has recently been considered in a new, more positive and plausible light. The Earth Mysteries researchers Nigel Pennick and Paul Devereux suggested the alignment of these ancient sites may be connected with "spirit tracks". Spirit Tracks, Ghost Paths and Fairy Paths are found all across Europe, and are all straight tracks joining important sites (be they ancient sites of varying kinds or graveyards).

This concept of straight tracks connecting sites, which the spirits may journey along, is found in many shamanic cultures, such as those in Siberia, South America, Africa and Australasia. These cultures all tend to have certain other elements in common, these including the use by the shaman of arrowheads and red cords to aid in healing. Arrowheads used with cords from the ill patient to trees to draw "evil" spirits out is a common concept among such cultures.

It seems to be an almost universal concept that straight lines facilitate spirit movement, and that likewise curved lines hinder them. Hence labyrinths can be seen as traps for spirits, preventing them from interfering with a person or soul on a mission. Examples of such use range from Baltic fishermen making a stone labyrinth on the shore to trap spirits who might hinder their fishing, to Feng Shui, the Chinese system of geomancy which uses curves to block or deflect spirits. In this light the use of the besom and other similar ritual brushes can be viewed as helping to create a sacred space which spirits cannot enter (like a circle with curved lines) or facilitating the encounter with spirits (by brushing straight lines).

There is only one way to work with Earth Energies, of course, and that is to go out and do it. Local maps of your area are a must for discovering old sites, the smaller ones of which are often not mentioned in books on ancient sites and sacred landscape (that is not to say that such books are not also valuable). Once you have located some sites, and decided to visit them, try and learn any local folklore about them. In Wales, for example, both the burial chamber at Tinkinswood and the mountain Cader Idris have the reputation that anyone spending Samhain night alone on (or in) them will end up dead, mad or a poet/bard (or possibly more than one of these!). These sort of local legends are often indicative of a strong focus of earth energies.

When you get to a site, it is better if possible to walk some of the way (if driving don't park right next to the site even if it is possible) to start to attune before you reach the site. A number of sites are on private land, and consideration must be given to the owners (often farmers) of this land and their livestock. Exploring the site and meditating are probably the best ways to get the feel of it. Whilst you should let your imagination have free rein, do not let it float too far away, or your intuition and instincts about a place are likely to be submerged in fantasy. During meditation you should get a feel for the type of energy in the place, and what sort of magickal work could be appropriately performed there. Some places have a strong death and transformation feeling (appropriate to Samhain), others a strong feeling of energy and growth (more appropriate to Eostra or Beltane), and so on. Rituals should always be performed in harmony with the place you are working.

Another important consideration at a site is trying to contact the site guardian, seeing if your intuition helps you contact it (or them). Often they are glad to be considered, and the contact is not too difficult. Sometimes they are hostile to certain things (like iron, see the next section for further details), which can be avoided once these are known. Site guardians respond well to offerings, the nature of which can be determined through contact. We can make offerings and libations, the nature of which we can adjust to suit the site and the season. Making offerings of food and drink you have prepared, as with bread or homemade wine, obviously has the benefit of giving back your own efforts and energies to the land. However, rather than always using red wine, it can be more appropriate to use drinks such as cider (the fruit of the apple, and remember Avalon means "Land of Apples") for Samhain, when it is appropriate as the fruit of wisdom and death and transformation (hence their use in apple bobbing, etc, at this time); hawthorn wine or mead for Beltane (the "May blossom"); barley wine for Lughnasadh is another obvious example with the ballad of John Barleycorn. Indeed appropriate drinks can be found for all the sabbats. Non-alcoholic drinks such as milk have often been used in the past, milk and honey being offered in ancient times to deities such as Pan and Artemis. Apples are very good as an offering for site guardians as well as more usual offering of bread and cakes. Finding out what the site guardians would prefer is the obvious course of action in all cases, just don't be surprised if they have sweet teeth!

Of course all the Earth is sacred, and you do not have to go to an ancient site to make a contact, or to contact nature spirits. Any woods, rivers, ponds, open land, etc can be as rewarding to be in as a stone circle, if approached with the appropriate respect and consideration.

Natural places also contain a wealth of plant and animal life with which we can learn to communicate, gain wisdom from, read auguries from, and in the cases of herbs and trees, use parts of them in healing, or in ritual work.

When gathering wild herbs for healing or ritual use, it is important to consider the environment. Do not gather rare herbs from the wild - use cultivated stock instead. Only take from nature that which nature has plenty of, and limit the amount you take to what you actually need. Most plants are more potent when the moon is waxing to full, as the sap is rising and the vital chemicals within are at their highest levels. Similarly, dawn is the best time of day to harvest most plants, when the dew is still on the plant, or for purposes of drying, when the dew has just evaporated. However, there are some variations on this, and different plants have their own most potent times. Harvesting the plant in the correct planetary hour and day depending on the planetary rulership of the herb may also be beneficial, if you want to go into that much detail, but is not strictly necessary - it is better to gather the herbs as you need them. There are many good books which give planetary correspondences of herbs (*Culpepers Complete Herbal* to name but one). It is also important when gathering wild herbs to make contact with the plant spirits, and to ask for their permission to gather them, and for their help in the work for which you wish to use them.

To do this, spend some time in meditation with the plants, being aware of your aura, and that the plant is within your aura, your aura and its aura merging. Call on the spirit of the plant. Feel your heart centre opening, and feel a connection from your heart to the plant. Ask your question (there is no need to ask it aloud, you are communicating with the plant on subtle levels) and wait for a response. Open yourself up, quieten down any mental chatter, and try to pick up any messages from the plants. Sometimes you will contact an individual plant, other times you will contact a guardian spirit of a batch of the plants. If you do not get a reply, try also making a connection with your throat chakra (communication) and your third eye (intuition). The reply may not be in words, but may be a strong feeling, or an image.

When you gather the herb, first stroke the part of the herb that you are going to pick (the same goes for when cutting a wand from a tree), visualizing the energy in the herb separating, so that there is energy within the part you are gathering, but you are not taking all the plant's energy. Visualize a gap in the energy, so that the point at which you cut or break the plant is "dead", and the plant will not be hurt by the cut. Next, seal the wound by gently holding the cut part of the plant and channelling healing energy to the plant. The tree meditation below may be used to gather energy to channel. If a whole plant is gathered, it is best to use a magickal tool such as a consecrated knife to loosen the earth around the roots before

142

pulling the plant out. An offering should immediately be made to the plant spirit (such as milk and honey poured onto the earth it has been pulled up from), and if the plant is in seed, return some of the seeds to the earth. Gathering of herbs should always be done with care and reverence.

In order to work with trees and tree spirits, we need to appreciate the trees and their qualities, and be prepared to meet them on their own level. As an integral part of nature, trees contain a harmony we have lost, and the first thing one can do is to practice exercises which emulate the trees.

Go out into a wood or park or your garden, somewhere with trees. Stand still and relax. Relax your shoulders, let your internal organs relax into your hips, let your weight sink firmly into the soles of your feet. Feel your feet becoming more sensitive, and your attention moving to beneath your navel. Remember the roots of the trees, and how deep into the earth they go. Feel the earth's energies, flowing into you through your feet, calming and nourishing. When you can feel this strongly, allow your heart to open and adopt an attitude of non-judgement - do not differentiate the world into subject and object. Feel your heart as the bud of a flower, being nourished by the root (i.e. your feet) absorbing energy from the earth. Practising this exercise helps one remove conditioning and develop a more self-aware attitude.

The Tree Meditation

This meditation is an empowering one, and may be done whenever you want to raise energy to direct for specific aims, e.g. healing. This exercise is important as it enables you to gather energy to use rather than using your personal power. Many people make the mistake of using their own energy for work such as healing, and end up drained and prone to illness themselves. Of course this exercise can also be used for work such as strengthening your aura, and helps develop your attunement to the subtle energies around us, and for earthing when you are feeling unearthed or out of balance.

Sit comfortably, and imagine yourself as a tree. Feel your body as your trunk, your arms as your branches. Then start to put forth roots from your feet, down into the earth. Deeper and deeper into the earth, through the

143

layers of rock, through the underground streams of water, through pockets of air within the earth, ever deeper until you reach the molten core, the fire at the centre of the earth. From the core, with every in breath, draw forth sparks of golden energy, up into your roots, drawing the energy up through your trunk and into your branches, which are visualized emerging from your head and shoulders, and which sweep back down to the earth creating a circuit of energy. Then feel the energy of the heavens, of the sun and moon and stars, on your leaves. With every out breath draw in the silver sparks of heavenly energy, drawing it down through your branches, through your trunk and deep into your roots in the earth. Continue drawing in energy, so that with each in breath you draw up gold sparks from the earth, and with every out breath you draw down silver sparks of energy from the heavens. Feel the two different energies meeting at your heart chakra, coalescing and being transmuted, empowering you with their energy. Feel the energy building up within you. When you feel sufficiently empowered, you may move on to the purpose of the empowerment. Energy may be channelled from the heart centre to the chakras in the hands (which are connected to the heart chakra) and directed out with the hands. Voice can be used to help in directing and releasing the energy, by vibrating a mantra or a wordless chant.

Exercise For Seeing and Contacting Nature Spirits

Go out into nature, to a site you have visited and felt an empathy with. Relax, and be aware of your surroundings. Close your eyes, and with your inner eye visualize your surroundings, until you can see it all clearly again. See the colours getting brighter, until you can see the auras of trees and plants, of rocks and all about you. When you can see all these clearly you may begin to see the spirits in your surroundings around you. Call to the spirits and ask them for a guide to help you explore the realm of nature spirits around you.

Wait for the guide to come, and spend some time getting to know this guide. Ask her or him for their name. This is similar to the inner guide pathworking in chapter 5, but this guide is specific to the world of nature spirits, and may be an elemental, faery or other kind of nature spirit. Ask your guide to help you explore the realm of nature spirits, and to make contact with them. Taking plant essences such as four-leafed clover or Green Bells of Ireland can help facilitate contact. Wild rose can help you open up and shed conditioning. Some of the herbs mentioned in Chapter 13 can also be used to facilitate contact.

2. Nature Spirits & Others

There are many types of spirits in nature, spirits of trees (hamadryads) and woodlands (dryads and fawns), streams and pools (nymphs), elementals (sylphs, salamanders, undines and gnomes), and others. All of these (apart from elementals) tend to be indwelling spirits of places, which guard and care for the place and plants and animals therein. Elementals tend to be personifications of their element, and as such may not always be so static in their locale. Faeries or "the Little People" are a bone of contention. There are many differing opinions on the nature and origins of faeries, such as their being the smaller more nature-based tribes (like Picts) who were largely wiped out by races such as the Celts. Others view them as ethereal beings who exist in an alternative dimension (or dimensions) accessible only through fairy mounds, and point to all the associated folklore.

The list of types of faerie is huge, from trolls and sprites to leprechauns and pixies. Most reputedly avoid human contact, and they are often mischievous (like Puck or Robin Goodfellow) if not hostile. They tend to dislike iron, a phenomena which seems to be common among nature spirits. This is one of the reasons why the horseshoe was placed above doorways in medieval times, the smith being a magickal figure through his transformation of iron. The World of Faerie (Tir Na Nog in Irish folklore) is supposed to be an entrancing world of great beauty, where time passes at a very different rate (generally considered to be much slower), another indication of the difference between the realms of men and the fay or faery.

There are other mythic creatures, beings of power, which may be contacted as well, the most notable ones being dragons and unicorns. Dragons are universally regarded with awe, although in the West the Christians have caused the dragon to often be viewed with fear through their centuries of propaganda. In the Orient where this process has not occurred, dragons tend to be viewed as noble and powerful beasts, lucky and beneficial to encounter. Dragons are associated with the power of the land, and symbolically are interchangeable with snakes and wurms (great wurms like the Midgard serpent of Norse mythology). Elements of the links of dragons with the land can still be seen today in mummers plays, and in the survival of references to them in books like the Mabinogion. In Wales, of course, the dragon's power has long been recognized and honoured in the Welsh flag with the red dragon (the English dragon is traditionally white).

The unicorn also has been the subject of propaganda, making it cute and loveable, so people do not see it as the powerful, independent and magickal embodiment of the spirit of freedom (including sexual). Unicorns can be seen as symbolising the power of the Horned God of the Wildwood (the horn is the erect phallus) and responding only to virgin (i.e. free and unbound women who have not had children) women, the appropriate priestesses of the Maiden Huntress aspect of the Goddess who also dwells in the woodland with the Horned God. The unicorn cannot be restricted or defined in too close terms, it is the animal of dreams, and of our unconscious.

These subjects are ones which require study and background reading, but more importantly, use of your imagination and perseverance, as with all magickal practice.

Chapter Thirteen

Herbs & Plant Lore

This lesson concentrates on the properties of psychoactive herbs, and how they may be prepared, and on flower and tree lore. It does not deal with the medicinal uses of herbs, the subject being vast, and many good books on the subject being available.

Psychoactive Herbs

Why take psychoactive herbs? Many people are uncomfortable about the idea of taking "drugs", though usually they are conditioned to be uncomfortable about either the (a) illegal ones or (b) those which they perceive might cause a loss of control, or they (c) feel they are pointless and duplicate a result which can be achieved without them.

To consider these points - firstly as most psychoactive herbs are not illegal (except cannabis, and dried or prepared magick mushrooms), the question of legality does not arise. Synthetic substances are almost inevitably illegal, being produced for escapist effects rather than to use as a sacrament. The issue of loss of control is one many people feel. If psychoactive herbs are used to create a desired effect in a ritual, the dosage must be carefully monitored. Many psychoactive herbs are poisons and can be extremely dangerous in anything other than the smallest quantities. With careful monitoring and use, herbs do not cause a loss of control. The only circumstance where loss of control may occur is when large quantities of psychedelic herbs (such as Fly Agaric or Magick Mushrooms) are taken to drastically alter consciousness, and in this instance a trusted magickally competent person should be present to oversee and act as a reference point to ensure your safety if necessary. On the issue of their use being pointless, we are discussing sacramental use to help produce a desired ritual result, not their recreational use. Sacramental use is not the use of a drug as a crutch, and does not detract from the pursuit of altered states of consciousness without using any psychoactive substances. Sacramental use can prepare you for the experiences of altered states of consciousness, and help by providing insights which might not otherwise be gained at that time. When using a psychoactive herb as a sacrament, you honour the spirit of the herb, and ask for its help to gain wisdom and insight. The sacramental use of herbs to alter consciousness is of course a time-honoured practice which has occurred and (in many places still does) in shamanic and so-called "primitive" cultures where the people are more in touch with the earth.

Using substances which are synthetic and have lost any connection they may have had with the earth or the spirit of the plant they came from (assuming they weren't made in a laboratory) can be seen as magickally questionable. We feel the use of substances such as opiates (heroin, morphine, opium, etc), barbiturates, stimulants (amphetamines, cocaine, etc) and designer drugs (ecstasy, etc) has no place in spiritual development, and will tend to have negative effects on the user, not to mention possible problems such as physical and psychological addiction in some cases. LSD has been used effectively in some psychotherapy experiments, but its use in magick is a two-edged sword and although it may allow times of sharp focus, it also tends to produce delusion and extreme vulnerability of the subtle body.

1. Psychoactive Herbs

Calamus - heightened sensations and mild stimulant.
Prep: Boil 2oz in 1 pint water. Strain and drink warm.

Damiana - general attraction and auric cleanser.
Prep: Add 2 tablespoons to 2 tablespoons de-stoned Saw Palmetto
          berries (not essential but preferable if obtainable) in 1 cup boiling
          water for 5 minutes. Strain and drink warm. For best effects
          repeat daily for several weeks.
2.   For a wonderful tasting aphrodisiac cordial, soak 1oz damiana in

1.5 pints vodka for 5 days. Pour off liquid, strain and filter. Soak alcohol-drenched leaves in 1 pint spring water. Pour off liquids, strain and filter. Warm water extract to 160°F and dissolve 1 cup honey in it. Add vodka extract to water extract, leave for 1 month and re- strain.

3.   Damiana is also used in the herbal high mix "Yuba Gold" which makes a very smooth base for non-tobacco smokers. Recipe is 4 parts Damiana, 4 parts Skullcap, 4 parts Passion Flower, 1 part Spearmint leaf, $^1/_2$ part Lobelia.

Fly Agaric - major psychedelic.

Prep: Fly Agaric may be consumed in several ways, but whichever fashion used, be sure to dry it first, an oven at about 170°F is recommended. This converts the Ibotenic Acid to the more psychedelic Muscimole, and evaporates out the more poisonous Muscarine.

1.   Eating dried mushrooms. Start cautiously with half a 6" mushroom and build up.
2.   Smoke dried mushrooms, added to a mix such as Yuba Gold. Add at least one 6" mushroom to the mix, and modify until you get it right.
3.   Tincture dried mushrooms in vodka, adding at least six 6" mushrooms to a pint of vodka, leaving for a month. Filter and drink.

Warning - extremely poisonous, build up dosage gradually and carefully

Galangal - relaxant, mild psychedelic in larger doses.

Prep: 2 tablespoons root per cup boiling water. Drink cold.

Kava Kava - stimulant and heightened empathy.

Prep: Eat root (gives a numb mouth).
2.   Blend 1 tablespoon lecithin and 1oz kava kava with 2 tablespoons coconut oil and 10oz water.

Kola Nut - stimulant.
Prep: 1 tablespoon powdered in 1 cup black tea or coffee (honey is recommended).

Lobelia - relaxant, psychedelic in larger quantities.
Prep: 1 pinch in peppermint or chamomile tea.
2.   Smoke neat.
Note: If made as a tea on its own, is good for inducing vomiting.

Magick Mushrooms - relaxant and psychedelic.
Prep: Dry well and ingest via eating, smoking or drinking tea. Start with does of about 30 and build up. 100 - 200 produces more psychedelic effects. Note: Make sure you can identify magick mushrooms before you go out picking, or you may end up poisoning yourself.

Mandrake - perceptions of astral plane and lucid dreaming.
Prep: Small quantities (max 30 grains) powdered root added to a glass of red wine.
2.   Add powdered root to ethyl alcohol (50 grains per glass of alcohol) and leave for 1 month. Dip herbal cigarettes or tobacco in the extract and let dry naturally, then smoke.

Warning - mandrake is extremely poisonous in any but very small doses
Note: Mandrake sold in shops is invariably White Briony (so-called False Mandrake). This may be used as described above with red wine for a pleasant stimulatory buzz.

Mormon Tea (Ephedra) - stimulant.
Prep: 3oz in 1 pint water brought to the boil for 5 minutes. Drink warm.

Morning Glory - psychedelic.
Prep: Wash seeds thoroughly (if bought, as seeds are treated with a

mercury compound, which is a residual poison that stays in the body). Grind well and soak in water for 1 hour. Strain and make a paste with fruit juice. Work on basis 2 seeds = 1 microgram LSD-25. For effect, use 150 - 200 seeds for 1 dose (may vary slightly from person to person).

Passion Flower - relaxant.
Prep: Smoke neat.

Skullcap - sedative and dream control.
Prep: 1oz in 1 pint very hot water for 20 minutes. Drink warm.

Thorn Apple (Datura) - alters perceptions, and lucid dreaming.
Prep: Smoke dried leaves with a herbal mix or tobacco. No more than 2g per session or 30g per week (if you are taking this much examine what you are doing!). Reduce dosage if blackouts or headaches occur (signs of low tolerance).
Warning, highly poisonous, DO NOT INGEST, using more datura than the quantities stated above may induce coma or cause death

Valerian - relaxant and sedative.
Prep: 1 tablespoon in hot water for 20 minutes. Drink warm. (Add honey, it tastes foul).
Note: Heightens physical sensation if taken prior to massage.

Wild Lettuce - astral and dream states.
Prep: Smoke (not very satisfactory). 2. Add 2oz wild lettuce to a pan of water. Heat (but do not boil) for at least 8 hours. Strain and put the liquid in a bowl. Leave the bowl in a warm dry place for at least 6 weeks. The funny smelling gunk left in the bowl is Lettuce Opium to be smoked.

Wormwood - inspirations and aphrodisiac.

Prep: Smoke the herb. May be extracted with alcohol and water, but is incredibly bitter, and you would be better off getting a bottle of Absinthe.

2. Trees & the Tree Alphabet

In the previous chapter we covered working with nature spirits and communicating with trees. This section covers some of the properties of the more common trees and also the Ogham Tree Alphabet (a late Celtic alphabet).

Some Tree Attributions

ALDER is a tree of birth. It is also the sacred tree of Bran, and is connected with the trickster spirits known as Fear Dearg, the Red Men, who help human beings escape from the other world. Alder is a water loving tree, with oily timber, used extensively for underwater foundations. The alder can help one to find spiritual protection in disputes, and oracular strength. Its sap is blood red and it is a tree of fire, used to free the earth from water.

APPLE is the tree of rebirth and eternal life, also a tree of wisdom. It is associated with choice and this may be between similar and equally attractive things. The act of choosing is what is important. When cut open, the apple contains the pentagram of life, and it is said that the ignorant should not eat its fruit. The crab apple is a protective tree like the hawthorn and blackthorn.

ASH is the tree of inspiration and rebirth. Yggdrasil, the Norse cosmic world tree, was an ash, and so this tree rules passage between the inner and outer worlds. The bunches of keys on the ash trees signify the power to unlock the future, but just as the seeds germinate only in the second year after falling to the ground, so the future can take time to unlock. In Celtic cosmology, ash connects the three circles of existence, Abred, Gwynedd and Ceugant, past, present and future, or confusion, balance and creative force. The ash provides a key to understanding the interconnectedness of all things.

BIRCH is the tree of fertility where our seed ideas find their points of conception. The white tree of purification sacred to the Mother Goddess. It is a pioneer tree and was the first to recolonise after the last Ice Age. It is also the first deciduous tree to put out leaves in spring time, and is thought to be the first wood upon which Irish Ogham was inscribed. Birching to drive out evil spirits or influences was used until recently, and it was thought that the New Year could not start until the Old Year was birched out. The Celtic Goddess Berkana is the Goddess of birch.

BLACKTHORN represents power in both the visible and invisible worlds. It gives strength to resist and defeat adversity, and to control or ward off supernatural and paranormal powers. It is good for overthrowing all resistance to ones will. It is also a tree for cursing and the thorns are used to pierce wax images.

ELDER is sacred to the Crone aspect of the Goddess. It is also connected with the Fates and the Norns, and signifies the three aspects of time. It is a tree of timelessness, or rather the unity of all time. According to some tree calendars, the Elder rules the thirteenth month, which is a short three day period ending in Samhain. Elder is linked to the eternal turnings of the wheel of life and death, and is a tree of regeneration. It regrows damaged branches readily and will root and grow from any part. The bark and flowers have healing properties, but the vapours emanating from the plantations of elder are reputed to bring disease and even death to those who have too much exposure to them.

FURZE or **GORSE** is in flower almost every month of the year, and is therefore a tree of continuous fertility. It helps one to carry on with ones work, despite surrounding conditions, and to stand out against the background, as the gorse does itself. It also represents a gathering together of energy or a skill at collecting.

HAWTHORN rules the awakening which must come after the dream state. It is also the Goddess's tree of sexuality. The name "Huathe" is said to mean terrible, referring to the Hag or Cailleach. It is considered to be a fairy tree and unlucky to tamper with. Hawthorn also represents cleansing and chastity, bringing protection from the inner magickal realms.

HAZEL is associated with the number nine, and the power of three times three. According to county lore, it fruits after nine years of growth. It is a tree of wisdom, and skill with words. Magickal wands are traditionally made of hazel. Hazel poles were used by the Vikings to delimit sacred enclosures in which combat took place, and hazel was used as a magickal shield. Salmon are associated with the hazel in Irish legend, swimming in the River Boyne under the overhanging hazel tree from which the nine nuts of poetic wisdom fell. The salmon ate the nuts of wisdom and hence became the salmon of wisdom. Hazel is also associated with meditation and mediation. Hazel embodies poetry, divination and the channelling of creative energies. It allows you to be a transformer of energies, aiding intuition.

HOLLY is a tree of fire, and strength in battle. It brings strength and power, but in a balanced manner. The wood of the holly was used in making spear shafts, and the holly guides one to find your strongest argument in a spiritual battle providing your cause is just. It gives the courage and vigour to fight with balance and unity, and to defend ones self against enemies.

IVY flourishes in many conditions. It is strong and difficult to destroy. It puts one in touch with ones inner strengths and abilities, and represents the inner journey. A plant of transformation.

OAK is seen as the most powerful tree, and is sacred to the major European Sky Gods such as Zeus, Jupiter, Taramis, the Dagda, Donar and Thor. The name "Duir" is related to the Irish "Dur" meaning hard, unyielding and durable. The word "Door" also comes from this word, and the oak represents the doorway to the inner worlds. The oak is central in the tree calendar, and stands between hawthorn on the left and holly on the right. Oak makes you secure and strong in your pursuits. The doorway to the inner self will be opened and you will be protected between the Hawthorn's feminine chastity and determination and the Holly's masculine vigour, courage and fighting strength. The oak represent primeval strength and the ability to overcome and survive.

POPLAR is a very hardy tree, able to grow in hostile conditions. It strengthens ones self-healing powers and represents mind over matter and the power of will overriding destiny. Poplar is said to have the power to protect from death and injury. Also associated with speech and language and referred to as whispering or talking trees. The wind, messenger of the Gods, makes the tree talk.

REED has its greatest power as a preserver. Pens were made from reed, which were used to preserve memory and knowledge. Ngetal is the ogham of written communication. Reed also represents the desire to search out basic truths.

Some tree calendars also include **ROSE**, but there is no ogham for this tree. Rose is a tree of love, passion and purity, but also pain and suffering. Connected with Venus and the Moon. Rose is a tree of virtue and persevering with ones quests.

ROWAN is the tree of quickening and is a magickal tree. Used for protection against psychic attack and is supposed to help develop powers of perception and prediction. Rune staves were often cut from rowan, and sprigs of rowan were placed over the main doors of houses to ward off the evil eye. In Wales, rowan was planted in churchyards to watch over the spirits of the dead, as yew is elsewhere. Rowan is also said to help keep your wits about you and retain control of your senses.

VINE, although not really a tree, is included in the tree alphabet. The correlation of this ogham Muin with the vine may be a late connection, and may originally have meant a thicket of any thorny plant. The vine is linked with the release of prophetic powers, letting go of inhibitions and letting subtle intuition surface and lead.

WILLOW is the tree of dreams. It is associated with the Moon and its powers, and the tree's power fluctuates with the Moon's phases. In divination, its power is greater at night than day, except when the Moon is visible during the day. The wood's flexibility reflects the tree's harmonious adaptations to the conditions of its environment. The willow is sacred to Lunar Goddesses, and offers protection against damp diseases. Salicin made from the bark is used in the treatment of rheumatic fever.

YEW is a tree of unity of life and death, sacred to Hekate. Yew guards against all evil and represents great age, rebirth and reincarnation. Often found in graveyards to protect the spirits of the dead and bring rebirth. It places one in direct contact with ones past. From this spiritual strength may be renewed and fresh vigour gained. Bows were made from yew, and it is also sacred to Ullr, the Norse Bow God. Yew is connected with the wisdom that was, is and always will be.

The ogham Ailim is translated variously as Silver Fir and Elm. The **SILVER FIR** is the tallest European tree, but is not indigenous to Britain. It represent long sight with clear vision of what is beyond and yet to come. It confers strength and healing, learned from ones past and present lives. The **ELM** is a tree of witchcraft, and in the Norse tradition the first woman Embla was made from an elm tree. Ailim is thought by some to be the Cornish Elm, which is a wayside tree, not found in woodland.

The ogham Ur is variously thought to be **HEATHER** or **MISTLETOE**. Heather is the symbolic gateway linking the earth and the spirit world. It is a lucky plant and brings freshness. It is connected with the morning dew. The honey bee gathering nectar from the heather was regarded as a messenger travelling through the gateway to the spirit world. Mistletoe is traditionally known as Allheal, representing the healing of all, and fresh fertilisation on solid foundations. Mistletoe growing on oak was held as particularly sacred by the druids as it was believed to contain the fertile life essence of the oak tree.

The Tree Calendar/Alphabet

To the Celts trees were very sacred, and the Celtic Lunar Calendar ascribes a tree to each lunar month. There were regional variations as to which tree fitted which month, and they vary annually. As a rough guide, the calendar starts with Birch at the first moon after Yule and runs through the first thirteen trees of the table below. Usually hawthorn, oak and holly should be the trees for May, June and July. The Celts also had an alphabet, the ogham, to which the trees were attributed, and a set of attributions for this is given below.

English	Gaelic	Let	Key Words
Birch	Beith	B	Cleansing, new beginnings
Rowan	Luis	L	Protection against magick, control of the

			senses
Alder	Fearn	F	Prophecy, spiritual protection
Willow	Saille	S	Feminine, night vision, lunar rhythms, fertility
Ash	Nuin	N	Passage between inner and outer worlds
Hawthorn	Huathe	H	Cleansing, chastity, protection, restraint
Oak	Duir	E	Solid protection, doorway to the mysteries, strength
Holly	Tinne	T	Victory, fatherhood, vigour
Hazel	Coll	C	Intuition, wisdom, poetry, divination, inspiration
Apple	Quert	Q	Beauty, wisdom, choice, immortality
Vine	Muin	M	Prophecy, letting go of inhibitions, instinct, emotions
Ivy	Gort	G	Spiral of the self and inner journey, transformation
Reed	Ngetal	Ng	Direct action, searching out basic truths
Blackthorn	Straif	Ss	Cleansing, cursing, fate, strife, punishment
Elder	Ruis	R	The end in the beginning, the beginning in the end, time, fate
Silver Fir*	Ailim	A	Healing, perception, regeneration (* or Elm)
Furze	Ohn	O	Individuality, strength through adversity, richness, fulfilment
Heather	Ur	U	Luck, freshness, entrance to the inner worlds
Poplar	Eadha	E	Self-healing, will overriding destiny, mind over matter
Yew	Ioho	I	Great age, rebirth, death, reincarnation, unity of death and life, contact with the past

Treesong

White from the ashes
Protecting from harm
A beginning in silence
To grow and be calm

Beith
Birch

The quickening flame
That guards all from charm
The blood-stained rune

Luis
Rowan

157

In the magician's palm
Fire and water
Alder
The blood red shaft
Alder
The sound of the raven
Ahead of the raft

Flowing with the tides
Saille
Of woman and moon
Willow
The gift of the seed
The goddess' boon

A key to wisdom
Nuin
With roots in the past
Ash
Growth through the worlds
Tells future at last

Power from beyond
Huathe
To be pure and aware
Hawthorn
Chaste and protecting
In a May maiden's hair

Green and enduring
Duir
The strength of the king
Oak
Doorway to wisdom
To summer from spring

Best in a fight
Tinne
The warrior's spear
Holly
The darkness is rising
Bringing strength to defeat fear

Tree of magick
Coll
And wand for the seer
Hazel
Like unseen water
Inspiration flows here

The star of knowledge
Quert
Love and rebirth
Apple
Fertile and heavy

Falls back to the earth
An aid to prophecy   Muin
Releases the sight   Vine
Harvests the omens
To grow by their light

The spiral dance   Gort
That taps deep within   Ivy
Gives knowledge of growth
You need to begin

Knowledge preserved   Ngetal
And direction found   Reed
Clarity and purpose
Are seen all around

The piercing thorn   Straif
Gives strength to persist   Blackthorn
See the unseen
And know when to resist

The shortest time   Ruis
Shows beginning and end   Elder
Though time may harm
She will also mend

A glimpse of the future   Ailim
Gives sight of the road   Silver Fir
Draws strength from experience
To lighten the load

Continuous flower   Ohn
Stands out like a star   Furze
Guiding the seeker
Links worlds near and far

All-heal gathered   Ur
With sickles of gold   Mistletoe
The spirit path

From times of old
The strength to endure   Eadha
A shield from woe   Poplar
The gift of the winds
Gives power to know

From winter's tide   Ioho
The bow shoots true   Yew
The fountain of time
Turns old into new

Joined in a circle   Koad
Faces raised to the sun   Grove
Through the moon's cycle
The dance is begun

The flash of lightning   Oir
Illuminates the way   Spindle
The passage from darkness
To the birth of the day

The sweetness of the centre   Villeand
The real self is shown   Honeysuckle
Achieving the way
The true worth is known

A foundation of wisdom   Phagos
With echoes of age   Beech
Methods well tested
Can break any cage

In the watery depths   Mor
Lie the secrets she brings   The Sea
Now hidden now seen
In a flying crane's wings

Plant Lore and the Language of Flowers

There are various myths and superstitions surrounding many herbs and flowers, and there is a language of flowers, originating in ancient times, which existed in different forms throughout the ancient world. The Chinese are said to have had a form of writing composed of flowers. The ancient Egyptians, and the Greeks too knew of the symbolism of flowers and herbs. There are British references to the language of flowers from medieval times, and it became very popular in Victorian times, and although used mainly to give messages of love or rejection, it can be used magickally.

Herbal talismans and pouches can be made containing herbs and flowers which symbolize the desired result. Floral and herbal crowns can be made to wear during specific rituals. The sabbats are obvious examples of rituals where such crowns may be appropriate; a crown of oak leaves to represent the Oak King for the Summer Solstice, for example, or a circlet of May flowers for Beltaine. Chapter 10 gives the magickal and mythical uses of some plants, in the section on essential oils. Here follows a list of other plants and the myths, superstitions and folklore associated with them.

Agrimony - To induce deep sleep. An eleventh century rhyme says;

> *If it be leyd under mann's heed*
> *He shal sleepyn as he were deed,*
> *He shal never drede ne wakyn*
> *Till from under his heed it be takyn.*

Bindweed - For binding! Use it for binding a poppet. Bind nine times with a length of the stem, winding it anti-clockwise, while saying "*I bind* (Name) *against or to* (whatever action is not wanted or wanted) *So mote it be!*" Then bury the poppet or image in a path where the person is sure to walk. In the language of flowers it means Fleeting Joys or Love Levels All. The lesser bindweed is a symbol of obstinacy.

Bittersweet - Good fortune and protection against black magick.

Burdock - A love potion may be made with the seed heads. Pound them in a mortar on the first day of the new moon, with some brandy, and leave in a quiet place uncovered for a few days, then cook it until it is thick. The original recipe also includes the private parts of a billy goat, hairs from a white puppy, and crocodile sperm - but these may be difficult to obtain!

Carnation - Affection. Garlands of carnations were worn by successful lovers.

Couch Grass - To entrance and spellbind an audience. Before dawn you should go to where the couch grass grows, and pull up some of its roots, saying "*As the birds wake and sing, so will I wake and sing, as we listen to them, so they listen to me*". Then wash the roots in running water and eat them. This should be done three mornings running during the waxing moon.

Cypress - Mourning, the funeral tree of the eastern world. The shade of the tree and its fragrance were believed to be deadly by the Greeks and Romans, and it was dedicated to Pluto. Shakespeare associated Cypress with murdering basilisk, lizards, stings, poison and gall, and "*all the foul terrors in dark-seated hell*" (*Henry VI*). Combined with marigold, it makes the emblem of despair.

Dahlia - Pomp, and "My gratitude exceeds your care".

Daisy - Innocence. Daisy roots were once believed to stunt growth, and were given to puppies to keep them small. They were also given by "fairy godmothers" to the lanky. It brings gentleness, and reconnection with childhood innocence. Daisies were placed under the pillow to bring pleasant dreams of absent lovers.

Fern - Gives the power of invisibility. One should use the seeds of a male fern, sought on St. John's Eve (June 23rd). If not gathered with the correct rituals, the seed will vanish while being carried home! Fern seed was also used in flying ointments.

Forget-Me Not - In the language of flowers, "*do not forget me*". They were also believed to cure the sting of scorpions and bites of poisonous snakes.

Geranium - The common scarlet geranium means stupidity, but different varieties have different meanings as follows:

Wild geranium (herb robert) - Steadfast Piety
Ivy geranium - Bridal favour
Lemon geranium - Unexpected meeting
Oak-leaved geranium - True friendship
Pencilled geranium - Ingenuity
Silver-leaved geranium - Recall
Rose-scented geranium - Preference.

Honeysuckle - Bonds of love, devotion and affection, generosity and gaiety, rustic beauty. It was used to ease bee stings, and it was said that if the juice were spread over beehives, the bees would not go away.

Lilac - A flower of death and presages of misfortune, often laid in coffins. It was said that should a lover offer lilac to his fiancee, the engagement will be broken off. Lilac also represents the beginning of summer, and the first emotions of love.

Lily - Purity. It was said to have risen from the grave of one who was unjustly executed, as a token of his innocence. For a man to step on a lily, means the loss of purity of the women in his household. The Madonna lily was said only to grow for a good woman, or for a house where the woman is the master. To dream of lilies brings good luck.

Lily of the Valley - Happiness. In Devon, however, it was considered unlucky to plant a bed of lilies of the valley, as the person who did so would die within the year. It was also unlucky to bring them into the house, or give them to a friend.

Ox-eye Daisy - Good luck, protection and power against lightening. In the language of flowers it is a symbol of obstacles, and patience. In Somerset it was known as the dun-daisy, from a supposed connection with Thor. It is also dedicated to Artemis, and used to cure women's complaints.

Orange Blossom - Saracen brides wore orange blossom as a symbol of fecundity. Christian symbolism has changed it into a symbol of chastity, to be worn only by virgin brides. *"To gather orange blossoms"* meant to seek for a wife.

Periwinkle - For love between couples.

Primrose - Primrose was anciently known as Paralysos, after a beautiful youth, son of Priapus and Flora who died of grief after the loss of his love, Melicenta. They symbolize young love.

Rose - Roses are said to have a mystic language and speak to your heart when contemplated. The different colours have different symbolisms:

> Orange - vigour and vitality.
> Pink - affection and warmth, innocent and pure love.
> Purple - calmness and spirituality.
> Red - love purified by suffering.
> White - peace.
> Wild - maidenly beauty and innocence.
> Yellow - joy and a sun-lit heart, but also jealousy and refusal.

Scarlet Pimpernel - A magickal flower giving the power to hear and understand the speech of birds and animals.

Thistle - Independence. Diosccoridus claimed that the root borne about one removes all diseases of melancholy.

Vervain - For love charms, protection, and healing. Gather it whilst reciting the following charm:

> All hele, thou holy herb Vervain,
> Growing on the ground;
> In the mount of Calvery
> There was thou found;
> Thou helpest many a griefe,
> And Stenchest many a wound.
> In the names of the Lady and Lord,
> I take thee from the ground.

Oh, Gods, effect the same
That I do go about.
In the names of the Gods, on holy ground
First I thee found;
In the name of the Lady and Lord
I pull thee from the ground.

Vervain was also used to protect against black magick, and an old rhyme says:

Vervain and Dill
Hinder witches from their will.

A sixteenth century love spell says; "*Rubbe vervin in the bale of thy hande and rubbe thy mouth with it and immediatelye kysse her and it is done*".

Vine - Intoxication, voluptuousness and repentance. The emblem of fruitfulness

Chapter Fourteen -

Healing

Healing is the essence of the Priesthood, whether it is healing the Earth, healing animals, or healing the bodies or minds of other people. By following the exercises and practices in the previous lessons, you can rebalance and heal yourself, and it is important that you feel balanced and healthy yourself before you attempt to give healing to others. Ensure that you feel good and that energy is flowing through you properly. Use the Chakra balancing yoga and bioenergetic exercises in chapter 4 to make sure you feel good. If you notice any imbalances, concentrate on healing yourself before you channel healing to others. Look after yourself generally - ensure you have a healthy diet, with plenty of fresh fruit and vegetables, avoiding too much processed or packaged food. Fresh air and exercise are also important, not just for physical well-being, but also for spiritual well-being. When you give healing to another person, draw on the energy of the Earth and the Heavens, don't drain your own resources, and also beware of people who will try to drain your energy. It is important to protect yourself, to keep your aura strong, and distinct from the other person's aura.

Here follows a basic outline of the healing process.

1] Ground and Centre yourself, making sure that you are feeling healthy and balanced.

2] Practice Pranic breathing, filling your body with the pranic energy gathered from all around you until you feel like you are buzzing with energy. The tree meditation can also be used here to draw energy up from the earth and down from the heavens (see chapter 12).

3] Visualize your own aura, making sure its boundaries are strong.

4] Visualize the other person's aura, keeping them separate from yourself, and being clear of the boundaries. See if you can see anything unusual, such as gaps or blocks in the aura, or strange colours. Look with your inner eye, being ready to listen to your intuition. See if you can sense any psychic or spiritual causes of their illness. Mentally try to contact the other person's spirit or higher self. This can be done by visualizing a line of energy from your third eye and a line of energy from their third eye, meeting above both your heads, and visualizing a glowing light there. See what you can pick up from this contact, and try to communicate with their spirit, silently telling them what you are going to do and checking their reaction. (If you feel that they are violently opposed to what you are planning, don't do it.)

5] Use your hands to channel energy. You may wish to use the bioenergetic exercise for the heart chakra (chapter 4) in order to help you actually feel the energy in your hands. Keep breathing, feeling the flow of Prana through you. Your heart centre transforms the Pranic energy to healing energy, and this travels out through your hands. Your hands may touch the person, or you may hold them a few inches away from the person, palms towards them, channelling energy through your palms. How you visualize this energy will depend on what you have seen in the other person's aura. You may use the energy to remove blocks from the aura, or to fill in gaps. You can visualize the energy as different colours as appropriate. Gold light, for example is energizing and vibrant. Green is balancing and harmonizing. You might also use mantra or intonation to help increase the flow of energy.

6] Seal the other person's aura, by visualizing it with a firm boundary. If they are open to it, ask them to visualize their own aura.

7] Visualize your own aura again, making sure you are separate and whole.

Absent Healing

There may be times when you want to send healing to someone who is far away. In this case, an object link, such as a photograph, lock of their hair, or other item can be used to help you tune into them. Follow the same process as above, but at point 4, call their spirit to you, to inhabit the object link. Visualize them there before you, and try to see their aura. Proceed as above, and when you have finished, send their spirit back to them. This is best done at night, when they are likely to be asleep, although it may be done at other times. There is no danger to them in calling their spirit to you - they don't have to come if they don't want to, and it will not be the whole spirit that will come, but a sort of spiritual double.

Healing is most effective when done within a sacred space such as a magick circle. You can silently cast a circle by visualizing a sphere of protection around yourself, and silently calling the elements in. Do not expand your aura to create the circle - this is fine for work on your own, but when working with a sick person you need to keep your aura separate from them. It is also a good idea to call on the Goddess and God for help, or choose a suitable healing God/dess form.

Healing and Alternative Medicine

Traditionally, witches and Pagan Priests and Priestesses make use of herbalism and other forms of natural medicine to aid in their healing work. Alternative medicine itself is a vast subject, and beyond the scope of this course. For those who wish to study these subjects further, there are many professional courses on offer from various organizations, such as the School of Herbal Medicine, etc. We have already given some information on the use of essential oils and plants, in chapters 10 and 13, but have not gone deeply into herbal medicine. There are also many good books around on herbalism. Crystals may also be used in healing, and the use of crystals in healing has been explained in chapter 11, Crystals and Power Objects.

There are however, many ingredients which just about everyone has in their kitchen which can be used in healing. There are also some common "weeds" which can be found in your garden, on wasteland, or in the countryside, which can be used safely by unqualified people. These herbs can be magickally charged to increase their healing potency. There follows a list of common kitchen and garden herbs, together with their therapeutic properties.

Aniseed - Expectorant, anti-spasmodic, carminative, parasiticide. Eases griping, intestinal colic and flatulence. May be used in bronchitis, and persistent coughs. For flatulent colic, mix aniseed in equal amounts with fennel and caraway. To use, pour one cup of boiling water over 1-2 tsp of the seeds and let it stand for 5 to 10 minutes. One cup should be taken by the patient three times a day. To treat flatulence, the drink should be sipped slowly before meals.

Basil - Antispasmodic, carminative, galactagogue, stomachic. Basil can be used for stomach cramps, gastric catarrh, vomiting, intestinal catarrh, constipation, and enteritis. Steep 1 tsp of the dried herb in 1 cup of boiling water. Take one to one and a half cups a day, a mouthful at a time. It can be sweetened with honey if taken for a cough.

Chives - Appetizer, digestive. Chives help to stimulate the appetite and promote the digestive processes. Use fresh.

Caraway - Carminative, antispasmodic, expectorant, emmenagogue, galactagogue, astringent. Used as a calming herb to ease flatulent dyspepsia and intestinal colic, especially in children. it will stimulate the appetite, and helps in cases of diarrhoea, as well as laryngitis, as a gargle. It can be used in cases of bronchitis and bronchial asthma. It is good to soothe period pains, and can help to increase milk flow in nursing mothers. Pour a cup of boiling water onto 1 tsp of freshly crushed seeds and leave to infuse for 10-15 minutes. This should be drunk three times a day.

Coriander - Carminative. Helps the digestive system get rid of wind, and eases the spasm pain that goes with it. Eases diarrhoea, especially in children. Stimulates the appetite. Pour a cup of boiling water onto 1 tsp of the bruised seeds and let it infuse for 5 minutes in a closed pot. This should be drunk before meals.

Cucumber - Demulcent, vulnerary, mild diuretic. The seeds of the cucumber possess anti-tapeworm properties. The juice of the cucumber is cooling, healing and soothing to the skin. For treatment of tapeworm infestations, 2 oz of cucumber seeds should be mixed with honey. This should be taken whilst fasting, and followed after 2 hours by a cathartic herb.

Dandelion - Diuretic, cholagogue, anti-rheumatic, laxative, tonic. It is good in cases of water retention due to heart problems, and may be used in cases of inflammation and congestion of the liver and gall bladder. It can be used for muscular rheumatism. It is also a good general tonic and purifying herb. Put 2-3 tsp of the root into a cup of water, bring to the boil, and simmer for 10-15 minutes. This should be drunk three times a day. The leaves may be eaten raw in salads.

Dill - Carminative, aromatic, anti-spasmodic, galactogogue. Dill is a good remedy for flatulence and colic. It will stimulate the flow of milk in nursing mothers. Chewing the seeds will clear up bad breath. Make an infusion of crushed seeds and use as caraway.

Fennel - Carminative, aromatic, anti-spasmodic, stimulant, galactogogue, rubeficient, expectorant. Fennel is good for flatulence and colic, and stimulates the appetite and digestion. It calms bronchitis and coughs, and increases the flow of milk in nursing mothers. The infusion may be used to treat conjunctivitis and inflammation of the eyelids (blepharitis) as a compress. Make infusion as for aniseed.

Feverfew - Anti-inflammatory, vasodilatory, relaxant, digestive bitter, uterine stimulant. Good for relieving migraine headaches. It may also help arthritis when it is painfully inflamed. It can ease tinnitus and dizziness. It relieves period pain and sluggish menstrual flow. It should **NOT** be used during pregnancy because of the stimulant action on the womb. One fresh leaf should be used three times a day.

Garlic - Anti-septic, anti-viral, diaphoretic, cholagogue, hypotensive, anti-spasmodic. Garlic is a good general tonic and effective against colds and flu. It may also be used for bronchitis and bronchitic asthma. It may be used as a preventative for most infectious conditions, digestive as well as respiratory. It reduces blood pressure and cholesterol levels. It is used in the treatment of threadworm and ringworm infestations. A clove of raw garlic may be eaten three times a day.

Ginger - Stimulant, carminative, rubefacient, diaphoretic. Ginger is good in cases of bad circulation, chilblains and cramp. In feverish conditions, ginger is a useful diaphoretic, promoting perspiration. As a carminative, it promotes gastric secretion and is used in dyspepsia, flatulence and colic. It may be used as a gargle for sore throats. Externally it can be used for fibrositis and muscle sprain. For an infusion, pour a cup of boiling water onto 1 tsp of the fresh root and let it infuse for five minutes. This can be drunk whenever needed.

Marjoram - Stimulant, diaphoretic, antiseptic, expectorant, emmenagogue, rubefacient. As a stimulating diaphoretic, marjoram is used in cases of colds and flu. It is a good mouthwash for inflammations of the mouth and throat. It may also be used externally for infected cuts and wounds. Headaches, especially when due to tension may be relieved by a tea of marjoram. A lotion may be used which will soothe stings and bites. For internal use, pour a cup of boiling water onto 1 tsp of the herb and infuse for 10-15 minutes. This should be drunk three times a day. For a mouthwash, use 2 tbsp of the herb with 1 pint of boiling water. Gargle with it three to four times a day.

Mint - Antispasmodic, carminative, diuretic, stimulant, stomachic. Mint is good for abdominal pains and flatulence. It is also good as a mild stimulant when one is feeling tired. It may be given for suppressed or painful urination. Steep 1 tsp of the herb in one cup of water for about 30 minutes. It should be taken frequently, a tablespoon at a time.

Mustard - Rubeficient, Stimulant, diuretic, emetic. Mustard is used externally as a poultice. The rubeficient action causes a mild irritation to the skin, stimulating circulation to that area and relieving muscular and skeletal pain. For feverishness, colds and flu, mustard may be taken as a tea, or sprinkled into a bath. It can also help chilblains and bronchitis. For a poultice, mix 4 oz ground mustard seeds with warm water to form a thick paste. Spread this on a piece of cloth and apply it to the skin for 1 minute. The skin may feel sore and red after this treatment, and olive oil can be applied to soothe it afterwards.

Nettle - Astringent, diuretic, tonic. Nettles are a good general tonic, and purify the blood. They are good in cases of eczema, especially nervous eczema, and as an astringent are good for nose bleeds and haemorrhage. Pour a cup of boiling water onto 1-3 tsp of the herb and infuse for 10-15 minutes. This should be drunk three times a day.

Oats - Nervine tonic, anti-depressant, nutritive, demulcent, vulnerary. Oats are good in cases of nervous debility and exhaustion when associated with depression. They are also good in cases of general debility, and applied externally are good for skin conditions such as eczema. They are most conveniently taken in the form of porridge or gruel.

Parsley - Diuretic, expectorant, emmenagogue, carminative. Parsley helps get rid of excess water in the body, stimulates menstruation (**DON'T** use during pregnancy) and eases flatulence. Make an infusion of 1- 2 tsp of the leaves or root with 1 cup of boiling water. This should be drunk three times a day.

Rosemary - Carminative, aromatic, anti-spasmodic, anti- depressive, antiseptic, rubefacient, parasiticide. Rosemary acts as a circulatory and nervine stimulant. It is good for the digestion, and for psychological tension. Externally it may be used to ease muscular pain, sciatica and neuralgia. Make an infusion with 1- 2 tsp dried herb with 1 cup of boiling water. This should be drunk three times a day.

Sage - Carminative, spasmolytic, antiseptic, astringent, anti-hidrotic. Sage may be used as a mouthwash for inflamed and bleeding gums (gingivitis), inflamed tongue (glossitis) or generalized mouth inflammation (stomatitis). It is good for mouth ulcers, and as a gargle will help in cases of laryngitis, pharyngitis, tonsillitis and quinsy. It is a good carminative in cases of dyspepsia, and reduces sweating when taken internally. It may be used to reduce the production of breast milk. For an infusion, use 1-2 tsp of the leaves with 1 cup of boiling water. This should be drunk three times a day.

Thyme - Carminative, anti-microbial, anti-spasmodic, expectorant, astringent, anthelmintic. Thyme is a good carminative in cases of sluggish digestion and dyspepsia. It can be used externally as a lotion for infected wounds, and internally for respiratory and digestive infections. It may be used as a gargle for laryngitis and tonsillitis, and eases sore throats and irritable coughs. As a gentle astringent it can be used in cases of childhood diarrhoea and bed-wetting. Make an infusion with 2 tsp of the dried herb and 1 cup of boiling water. This should be drunk three times a day.

Herbs can be mixed together when making preparations, and you can bless and consecrate each ingredient as you add it. Rhyme can be employed as you add the herbs, e.g. *"Rosemary ease muscular pain, feverfew, make the inflammation wane"*. You can then channel healing energy into the mixture. Similarly, essential oils may be mixed and charged with healing energy.

If you use other more physical forms of therapy, such as massage, shiatsu or reflexology, the effectiveness of these methods can be increased by channelling healing energy at the same time. Similarly, energy may be channelled into the acupuncture points if you practice acupuncture or acupressure.

It is important when giving healing, that you do not deplete you own energy, but that you draw in energy from around you, and channel it. It is also a good idea when healing another person, to help them to help themselves. They should not become dependent on you for healing, as this will not help them in the long run, and it may be a drain on you. It may feel good at first to be needed and relied on by them, but the novelty will soon wear off. Help them by giving them advice on sealing their own auras, centring themselves, and on simple remedies they can use.

Chapter Fifteen -

Developing the Magickal Personality

"I for my part, knew how little the true adept needs for his magic, but I had to work upon men's imaginations, and for that I needed a stage setting...and to this end I had to have about me that which should suggest the great days of the past when the cult to which I belonged was at the height of its power...And so, little by little, I had collected ancient things from the old temples...I also used colours for my background, knowing their power over the mind - over my mind as well as over the minds of those who came to visit me. There is a science of colours...for my purpose I use the pale opalescent moon-colours on a base of silver; the purple that is a plum- colour, and the reds that are magenta or maroon, and the blues of sea-water and the sky at night; never the strong primaries such as a man uses when he is a magus. Always the shadowy, blended colours are mine, for I am the shadow in the background.

As for my body, I had made that to be an instrument of my personality, training it, suppling it, learning its arts and powers. Nature had not been unkind, but she had not been lavish, and I had to make of myself something that I could use for the purpose I had in hand...I am bold, even rash, in the matter of lipsticks, and I love long ear-rings. It would require Huysmans to do justice to the ear-rings I have possessed - jade, amber, coral, lapis, malachite for day; and for the night I have great jewels...I wear my own fashions, and they come from the "soft furnishings" as often as not, for there is a richness in the great breadths of the draperies that one does not find in the dress materials...I like rings, too, so big that I can hardly get my gloves on over them; and bracelets like fetters on my wrists. My hands are supple with ritual...and I wear my nails long to match my tiger teeth. I like my shoes to be very soft and light and supple, like gloves rather than shoes, so that I can move in them without sound...I know the meaning of movement - how it should flow like water. I know too how the body should swing and balance from the waist..."

(from *Moon Magic* by Dion Fortune)

The above passage, from Dion Fortune's magickal novel *Moon Magic*, gives a description of how her character, Vivien Le Fay Morgan, has developed her magickal personality. She chooses clothing, colours, jewellery, and even the way she moves her body, and speaks, in a conscious way, to project her magickal personality. The way we dress, and how we look, not only tells others a lot about ourselves, but also affects the way we feel about ourselves. When we take our clothes off to work rituals sky clad, we are casting off our social selves, and coming to a more natural state, closer to nature. Putting on ritual jewellery, which is associated with the magickal personality helps one to transform into the Magickal Self, or to identify more strongly with it. If you work robed, changing into a robe is also a way of changing one's identity to that of the magickal personality, and this should be done consciously.

There are different viewpoints as to the place of the Magickal Personality in everyday life. In the passage quoted above, Vivien Le Fay Morgan consciously lives her magickal personality. However, firstly, this is a work of fiction, and secondly, there are dangers in this if one is not well earthed. W. E. Butler, in *"The Magician, his training and work"* (pp 122-127) says that the magickal personality should only be assumed consciously, for works of magick, and then should be positively dismissed by the operator, and returned into subconsciousness. However, he does say that although the magickal personality is dismissed, it will continue to operate indirectly on normal consciousness. In this way, one might find that the more one works with the magickal personality, the more like it one becomes in daily life. It is extremely important then, to ensure that one has a positive image of the magickal self. Butler instructs students to practice meditating on Love, Power and Wisdom, and to try to think and feel as if one is the embodiment of these qualities, first one at a time, then putting them all together, and this is good practice to ensure a positive magickal personality.

Butler talks about building the Magickal Personality from scratch. However, one may already have an image of one's Magickal Personality which one wants to develop further. We all have various sub- personalities, or inner selves, which interact with each other, and with the external world. When exploring these inner sub-personalities, many people find that they have an inner Priest/ess type figure, or Shaman, or Wise Person. Other common sub-personalities are the child, the warrior and the King or Queen. Pathworking can be used to discover one's sub- personalities, and then body and voice work can be used to get to know them and manifest them.

Sub-Personality Journey

Close your eyes and relax. Concentrate on your breathing, and feel deeply relaxed. Imagine yourself waking up in a summer meadow, and in your mind's eye, stand up and look around you.

Notice what is around you, the type of meadow you are in. How long the grass is, what type of flowers there are, and any insects, birds or animals. You notice a path leading away from you, and you begin to follow it. Notice whether it is straight, crooked, wide or narrow, neat or overgrown. Follow it until you come to a gate, behind which you can see a house. Notice what the house is like - how big, how many floors, whether old or modern. Open the gate and go through, and stand outside the house for a few moments, looking carefully at the house, and listening for any sounds. Now, open the front door, and go in and explore, but do not meet or see any of the inhabitants. Just look at the furnishings, and the contents of the house. Explore every room.

When you have finished exploring, come out of the house again, and stand outside the front door. Now call to your sub-personalities, ask for two or three of the sub-personalities which are most familiar to you to come out. Greet each of them, ask them their names, and try to get to know them a bit. Then call some more out, ask for two or three of your less familiar sub-personalities to come out of the house and make themselves known to you. Talk to them, and get to know them a bit. Watch the interactions of the different sub-personalities with each other, and notice if there is any antagonism between any of them. Choose the two who get on least well with each other, and watch them. What symbol is there for a compromise between them. You may find that body work will help here. Through movement, physically get into being one of the two antagonistic sub-personalities, and then the other. Feel what it is like to be each of them - what you are like when you manifest each of them, then find a symbol for the compromise, and make that symbol with your body. Keep your eyes closed whilst you are doing this. When you have found the symbol, say goodbye to your sub-personalities, and watch them go back into the house, then in your imagination, turn and walk back to the meadow, lie down, relax, then wake up again back in your own room or meditation space.

Try to draw what you have seen, rather than write a report of your visions, as the unconscious speaks in images, and the pictures will be useful to refer to time and again to do further work with.

You may find that a Priest/ess type figure has emerged as one of your sub-personalities. They may take many forms, such as a Chinese Sage, an Egyptian Priestess, an African Witch-Doctor, a Siberian Shaman, etc. If no such figure has emerged, try the journey again, this time specifically asking for your inner Priest/ess, or Magickal Personality to come out of the house.

Second Sub-Personality Exercise

Visualize yourself in the meadow again, but this time you are standing in the centre point of a white circle. Individually, each of your sub-personalities comes in to the circle, and you ask her or him "What do you want from me?", and listen to their reply. Then, tell them what you want from them. See one sub-personality go out of the circle before another comes in. When you have spoken to all of them, see a pillar of white light surrounding you and reaching up to the heavens. Float up the pillar until you meet another being at the top. This represents your higher Self. Your sub- personalities are all gathered around the edge of the circle down below. Notice what they are doing, and how they are interacting. Talk to the wise being about the meaning of it all. When you have gained some insight, float down the pillar again, and come back to normal consciousness. Record your experience through writing and drawing.

The sub-personality journeys can lead to greater self-understanding, and you may notice when different sub-personalities are acting in your life. For example, you may have an inner child, who manifests when you are frightened, miserable, or playful, or your Priest/ess may manifest when you are feeling confident and self- assured. Some of your sub-personalities may be in animal form, or be mythical creatures, such as a dragon, minotaur or gryphon. You can get to know each of them experientially through acting them out, using body posture, movement, voice work and key phrases that they might use. When you know your sub-personalities, you can call on them to help you. For example, if you are feeling frightened, and are manifesting your inner child, you can call on your inner warrior (if you have one) for strength, or your Priest/ess for confidence and guidance.

You may have more than one Magickal Personality, for example, an Atlantean Priest/ess and an African Shaman, or you may have a warrior type figure who also appears to have some magickal power. You should work on getting to know them all, but in magickal work, concentrate on just the one main Magickal Personality. When you feel that you are fully manifesting this one, you can begin to work on another in your ritual work. You can also try working with the Wise Being at the top of the pillar of light, but this may be more difficult as it may be more abstract and less personal. Work with the sub-personality first.

Channelling the Magickal Personality

Think about the type of robes or clothing your magickal personality wears, and any jewellery or other distinctive features. Try to get robes and jewellery as close as possible to that which you see your Magickal Personality wearing, and have these and any other props close at hand, when you perform this ritual. Begin this ritual sky-clad, and without jewellery. Cast a circle, and then meditate on your magickal personality. Put on the robes, clothing and jewellery of your magickal Personality, and think yourself into it. Use your body to express it, getting into the body posture, facial expression, and feel of the Magickal Personality. Begin to speak as your magickal personality, in its voice, starting by saying sentences which you have heard it say in inner journeys, then letting words flow. Give it freedom to express itself in speech, movement, sounds, maybe even dance. When you have had enough, remove the clothing, and close the circle. In future, you may find that donning the robes and jewellery is enough to transform you into your magickal personality, or just wearing the jewellery, and working sky-clad. You will also be able to transform yourself into your magickal personality without any props.

It is important that the sub-personality you are working with is in fact your Magickal Personality, and is a positive figure. The Magickal Personality is a sort of perfected you, and should manifest Power, Love and Wisdom. The more you work with this figure, the more you will manifest these qualities in your life, but do not try to be exclusively this being all the time. Your other sub-personalities need expression too, and are there for a reason. Do not try to destroy them or repress them, but look at how they can support each other, and express their positive sides. Sub- personalities which seem totally negative can also be the source of creativity and strength (like the Shadow archetype). Similarly, "good" ones can have a darker side. Sometimes, two opposing ones are just two sides of the same personality. Even your inner Priest/ess may have an alter-ego which appears in another form, but is connected. This may manifest negative Power (power over others), cunning, spite, malice and egotism, or sickly love and false compassion. It is a good idea, therefore to practice meditating on the three basic aspects of life; Power, Love and Wisdom. Meditate on each one in turn, and then try to manifest it. Feel Power in all its forms, and let it surge through you. Then do the same with Love, then Wisdom. Always do this in balance. Work equally with all three qualities. Finally try to manifest them all at the same time. Put these together with manifesting your Magickal Personality in rituals. It is a good idea to begin the meditation work on Power, Love and Wisdom before you do the sub-personality work, so that you have built up a good foundation, and will recognize your true Magickal Personality.

Magickal Names

As a magician and priest/ess it is important that you also find the magickal name(s) that correspond to your magickal personality(s). The name of a person or personality carries the essence of the person(ality). When you do work with magickal personalities, also work to discover your name(s). Names may come during meditation, or as a flash of insight during assumption of deity or in other altered states. Magickal names are a very personal thing, and should not be revealed to others, unless the name corresponds to an appropriate personality, e.g. a magickal personality for working in a group may be different and have a different name to the one you use when by yourself. In this respect a magickal name is a powerful secret, and should only be shared with others if they are people you have a bond of love and trust with.

Use of a magickal name during ritual can enhance the power and focus of a ritual, e.g. by use as a mantra, or as a proclamation or exclamation. In the same way as different magickal personalities may be appropriate to different types of work such as solo or group work, so also they may be appropriate to types of magick and used accordingly. Examples would be the use of a shaman type personality for working with nature spirits, a priestess for work with deities, a magician to results magick, etc. It may be the case that you develop one overall magickal personality, of which the other personalities are aspects, and as such the personality used will depend on the work undertaken, and the overall personality would be used for general work.

Chapter Sixteen -

Self-Initiation

Initiation is a process of "death and rebirth" - the old self dies, and the new and magickal self is born. A rite of initiation marks a serious commitment and dedication to the path, and should not be taken lightly. Having worked through the course, thus far, you should have noticed subtle (or not so subtle) changes in your self, and you may wish to mark this, and affirm your commitment to the path with a self- initiation ritual. Initiation is a process which happens over time, and the rite itself should be preceded by daily practice, building up in intensity as you approach the day of the rite, with the initiation rite being the culmination of this ritual practice. As the rite marks a rebirth, into your witch self or magickal self, you may wish to obtain a new magickal item or items for it. This could be a piece of ritual jewellery, such as a pentagram pendant, or amber and jet necklace (the traditional witches necklace), or a cord you wear around your waist. Some people choose to mark their initiations by having a tattoo in a magickal design, personal to themselves. It is also good to have a magickal weapon which you will consecrate at the end of the initiation rite. A ritual dagger, or athame is the general tool.

Self-initiation can be very empowering, and can produce a feeling of "walking on clouds", and it is very important to earth oneself afterwards, and then to have a rest from magickal work for a period of between a week and a month. Simple daily meditation may be practised during this period, but avoid intense magickal work. Time is needed to assimilate the experience, and the initiation process should be undertaken at a time when you do not have too much outside stress, and are able to take time for yourself. It should be stressed that self-initiation is not the same as initiation into a coven, and should you wish to join a coven at a later date, you would still have to go through a probationary period and coven initiation, if accepted.

When you decide that you want to do a self-initiation, plan the date of the ritual at least a month in advance, choosing a suitable time, perhaps consulting astrological tables, or at least the phases of the moon. It is best done on a waxing or full moon. The preparation beginning at the new moon. Make sure that you have a day off work for the initiation itself. You should already be doing daily magickal work based on the previous chapters, and you may already have decided on a magickal or witch name. If you haven't yet decided on your witch name, find one through meditation and pathworking in the daily ritual leading up to the rite of self-initiation. An outline of the preparatory work and initiation ritual are give here, but the actual ritual may be added to and personalized.

Begin preparing for the self-initiation by performing a daily ritual in which you contact your inner guide. Begin by creating a sacred space. Purify the area with incense and sprinkling salt water. Visualize a sphere around yourself, and call on the powers of the four quarters, visualizing the elemental landscapes. Call on the Goddess and the God, by whatever names you prefer to call them, and call on the Old Ones (see Chapter 24). Declare to the Elements, the Goddess, God and Old Ones that you are embarking on the path of initiation, and ask for their help in preparing you. Ask them to send you an initiator when the time comes.

Spend some time in meditation on the meaning of initiation, and opening yourself up for any messages from the Goddess and God. Carry out the "inner guide journey" (see chapter 5), and meet with your inner guide. Talk to her/him about initiation, and ask her/him to be your sponsor. Listen to what your guide has to say. When you come back from the journey, reaffirm your intention, before thanking the Goddess, God, Old Ones and Elements, and closing the circle.

The intensity and duration of this practice should be increased daily, and you may include other appropriate magickal work in the ritual. At least an hour a day should be spent performing this ritual in the week leading up to the self-initiation rite. Make vows when you start doing the preparatory rituals, that you will perform it every day, and about the duration of the practice, and stick to the vows. If you break the vows at any time, you should not proceed to the self- initiation rite. Make sure that the vows you make are realistic! It is better to make less demanding vows than to make highly demanding vows and not live up to them. When you have completed the preparatory work, and have reached the day you have set for your initiation, proceed as follows.

The Initiation Ritual

Spend the day in quiet meditation and fasting. Drink only pure water, or if you really cannot do this, allow yourself a small quantity of apple or grape juice. And do not smoke or take drugs! If you are on prescribed medication, consult your doctor. If the medication is short term, wait until you have finished the course of medication before doing the ritual. If possible, go to a sacred site or wild place and attune yourself with nature. Communicate with the nature spirits, and ask for their blessings. Think about the vows that you wish to make in your initiation. Think of a vow to yourself, one to the Goddess and God, and one to the Earth. Before you start the ritual, have a purification bath. You may put essential oils, herbs or sea salt in the bath.

Whilst in the bath, meditate on purifying your aura. See your aura as grey and dirty, but gradually becoming lighter and cleaner, until it is brilliant. When you emerge from the bath, allow yourself to dry naturally. Do not use a hair dryer, or rub yourself with towels. Rub your entire body with oil. This may be olive oil, grapeseed oil, or other vegetable oil, scented with pure essential oils of your choice. Perform the ritual skyclad.

Have an altar set up, with an altar cloth on it, with a chalice of wine, a piece of bread or cake on a platter, a censer, two altar candles, some anointing oil, your athame or other tool, any ritual jewellery which will be put on at the end of the ritual to mark your initiation, and two small dishes containing sea salt and water (from a spring or sacred well if possible). You may also wish to have images or statues of the Goddess and God on the altar. Light the candles and the incense, and purify your ritual space. Hold your hands over the water dish and say:

"I purify you, Oh water, in the blessed and mighty names of the Goddess and God", visualizing it glowing with white light.

Do likewise with the salt, then tip some of the salt into the water, and mix it in with your fore-finger. Sprinkle the salt water around your ritual space. Visualize a circle around you.

Call on the elements, then on the Goddess, God and Old Ones. Declare your intent, saying something like:

"I (ordinary name) *am prepared for initiation. I have followed the path and fulfilled my vows, and I now call upon the Goddess and the God and the Old Ones to confer on me initiation. I ask for the blessings of air, fire, water and earth"*.

Spend some time in meditation, and pranic breathing to gather energy and achieve an altered state of consciousness. You may also wish to use a mantra or chant. Proceed with the inner guide journey as above, and meet your inner guide. You may find that they look slightly different, or are dressed differently, in preparation for your initiation. Ask again for initiation, for your guide to be your sponsor, telling her/him that you are properly prepared and ready. Wait for an initiator to come, and see what happens! In some cases the inner guide might perform the initiation. In other cases another figure may appear. Others still may experience a lightening flash or a sudden expansion of consciousness. It will be a personal and individual experience. When you feel that it is over, thank and take leave of your guides and come back from the journey.

When you are ready, stand before the altar, and anoint yourself first with oil, then with salt water and lastly wine, saying:

"I am reborn into my true and magickal self, and I take on the name of (Witch name). *I ask for the blessings of the Goddess and God on my endeavours, and I vow (make your vows)"*.

When anointing yourself you may wish to anoint your chakras, or anoint yourself with a circle, pentagram, or personal symbol. It is good to write down your vows in your magickal diary, and sign the entry with your witch name. You might wish to sign it in blood (menstrual, or prick your finger with a pin). Present yourself to the Old Ones, and to the quarters, stating that you are now an initiate on the solitary path. Consecrate your ritual jewellery with the four elements (incense, water, salt and candle flame), and anoint it with oil for spirit before putting it on. Consecrate your athame or other tool in the same manner, then hold it to your heart, feeling a link with it, and filling it with your energy. Hold it up to the moon and stars, and ask for the blessings of the cosmos on it, then touch it to the ground, and ask for the blessings of mother earth. Lastly, consecrate the wine and cake by touching your athame to them, and channelling energy through it. Drink and eat, earthing yourself, then thank the Goddess, God and Old Ones, and close the circle. Write up your experiences in your magickal diary. Refrain from ritual for at least the next week, whilst you integrate the work.

Chapter Seventeen -

Spell and Ritual Construction

What is the difference between a spell and a ritual? A spell may be part of a ritual, and is used for results magick, i.e. achieving a specific result. Results magick can be very beneficial to magickal development, as repeated success in your magick helps strengthen the will and demonstrate the reality which replaces faith. Results magick usually works on a principle of attraction (things you want or preferably need), repulsion (getting rid of unwanted influences, traits, etc) or direction (to gain clarity and insight, help other people, places, etc). When doing results magick, one needs to be realistic in the intent of the spell, e.g. spells for a million pounds do not tend to work, because the number of ways you could get that sort of money are very limited, and the amount of energy that would be required to create sufficient change for this (via say a pools win) too massive to be generated. Results magick to attract things tends to work best when you provide a number of avenues for the magick to work along.

Rituals tend to be more diverse than spells, and may be for self-development, group development, or focusing on a spell to enhance its potency. Spells are usually fairly simple, but rituals can be quite complex and take a lot of time. Rituals tend to be repeated, and spells more performed as individual occasions for specific results. Rituals are more useful for results magick to create sustained change over a period of time, such as work on traits, self-empowerment, healing the land and other such themes.

Having decided to do a ritual or spell, the following process is usually followed:-

1] Intent

2] Preparation & Planning

3] Purification

4] Creation of Sacred Space

5] Invocation

6] Raising Power

7] Directing Power towards Intent

8] Earthing

9] Closing

10] Writing Up

1] When planning a spell or ritual, the first consideration is the intent, what do you wish to achieve through the use of techniques of raising and directing energy in accordance with your will? The intent of a ritual or spell is the essence running through the process, and you must be precise and concise in defining your intent. If your intent in any way imposes on the will of others, you must question your motivation for doing so. For example, it is morally negative to try to make a specific individual love you, but making yourself more attractive to gain attention is fine as it does not impose on anyone's will. There is nothing wrong with using magick to improve your situation, to find a better place to live, better work, to try and attract a partner, etc. The key is going about getting these things in a way that does not impose on the wills of others, usually by strengthening aspects of yourself and working with energies which attract the things you will to attain.

2] When you have decided on the intent of the ritual, you have to decide what techniques you will use to raise energy. When using any tools or substances, they should have a sympathy with the intent of the ritual, for example if you do a ritual to help you attract work, you would probably decide to use Jupiter, and hence appropriate symbolism, like the colour blue, cedar oil, hyssop herb (the lists in earlier lessons of herbs, oils, crystals, etc, may be referred to advantageously). The more you can put into the preparation of a ritual, the better. Using incense you have made, home-made wine as a sacrament, and anything else you have put energy into, all helps increase the energy of the ritual.

3] Purifying yourself before a ritual is always helpful, setting you in the right mood and frame of mind to perform magick, and reminding your conscious (and unconscious) mind that what you are doing is consciously creating change by working magick. Bathing is the usual form of purification, this may be ritualised by performing chants or mantras in the bath, and by doing a meditation/visualisation of purification whilst in the bath (seeing the water washing away any negativity and leaving the aura cleansed). Appropriate oils may be added to the water so you are suitably fragranced for the ritual. It is preferable to allow yourself to dry as naturally as possible, so whilst using a towel is fine, try not to use a hairdryer, it is distracting and tends to disperse energy away from the intent. Exercises such as the chakra exercise and the tree meditation (given in earlier chapters) may also be used to purify yourself (particularly if you are outdoors and not in a situation where bathing is possible).

4] There are various ways to create Sacred Space, but they all tend to run in a similar way. The area is generally purified, which may be done with the elements (taking a candle, incense, water, salt, etc around the space), by using an instrument like a drum or rattle, by clapping or sweeping with a broom (widdershins to indicate the banishing of any negative influences), or other such methods. When the space has been cleared it is ready to have the circle cast. A circle is a space between the worlds, free from outside influence, and influenced only by the will of the individual(s) in it and any influences they may have invited into it (deities, elemental energies, etc). Casting the circle symbolises stepping outside the normal modes of perception and action, and working magick and opening oneself to direct mystical and magickal experience. For this reason it is important that the space has been cleared, and the individual(s) ground themselves so as not to bring the stresses of mundane life into the circle. One should always perform some sort of grounding before casting a circle to centre oneself and prepare to do magick, and let go of anything inappropriate in the sacred space between the worlds.

Before grounding you may wish to do simple bodywork to let go of stresses held in the body, such as shaking the arms and legs, flopping (stretching on to tiptoes breathing in and raising the arms and then flopping down so you are bent double forcing the breathe out with a sound), breathing the stress out, etc. Exercises such as the tree exercise in chapter 12 and the breath meditation with white and black light in chapter 1 may then be performed to purify and centre the self. You are then ready to purify the space with methods such as those mentioned in the previous paragraph.

Casting the circle normally starts in the east (the place of beginnings) moving deosil (clockwise) round through south, west and north and back to east. Some people prefer to start from the north when casting the circle, as the north is often considered the place of deity. As long as you are consistent and return to the quarter you began in so a full circle is inscribed there is no reason why you cannot start in any quarter, though east is the norm as the beginning. As you move around the circle visualise a circle of blue light being formed by your hand, wand, dagger, sword or whatever you are using to inscribe the circle.

If working outdoors it is preferable to inscribe the circle on (or close to) the ground as you are drawing nearer the midpoint of the sphere (remember a sphere extends as far below you, into the ground, as it does above you), if indoors it is easier to draw it in the air more at waist or shoulder height, so you avoid furniture and do not have to bend over awkwardly. As you start to inscribe the circle, see the blue line of the circle flaming upwards and downwards, the flames expanding and making the body of the sphere, so that as you walk round the circle the flames are expanding to form a dome overhead and also underneath. If there is more than one person present, all others present should visualise this process happening as the circle is cast. When you have returned to the quarter you started in the sphere should be complete and the blue flames be all encompassing with no gaps or holes in the flames. When outdoors and in nature it may not require much effort to purify the area before casting the circle, the land being sacred anyway.

5] Having created a sacred space, it is usual to invoke energies to aid in the ritual. After the casting of the circle the elements are invoked. As with circle casting the elements are usually invoked from the east (air) first, moving deosil round the circle. To invoke an element stand at the appropriate quarter and draw an invoking pentagram, and visualise the elemental landscape (see Chapter 6) or different manifestations of the force of the element (such as winds and tornadoes for air, fire and volcanoes for fire, etc). Call to the spirits of the element and ask them to join you in the circle, with words such as "*Powers of the East, Spirits of Air, I invite you to join me in this circle. Come and be about me that I may know you better and share your qualities of (see Chapter 6 for appropriate qualities) with me. In the name of love I bid you hail and welcome.*"

Appropriate aspects of the Goddess and God are then invoked. Remember that although all Goddesses may be one Goddess and all Gods one God, they both have many faces. Thus there are many aspects to work with, and the choice of deity is usually dependent on the nature of the ritual and your personal sympathies. To invoke a deity, it is preferable to have created a link first. This may be achieved by researching and reading all you can about the deity, by wearing appropriate scents, items, etc; by meditating on the deity and her/his deeds, and so on. Having created a link with a deity beforehand means you are more likely to create a good link in the ritual and hence benefit from the energy of the deity (or deities) entering the ritual as well (be it in the form of energy, inspiration or whatever).

6] In both spells and rituals, the energy raised must be focused and then released or directed towards the desired end. Techniques may be either static (such as meditation, pranayama, visualization, using herbs, oils and incenses) or active (dancing, drumming and playing instruments, mantra and chanting, sexual activity, etc) or (commonly) a combination of the two. Rituals often have an active component (or several) in them to raise energy.

7] At the climax of a ritual or spell you direct Power towards the intent. This is generally done by visualizing the power being directed from yourself, as a beam of light (appropriately coloured) or cone of power. Depending on the spell or ritual the energy may be focused into something (candle, cord, crystal, yourself, etc) or towards something/someone (such as for healing, protection of other people/places, etc). During a ritual you will feel the energy levels rise, and the energy should be released at the moment when it feels right. This quickly becomes apparent when you do rituals, there is a build-up as of static charge, and you know the right moment instinctively. It can help if you visualise and see the energy building up as the ritual does, and be useful at times to release the energy with a sharp gesture or sound.

8] After you have done a ritual, it is important that you return yourself to a grounded and balanced state. Having shifted your consciousness through raising energy, and released the energy appropriately when in an altered state, you should then return to a centred and earthed state. This can be done by putting any surplus energy into the earth (which can always do with it); feasting also helps earth you, and grounding gestures like stomping your feet are good (as they release the energy into the ground automatically).

9] When the ritual is over and you have grounded yourself, it is time to close the ritual down. This is often done by reversing the actions you did in the creation of the sacred space. First you say goodbye and thank you to any deities you have invoked, and to the elements. Then the circle is opened and the ritual over.

10] After a ritual or spell has been done, it is important to write up what you did, what you felt and saw, impressions, etc. This helps you assess how well your work went in future times, and keep track of the techniques you use and how you feel about them. After a while patterns tend to emerge and you can see the type of techniques and exercises that work best for you, and develop your own style of working.

For spells, techniques like sigilization, talismans, candle and cord magick are very simple and effective ways to produce results. Sigilization and talismans are covered in the next lesson. Cords may be used very effectively with knots being used to formulate or disperse intent and/or energy. After generating energy, tying a knot to symbolise your intent, and naming your intent as you do so is a good way to formulate a spell. The knot is left in the cord and the cord placed somewhere away from sight, preferably wrapped in silk or a charm pouch. To get rid of something you don't want in your life, the knot should be tied at the beginning of the ritual, again naming what the knot represents and untied at the climax, to dispel the unwanted influence (sending it where it belongs), preferably with a sharp sound like a shout, clap or call. Obviously you would use a cord coloured appropriately to the nature of the ritual. Techniques like dancing and chanting go very well with using cords.

Raising energy and storing it in a candle, and anointing the candle with an appropriate oil and naming your intent as you do so is another simple and effective technique. The candle may either be allowed to burn down, sending the energy on its way, or burned for periods of time, repeating the ritual each time. Whether doing a ritual once or repeating it, it may also be enhanced by doing it when the appropriate planet(s) is/are well aspected, and on the appropriate day. Magick for growth and creation is generally performed on the waxing moon, and purification and banishing/removing on the waning moon.

Planetary Correspondences

Sun - individuality, will, wealth, success, advancement, power, friendship, growth, healing, leadership.
Metal - gold, colours - gold & orange, number - 6.

Moon - intuition, dreams, mystery, cycles, birth, fertility, psychic ability, secrets.
Metal - silver, colours - silver & white, number - 9 & 13.

Earth - manifestation, perseverance, strength, endurance, solidity, awareness.
Metal - not usually attributed, colours - brown, green & black, number 10.

Mercury - knowledge, healing, intelligence, communication, business, memory, creativity, science.
Metal - mercury, colours - orange & yellow, number - 8.

Venus - emotions, love, fertility, attraction, art, harmony, pleasure, sexuality.
Metal - copper, colours - green & rose pink, number - 7. Mars - strength, ego, conflict, revenge.
Metal - iron, colours - red, number - 5.

Jupiter - devotion, religion, authority, honour, truth, law, philosophy, humour, politics, responsibility, leadership, business.

	Metal - tin, colours - blue & purple, number - 4.
Saturn -	self-discipline, wisdom, time, formation, limitations, death, history.
	Metal - lead, colours - black & brown, number - 3.

Uranus -   invention, higher self, change, magick.
               Metal - tungsten*, colours - purple, number - 11.

Neptune - psychic powers, mysticism, compassion.
               Metal - titanium*, colours - grey & sea green, number - 2.

Pluto -   regeneration, transmutation, death.
               Metal - platinum*, colours - black & white, number - 1.

* These attributions are our own, based on experience, the others are traditional ones.

Example Spell for getting a Job

You will notice the symbolism is largely Jupiterian - Jupiter being associated with expansion and works to improve ones lot, with a little solar and earthy symbolism in the ingredients, both of which are associated with wealth (patchouli is often used for wealth spells). You will need the following ingredients - a blue candle, any of the essential oils listed below for purification, patchouli essential oil, incense (frankincense mixed with a touch of saffron would be good, but frankincense will suffice if you cannot get the saffron).

Ritually bathe and purify (essential oils such as chamomile, lavender and sandalwood would be good in the bath).

Cast a circle and call on the elementals in turn to come and aid you in your spell.

Call on the Goddess and God in appropriate forms you are happy with (for example Ganesha as remover of obstacles and god of business endeavours, and Lakshmi as goddess of wealth would be appropriate, or Hades and Persephone as associated with wealth and fortune) and ask for their blessings.

Hold the candle in your hands and visualize your circumstances changing and improving, visualize the sort of job you want. As your images become clearer and more defined etch the planetary symbol of Jupiter onto the candle about a third of the way down with the point of a knife. Continuing the visualization begin a wordless chant, making vowel sounds or humming as the feeling takes you. Focus the energy into the candle. After a few minutes anoint the candle with patchouli oil (as you do this concentrate on your job situation improving in the desired manner), starting at the middle of the candle and moving up the candle, then moving from the centre to the bottom of the candle, and then a flowing stroke from the bottom of the candle to the top and then back to the bottom again saying:

> *"From above to below*
> *Flows the pattern of perfection*
> *From desire to manifestation*
> *Flows the pattern of magick*
> *From within to without*
> *Flows the pattern of my will"*

Light the candle as you reach the last line (ideally so the flame takes as you say "my will"). Then visualize a blue cord of energy around the candle and make a tying gesture with your hands saying:

> *"I call on Earth to bind my spell*
> *Air to speed its travel well*
> *Fire lend Spirit from above*
> *Water quench this spell with love*
> *By all the power of three times three*
> *This spell bound around shall be*
> *To bring no harm nor return on me*
> *As I do will so mote it be"*

The spellbinding is performed so that you attract what is right for you rather than impose on the will of others.

Feast as desired.

Thank Goddess and God and say farewell. Thank elements and say

farewell.
Close circle.

The candle is left to burn down and the spell will then begin to manifest down from astral to physical.

Chapter Eighteen -

Voice Work & Body Work

Voice Work

The voice is one of the most important magickal tools we possess, yet it is often neglected in magickal training. Sound is transmutable energy, which can be used in many ways in ritual and magick. The voice is one of the most versatile tools, doesn't cost us anything, is natural, and we all have one. Developing the way that you use your voice is also an impiortant part of developing the magickal personality.

Firstly, the voice may be used to clear yourself of tension, stress or trapped energy, especially when combined with body work. Screaming, shouting and stamping are known to be therapeutic. This can be used to deal not only with tension and problems from the day, but with the help of a therapist (or Priest/ess or Shaman/ka) blocks and problems from the past. This is known in psychotherapy as catharsis. Here, old, unexpressed feelings and emotions, which have been festering within are finally let out, with voice, body and the emotions all fully engaged. This releases a lot of trapped energy, as when emotions are repressed, not only do we not have the use of the energy of the emotion, but we also use a lot of extra energy in keeping it repressed. When it is released we may find ourselves filled with energy and vitality which we did not know we had.

Using the voice in different ways can help put us in touch with our emotions. Each emotion has a different "wavelength" which can be studied, and imitated with the voice. For example, anger is sharp and abrupt, it builds up to a peak quickly, hits home, and then levels off. Saying "No!" loudly and sharply, can get us in touch with anger. Often we do not allow ourselves to fully experience an emotion, and a half experienced emotion can cause all sorts of problems, as it doesn't entirely go away. There needs to be fore-contact, i.e. a build up to contact with the emotion, followed by full contact with the emotion, and finally, withdrawal and letting go. "Sentic forms", i.e. the wave patterns which different emotions have, can be used to experience "sentic states" (see *"Sentics, the Touch of the Emotions"* by Manfred Clynes, unfortunately now out of print, but may be available through libraries or second hand book shops).

The following are the different wave forms for the different sentic states, as protrayed by Clynes, who developed the work of Richard Borofsky.

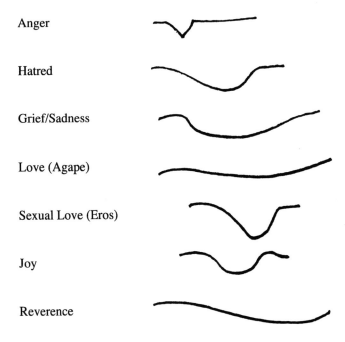

Anger

Hatred

Grief/Sadness

Love (Agape)

Sexual Love (Eros)

Joy

Reverence

A more controlled way of using the voice and boy to release stress and tension is the yogic body flop. This is a good exercise to do prior to a ritual, as it helps to remove the stress of the day, and put you in the right frame of mind for the ritual. It is especially good for those occasions when you do not have the time for a ritual bath prior to your magickal work. A description of the yogic body flop is given in chapter 1.

Another way the voice can be used is to achieve an altered state of consciousness. Chanting mantra can be used to this effect. Repeating a single sound over and over again produce a trance state, and sometimes the loss of self. Chanting mantras in a group can be particularly effective, as the different voices harmonise, and become one continuous sound. Participants may feel that they become one with the sound. Different sounds have different energies, which in turn have different effects on consciousness. The most famous mantra is the Om or Aum, which is said to be the sound of the universe. It can thus be used to gain transcendence, and achieve oneness with the universe. Other mantras are included in chapter 2.

Voice work can also be used to aid shamanic transformation. For example making animal sounds, roaring, grunting, etc, to transform one's consciousness into that of an animal. This is a useful technique in working with power animals and animal guides, and to aid astral projection in animal form. We could also learn to channel our inner guides more effectively by thinking about how they talk, the words they would use, tone of voice, speech patterns, etc, and imitating them, until we feel ourselves transforming into our inner guide. Again, all these techniques are more effective when combined with body work. The same technique can be used to explore our sub-personalities, and to become the magickal personality.

When invoking deities, we are using our voices to bring the divine energy to the magick circle or temple. The way in which the voice is used can greatly influence the effectiveness of the invocation. The voice is an instrument of our will, and helps to put our will into action. The intonation and vibration of divine names can be very powerful in bringing the divine power to us.

The voice is also used to raise power in the circle. Sound is energy, and that energy can be used to give impetus to our magickal work. Again, this can be combined with bodywork - chanting and dancing is an excellent way to raise power. It may be combined with other methods of raising energy, such as pranayama, visualisation, etc. Similarly, once the energy is raised, the voice can be used to direct it to the right place, again in conjunction with visualisation, breath, and body work. This may be done by using a command word, such as "Go" or "Heal", or by using a barbarous word and putting power into it whilst concentrating on the intention. Barbarous words are words which do not have any obvious meaning, but contain inherent power in the sounds of the syllables. Medieval grimoires are full of such words (which may be mistranslations of older actual words), as are translations of some older texts, such as Ancient Egyptian and Coptic texts. Examples of barbarous words are words such as Ompehda and Bahlashti.

Voice work can also be used to help us build rapport with others, and in a more negative sense, to enable us to manipulate others. Neuro Linguistic Programming (NLP), which is now widely taught to both sales people and people in the helping professions teaches methods of indirect hypnosis using speech and body language. In effect this means that you can learn to hypnotise people without them knowing you are doing it. This is done through subtly imitating a person's body language and speech patterns, using the type of language they use, speaking at the same pace, and adopting their tone of voice and mannerisms. Once you have practiced this enough, and the person has become very relaxed with you, you can make a subtle change, such that you begin to take the lead in conversation, rather than following them. Speeding up and slowing down the speech, and using words which the person associates with relaxation, can produce a trance in the other person. To do this requires a careful study of the other person's speech, mannerisms and terms of reference, and needs training and practice.

Voice work then, can be used effectively in all stages of magickal work, from preparation for ritual, to invocation, raising of power, trance induction through to directing and sending of the energy. In group rituals another important use is in communicating the intent of the ritual, as well as the format of the ritual to all participants. Outside of ritual, the work continues, with bringing the magickal personality through in daily life, and using the voice to influence others (preferably not in a way which will infringe on their rights or will).

Body Work

Body work too, can be used to clear oneself of tension and blocks, to help us to get more in touch with our emotions, to achieve an altered state of consciousness, to aid shamanic transformation, and to raise energy within the magick circle. Dancing can be used to achieve an altered state of consciousness, and to raise power. Scourging and binding the body can also be used to achieve an altered state. Ecstatic dancing is used widely in Shamanic traditions, and more controlled body movements and postures are used in other traditions, such as yoga and the martial arts. Using one's body to imitate an animal, forming yourself into the shape of the animal, crawling, leaping, etc. helps us to get into the animal state of mind, enabling a shamanic transformation. Again, using the body posture chartacteristic of an inner guide, or sub-personality can aid us in channeling the guide, or becoming more in touch with the sub-personality. The magickal personality may be imitated in a similar way, until the magickal self becomes the natural you.

In order for the energy to flow properly, we need to be comfortable and happy in our bodies. We need to be able to listen to the messages our bodies give us, and to express ourselves through our bodies. Yoga, dancing, Tai Chi and the martial arts are all excellent forms of body work. Practising any of these helps to unify the mind and body, such that they flow together harmoniously. The mind and body canot be totally seperated, each affects the other. Our attitudes, thoughts and emotions can affect our bodies in a negative way producing psychosomatic illnesses, which can lead to more physical illnesses, such as arthritis and even cancers. In a more positive way, an untroubled mind may show forth in a vital and healthy body and good posture.

Stanley Keleman, in his book "*Emotional Anatomy*" describes individual shape as a "dynamic interaction between personal emotional history and genetic shape". This is an ongoing process in which thoughts, emotions and experiences are embodied. Structure (our personal form) is seen as ordering the events of our existence. Keleman describes the creation of human shape, beginning with the molecules and cells which form the embryo, and argues that a given shape is changed by a person's emotional history, the marks made by love, disappointments, insults and assaults, the challenges and stresses of existence. He describes four basic patterns of somatic distress - rigid, dense, swollen and collapsed. The rigid type has a braced, overfirm and aggressive stance, which reflects emotional qualities such as anger, fear, pride, cruelty and an authoritarian personality. A person exhibiting this type of somatic distress needs to "destructure", to

RIGID
OBEDIENT
CONTROLLED

DENSE
DEFIANT
SHAMED

SWOLLEN
INVASIVE
MANIPULATIVE

COLLAPSED
COMPLIANT
COMPROMISING

unbrace themselves, challenge their actions and soften up. Body work needs to concentrate on shortening the body, feeling the centre of balance at a lower point on the body, reaching out, moving fluidly, etc.

The dense pattern of somatic distress shows forth in a compacted, pushed down, over-firm and pressurized body stance, reflecting emotional qualities such as suspicion, doubt, possessiveness, stubbornness and humiliation. It may indicate a passive-aggressive behaviour pattern. The person needs to soften the outer wall of the body, relaxing the outer muscles, lengthen, elongate and decompress the body and resotre rhythmicity.

The swollen type appears puffed out, inflated pear- shaped, and jelly like, reflecting a manipulative and invasive personality and feelings of dissatisfaction, self-absorption, inferiority, narcissism and lacking boundaries. The person needs to deflate their body, organise their boundaries, using their body wall, and give structure by firming and filling in.

The collapsed type appears sunken down, caved in and formless, reflecting feelings of weakness, disappointment, resentment, being a victim, and withdraal. The person needs to stand more upright, build an inner support strucutre working with their inner connective tissue, and to build rhythmicity, excitation and pulsatory vitality.

The above descriptions are extreme, and a person may display a mixture of these somatic distresses at a given time, or you may notice that people you know display one or other of them all the time to some extent. Bioenergetic exercises (such as those given in chapter 4) and massage can be used to help restore balance, but it may require a trained Reichian (or other bodywork) therapist to help. There are, however, some simple exercises which can be done on a daily basis to help balance the subtle energies in the body, and to energise and balance the chakras (see chapter 4).

Chapter Nineteen

Skrying and Other Forms of Divination

Skrying has been mentioned in chapter 11, and we will now consider it further. Skrying is probably the oldest form of divination, and may be performed in many mediums - e.g. mirror, crystal, bones, water, flame, oil, clouds, entrails, etc. A key to becoming proficient in skrying is practice - this really is a skill that only comes with practice (unless you are extremely lucky and have a natural talent for it). Skrying is quite a passive form of divination, in that you look for images and symbols in the medium you are using, be it a mirror, candle flame, bowl of water (and/or oil), etc.

Before skrying you should always ground and centre yourself, and try to ensure your surroundings are quiet and harmonious, and likely to remain so for the duration of your work. Practice pranic breathing and focus your attention on your breathing. When you are well focused, turn your attention to the medium you are using (in this instance let us say a crystal ball). Hold your attention on the ball and do not let it waver.

After a while (and it may be a while!) you will see the ball starts to "cloud over" inside (usually with a white sort of mist), and this mist clears to reveal images. Making sense of the images is another matter! You may find it takes a number of attempts to reach the stage where the "clouding over" occurs, this is to be expected. If you are skrying indoors, such as in a temple, have only one candle as illumination, as you will find this sets the mood better and enables better perception of imagery in the ball. This technique works well with mirrors, crystals and fluids in a bowl (like water and oil). You may find it helpful to drape a cloth around the medium (unless it is a candle!) to prevent reflections of objects around the room from appearing in your medium and giving you a false impression of what you are seeing (or not!). If you are skrying in a candle or cloud, they will not mist over, and you may either find spontaneous images coming to you, or you may see images in the shapes made by the dance of the flame or drifting clouds (like you used to as a child). It is important to remember that when you are skrying the images may come in the form of symbols, and symbols always have more levels than you consider!

Another technique that could be considered skrying is psychometry. Psychometry is where you hold an object that belongs to somebody and receive psychic images connected with the object and its past and use. Psychometry also requires much practice, and if you try developing a skill in it you may find a lot of the images you get when psychometrising objects for people are quite abstract, and the people concerned will not see any relevance in what you see. Do not be put off by this, as time goes by and you practice, you will become more proficient at getting clear images and being able to interpret them appropriately.

There are many forms of divination, the most commonly used probably being the tarot, runes, I Ching, and geomancy. As there are numerous books written on each of these subjects which cover the material admirably, we leave it to you to further research them and discover which you feel a sympathy for and desire to work with. We would recommend finding one form, such as runes or tarot, and concentrating on it and developing a proficiency before moving on to another type of divination. By proficiency we mean at least a couple of years fairly intense work with the system you choose.

Recommended Reading

Geomancy - "*Terrestrial Magic*" by Stephen Skinner is a good comprehensive read.

I Ching - "*The I Ching or Book of Changes*" translated by Richard Wilhelm. The classic translation and for us still the best. To really appreciate the I Ching a study of Taoism is recommended. Reading a copy of "*The Tao Teh King*" first is definitely helpful, and also gives a lot of insight into the mystical path and mystical experience.

Runes - there are two essential works which negate the need for the other more mediocre or general books around. These are *"Leaves of Yggdrasil"* by Freya Aswynn and *"Futhark"* by Edred Thorsson.

Tarot - there are many books available on the tarot. We would recommend *"The Tarot"* and *"The Book of Tokens"* by Paul Foster Case, *"The Golden Dawn Tarot"* by R Wang, in that order.

Chapter Twenty

Talismans: Construction & Use, Sigilization Techniques

1. Talismans

Talismans could be described as magickal foci to attract energy on a specified wavelength to achieve a desired intent. Talismans using symbols, letters and sigils are usually constructed on virgin paper (preferably parchment, vellum or papyrus bought specifically for the desired purpose). As with any ritual the more effort put into the preparation the better, such as the use of a magickal ink. This could be a resin such as dragon's blood, or your own blood is very powerful (menstrual blood particularly so), though this is a matter of taste as some people are unhappy with its use. The use of any blood other than your own cannot and should not be countenanced. A power object such as a crystal, rock, piece of wood or bone may also be charged up as a talisman, with symbols or sigils being carved into it. Staining the carvings with magickal inks is a good empowering technique, as is anointing the talisman with a suitable oil afterwards. When making a talisman the shape should also be considered, e.g. it may be appropriate to make the talisman triangular, square, or circular, etc. The following list is a checklist for constructing a talisman:

a) The intent of the talisman.

b) Material to be used - paper or other.

c) The ink to be used.

d) The symbols and/or sigils and/or letters to be used.

e) The timing of the creation.

f) The ritual to go around its creation, e.g. what energy raising techniques are you going to use prior to the creation of the sigil to empower it, etc.

After a talisman has been constructed, it should be placed either on your person (preferably wrapped in silk, such as in as pouch if it made of paper) or somewhere where you will spend a lot of time close to it and benefit from its effect, such as under your pillow. If you were creating a talisman to attract energy to a place, such as a site, you may bury the talisman to attract energy to the place to be directed appropriately.

2. Techniques of Sigilization

A simple and effective form of sigilization involves the formulation of a sentence of intent, such as "*It is my will to have the cunning of a wolf*". Each duplicate letter is then removed, leaving one of each letter that is in the sentence, in this case, the letters A, E, H, I, L, M, O, S, T, V, W & Y. A pictographic sigil is then made using these letters, combining them to form a sigil which on looking resembles nothing to do with the statement of intent. This sigil is then placed somewhere where you will frequently see it, such as on a door. Every time you see the sigil you reinforce the intent which has been fired into your unconscious mind at its creation in a ritual.

A magick square is a square of numbers where each horizontal line, vertical line and diagonal add up to the same number. The square for a planet has sides the length of the number usually attributed to the planet, such as 3 for Saturn, 4 for Jupiter, etc. When using magick squares to form a sigil, a word to represent the desired intent should be formulated. Traditionally Hebrew is often used, but English (or any other language you desire) works just as well, and is the language concentrated on here as it is our mother tongue. Each letter has attributed to it a number between 1-9. The word can then be seen as a list of numbers between 1-9, e.g. Wisdom would be 5,9,1,4,6,4. The first letter is chosen as the starting point on the appropriate planetary kamea, marked with a small circle and a straight line drawn to the next number on the square, onto the next, and so on until the last letter is reached. The figure drawn then represents the word as a sigil to be drawn on a talisman.

A, J, S	1
B, K, T	2
C, L, U	3
D, M, V	4
E, N, W	5
F, O, X	6
G, P, Y	7
H, Q, Z	8
I, R	9

The Kameas or Magick Squares

Saturn

4	9	2
3	5	7
8	1	6

Jupiter

4	14	15	1
9	7	6	12
5	11	10	8
16	2	3	13

Mars

11	24	7	20	3
4	12	25	8	16
17	5	13	21	9
10	18	1	14	22
23	6	19	2	15

```
Sun       6  32   3  34  35   1
          7  11  27  28   8  30
         19  14  16  15  23  24
         18  20  22  21  17  13
         25  29  10   9  26  12
         36   5  33   4   2  31


Venus    22  47  16  41  10  35   4
          5  23  48  17  42  11  29
         30   6  24  49  18  36  12
         13  31   7  25  43  19  37
         38  14  32   1  26  44  20
         21  39   8  33   2  27  45
         46  15  40   9  34   3  28


Mercury   8  58  59   5   4  62  63   1
         49  15  14  52  53  11  10  56
         41  23  22  44   8  19  18  45
         32  34  35  29  25  38  39  28
         40  26  27  37  36 30 3   1  33
         17  47  46  20  21  43  42  24
          9  55  54  12  13  51  50  16
         64   2   3  61  60   6   7  57


Moon     37  78  29  70  21  62  13  54   5
          6  38  79  30  71  22  63  14  46
         47   7  39  80  31  72  23  55  15
         16  48   8  40  81  32  64  24  56
         57  17  49   9  41  73  33  65  25
         26  58  18  50   1  42  74  34  66
         67  27  59  10  51   2  43  75  35
         36  68  19  60  11  52   3  44  76
         77  28  69  20  61  12  53   4  45
```

Chapter Twenty-one

Magickal Tools: Types & Consecration

What are magickal tools? Magickal tools are items made or personalised to act as a focus for the mind and for subtle energies, and to symbolise the qualities of those subtle energies. As the name implies, they are meant to be used. The most well known tools are the elemental ones - pentacle (or disk), dagger (or athame), wand, cup and sword. There are many others such as musical instruments, the censer, etc, as listed below:-

Earth

Pentacle - a disk or platter, symbolic of the solidity and endurance of earth. The traditional pentacle in magick has a pentagram representing man (the microcosm) on the front and a hexagram, representing the universe (the macrocosm) on the obverse. This also emphasises the primary magickal axiom *"As Above, So Below"*. Many pagans and witches use a wooden platter as the pentacle, emphasising its use as the sustaining principle to hold food, usually bread, cakes or fruit.

Drum - the drum also represents earth as the shaman's symbol of the world, often decorated to illustrate the experiences, affiliations, perceptions, etc of the owner. The drum is an excellent tool to help induce trance, both by sustained playing and also by using tapes of drum music as a background to meditative or ecstatic states.

Air

Dagger - some say the dagger represents fire, but we find the attribution of air more appropriate. (Indeed the attribution of fire can cause problems when working with the tarot where wands are fire). The dagger represents the power of the mind, the decisive cleaving power of clarity and focus. The dagger is often used in invoking and banishing rituals, as it is an active weapon to be wielded. The dagger is also used as a tool to etch sigils in candles, chop wands, cut food, etc, and should be functional not ornamental. Witches get round this by having the athame (black-handled knife) to wield and direct, and the burin (white-handled knife) to use practically.

Flute/Pipes - wind instruments are of great use to work with air, calling up the powers of air, and being able to provide pleasant sounds to maintain calm or wild tunes to frolic to.

Censer - holds the incense and enables one to smudge oneself. The stimulatory properties of smell in ritual should not be ignored, as smell is one of the strongest prompts to the unconscious available.

Fire

Wand - representing the power and force of the wielder, the wand is a tool of command (cf the traditional sceptre or rod). Wands may take many forms. As well as the traditional attribution of fire (some say air), it may be attributable to any element as a focus to direct the energy of that element using an appropriate wood. E.g. willow for a water wand, oak for earth, and not forgetting of course the caduceus, which is appropriate to air as the symbol of healing.

Spear - often attributed to Mars and the Sun, the Spear also represents power and force.

Stave/Stang - although here attributed to Fire, the Stave may also be attributed to Spirit, being used to direct the will and do such things as casting the circle, as a sword. It is a very useful tool for outdoor work, being easy to carry without attracting attention (like a sword might, for example). The same use and convenience is true of the stang, which also represents the Horned God (with 2 points) and the Goddess (three points).

Rattle/Sistrum - the rattle is often used as a cleansing or banishing, and both are good for their invigorating qualities.

Water

Chalice/Horn - holds the wine, water or appropriate sacrament. Symbolic of the womb of the mother, and of the receptive principal. May also be used for skrying in.

Rain Pipe - the sound of the water pipe is an excellent call to the element of water and has a soothing quality as one would expect.

Trident - may be Neptune and Spirit as well. Like the stave, a trident may be used to direct energy.

Spirit

Sword - some attribute the sword to air or fire, but for us it is active spirit. By size alone, it is of a larger scale of magnitude to the other elemental tools. The sword symbolises the will of the wielder, and is used to command and direct.

Cauldron - as a combination of all the elements, the cauldron to us also represents spirit, as the place from which the elements are formed and to which they eventually return. It is the source of wisdom.

Bell - represents the Vault of Heaven, and the chime suggests purity.

Other Tools

Belt/Girdle - traditionally Venusian, the belt or girdle represent the power of Love, the motivating force of the universe.

Besom - for purifying. The besom is used to sweep the circle, to keep places clean. Also a symbol of the union of the Goddess and God as the Her yoni (the brush) and his Lingam (the rod). Represents spirit flight as the witches mount.

Cords - used for purification (being "properly prepared" in a Witches circle) and for cord magick.

Crystal Ball - for skrying and may also be used for focusing energy, spheres (along with eggs) being the best shape to contain energy.

Magick Mirror - for skrying, the mirror is lunar in its use of reflection. Magick mirrors are usually painted black, and often have accumulators with metals or herbs representing the seven classical planets used in their construction. See the excellent and inexpensive "*How to Make and Use Magick Mirrors*" by Nigel R Clough for full details.

Necklace - represents the power of the Goddess, the Circle of Rebirth. Symbolic of the yoni, attributions may be as appropriate depending on what the necklace is made from.

Robes - robes represent the change into the magickal personality, we change out of our everyday clothes and into a robe to perform ritual. Hence they indicate the change in our state and our conscious decision to move out of the mundane and into the magickal worlds.

Scourge - is a tool of discipline. May be used to generate energy (through light scourging of the back and buttocks, which stimulates the Muladhara chakra) as well as symbolizing the need for mental discipline.

Sickle/Scythe - are Saturnian in nature, and may be used to harvest herbs and plants, and they symbolize time and its power to reap the harvest of life.

You may often read about making your own tools, and how it is preferable to do so. This is true if you have the skills to do so, but if you do not then buying them is the obvious solution (you should at least make your wand though). Obviously when you make your own items the process of empowerment begins at an earlier stage than when you buy something, and will have more of your charge attached to it. It is a magickal tradition that you never haggle when buying something to be used for magick, as this is considered to disperse energy and detract from your intent. There is a plethora of suppliers around now, although many items may be found in places such as craft and antique shops. When purchasing magickal tools, follow your instincts on things that feel "right".

Magickal Tool Consecration

Once you have purchased a magickal tool, you will need to consecrate it, ready for use in ritual. A simple consecration ritual is given below as a guide, but do feel free to modify and adapt this to your own preferences.

Have salt (or a crystal) and water (not tap) ready in small bowls, candle, incense and censer, and a suitable oil (depicting spirit) on the altar ready.

Ritual Bath.

Ground yourself.

Cast circle.

Call on elements in turn at the appropriate quarter (starting with Air - East and moving round clockwise (deosil) to Earth - North) and ask for their blessings and energy.

Call on the Goddess and God in turn in whichever aspects you know them best (it is preferable if possible to call on aspects which match from the same pantheons, such as Isis and Osiris, Kali and Shiva, etc) and ask for their blessings and energy.

Pass the item through the incense smoke (if it is large you may move the censer around it and blow smoke over it as well as you do this), saying:

"I purify and consecrate you with the power of the element of Air." As you do this visualize winds blowing over the item, removing any impurities.

Pass the item through a candle flame, saying:

"I purify and consecrate you with the power of the element of Fire." As you do this visualize fire caressing the item around its edges, burning away any impurities.

Sprinkle the item with water, saying:

"I purify and consecrate you with the power of the element of Water." As you do this visualize water flowing over and around the item, washing away any impurities. Sprinkle the item with salt, or touch the crystal to it, saying:

"I purify and consecrate you with the power of the element of Earth." As you do this visualize the item being surrounded with earth, absorbing any impurities. Anoint the item with oil, saying:

"I purify and consecrate you with the power of the element of Spirit." As you do this visualize gold light imbuing itself in the item.

Thank and say farewell to the God and Goddess.

Thank and say farewell to the elements (in reverse from North anti-clockwise (widdershins) to East). Open circle.

You may wish to wrap items which are not being left on an altar in silk, to preserve the charge on them. Do not allow anyone else to handle your magickal tools. Your tools represent a unique extension of you as manifest in your magickal self, and as such should only be used by you in ritual, and not by anyone else.

Chapter Twenty-two

Telesmatic Images, Deity Assumption & Mandalas

Telesmatic Images

A telesmatic image is one built up from the attributions of the letters in the name of the form of the image. The technique comes from the Golden Dawn system, and is generally used to depict Angelic forms based on the Tree of Life, and in rituals such as the Lesser Banishing/Invoking Pentagram (see Appendix 2). Although the technique can be used for other deity forms, it does not always translate so well, and experimentation may be required to find suitable forms.

One of the great values of this technique is that it enables you to build up an image for any word, such as one used in a sigil or talisman, and give it a form. It also encourages you to practice visualisation of complex images in a precise manner. It should be noted, though, that this technique is often used to form a divine image, and so the precision of the image is vital, as incorrect form may lead to not quite getting the contact you wanted, which may be a not very pleasant surprise if the current contacted is inappropriate to the nature of the work you are doing.

If this technique is used with a sigil or talisman, the telesmatic image formed may be visualised (for instance) on the talisman as part of the empowerment, or it may be used to give form and image to the thought form.

Hebrew	Letter	Attribution
Aleph	A	Spiritual, winged, slender, male
Beth	B	Active, athletic, male
Gimel	G	Beautiful, full, changeable, female
Daleth	D	Beautiful, full, female
He	H, E	Fierce, strong, fiery, female
Vau	V, U	Steady, strong, heavy, male
Zain	Z	Thin, intelligent, male
Cheth	C, Ch	Full, female
Teth	T	Strong, fiery, female
Yod	I, J, Y	Delicate, female
Kaph	K	Large, strong, male
Lamed	L	Well proportioned, female
Mem	M	Dreamy, epicene, female
Nun	N	Determined, male
Samekh	S	Thin, expressive, male
Ayin	Aa, O, Ngh	Heavy, male
Peh	P, Ph	Fierce, strong, female
Tzaddi	Tz	Thoughtful, full, female
Qoph	Q	Full, male
Resh	R	Proud, dominant, male
Shin	Sh	Fierce, active, male
Tau	Th	Epicene, male

By male and female, we mean rather masculine and feminine, though when applied to body parts they may be "converted" into attributes such as fullness, athleticism, litheness, etc. It is also worth noting that many of the Archangels names end with -AL or -EL, a combination of male and female letters, which is indicative of the fact that angelic (and indeed divine) forms combine both male and female, and transcend gender. Thus most names will be a combination of male and female, with one being dominant due to more of that "gender". The first letter of the name is considered to be the head, and the last to be the feet, the remainder making the rest of the body.

A note on size - Angelic forms may be visualised about reasonable human size (6'), Archangelic forms about 8'- 10', and Deities huge and towering.

Example

Raphael -   RPAL (Hebrew)

Head   -   R - Proud dominant masculine
Upper Body -   P - Strong, resolute, feminine
Lower Body -   A - Slender, masculine
Feet   -   L - Well proportioned, female

Male = 2, Female = 2 - Androgynous form

Raphael is the Archangel of Air, so the image would be of a male looking figure (as head is masculine), with a strong but lithe torso, slender muscular legs and small but well proportioned feet. As Archangel of Air, the robe colour would be yellow, and s/he would bear the tool of air, i.e. a sword (although this would be expected to be the dagger, it is more the attributions as considered for the tarot suits).

Example

Shiva - ShIVA

Head   -   Sh - Active, male
Upper Body -   I - Delicate, female
Lower Body -   V - Steady, strong, male
Feet   -   A - Slender, spiritual, male

Male = 3, Female = 1 - Male form

So the form could be seen as a huge man, with a keen active and beautiful face (Deities are usually beautiful after all!), with a slender torso, firm strong legs and slender feet. From depictions Shiva is shown with blue skin, and wearing a tiger skin loin cloth, and bearing a trident.

From the example it can be seen that one needs to consider the attributions and known forms, as the Hebrew does not always translate that well, so unless research is done and ones own attributions worked on, this technique may not always work so well with non- Hebrew forms and other attributions should be included as appropriate. E.g. Pan would have A attributed to the upper body and N to the lower. The N on the lower body would in this instance equate to the furry lower body and large phallus.

Assumption of Deity

When you have become accomplished at the creation and visualisation of telesmatic images, you may wish to progress on to one of the keystones of magick, which is the assumption of godforms. By assumption we mean the visualisation externally of a deity, which is then brought into and merged with your being, so that you become infused and enthused with the deity and her/his energy. If you do intend to assume godforms, it is worth spending time researching the deity in question to discover existing symbolisms, correspondences, means of worship, etc, as well as doing meditation and attempting to form a link with the deity through use of the appropriate symbols and forms.

Before you visualise the deity and assume its form, raise energy through offerings (such as a mandala), appropriate mantra, meditation and any other appropriate techniques. You should then start the assumption by visualising the deity in front of you. There are several ways all of which work equally well for different people, so try them out and see which suits you best. One way is to visualise the deity the same size as yourself, and then moving towards and into you. Another is to visualise the deity very large, but getting smaller as it approaches you so it is the same size when you merge. A third way is to visualise the deity very large, and increase in size to its size so you merge as a "giant" (the deity may also shrink a bit to meet you "in the middle" as it were if you so desire).

As the deity merges with you feel the energy of the deity flowing through you, explore the differences it brings, in perception, attitude, senses, power, love, etc. Perform any spells or rituals you may have planned and feel appropriate in this form, and then start the process of cutting off your link from the deity (if it has not already left). You may find the feeling of the presence of the deity fades naturally any you can enjoy the "afterglow" as the deity returns to its more usual form/place. If the deity has not left by the time you wish to close the ritual begin by visualising the deity leaving your body, and see it becoming larger as it moves away, offer love and thanks and bid her/him farewell. You may wish to earth yourself after this if you do not feel totally centred, try stamping your right foot hard three times in quick succession. If you still feel residual traces of the deity and do not feel they are appropriate, do an earthing exercise and put the surplus energy into the earth. Unless you are doing a devotional practice with a deity, it is usually inappropriate to invoke and assume a godform and then not cut the link after ritual. To operate in the mundane world whilst in an assumed godform may cause you to start having experiences of a bizarre not to say possibly unpleasant nature and is strongly discouraged.

Mandalas

A mandala (Sanskrit) is a symbolic representation of the universe, in the same way as a yantra is a symbolic representation of deity. Although deities may of course represent and be the universe, with mandalas we are considering the universe both as microcosm and macrocosm, so a mandala may also represent a person, and their state of being.

The use of mandalas as an offering can be a very powerful technique and good for encouraging the mystical side. A mandala is created as a symbolic universe, and then that universe is offered to a deity. As the creation of the mandala is designed to be pleasing to the deity it is offered to, so too should it be pleasing to you, the maker. Use things and colours which please you, such as crystals, feathers, beads, bones, paints, etc. In this manner you are putting something of yourself into the mandala and offering that part of yourself as part of the ritual. Also, by putting something of yourself into the mandala, you are embodying one of the great magickal axioms - "*As above, so below*", by the reflection of you, the microcosm, into your creation, the symbolic macrocosm.

It is important when you make mandala offerings that you destroy the mandala after the ritual is over. The energy that you put into the creation of the mandala has been offered, the physical form of the mandala is now effectively an empty shell. By the destruction of the mandala you give the final blessing to the rite, by cutting off from the energy you offered, thus ensuring its selfless nature as devotion and trust in the deity. If you look around the world this theme is echoed in very different cultures, from Tibetan mandalas to Amerindian sand painting.

Although often symmetrical, mandalas do not have to be so. The drawing of a mandala can be a powerful act, and when drawing one you should give free rein to your intuition, and let whatever colours and symbols come to your mind be expressed in the mandala. Where possible the mandala should be drawn in one session, to allow free flow. A mandala is a form of self expression, and subsequent examination of the mandala may reveal much about your state of mind and being. Look at the colours and symbols you have used, and consider what they mean to you - did you use animals, shapes, etc, are there any significant numbers in it, repetition or contrast, for example.

Drawing a series of mandalas over a period of time (such as monthly over a year) can give insight into the changes you go through in that time, as themes change with you. Persevering with mandalas over a period of time may reveal such things as totemic animals, particular plants or trees to work with, colours as states of being, etc.

Manðala Offering to Tara

Tara is the Indian and Tibetan Buddhist Goddess of Compassion. Performing this practice regularly can help to develop the quality of compassion.

You will need a plate or platter, about 10 inches in diameter, a bowl of grain, some "precious objects" such as jewellery or crystals, including one object especially precious to you, and three rings about 8", 5" and 2" in diameter respectively. The rings can be made of metal, wood, cardboard, cord, or any appropriate material. As you create the mandala with these materials, visualize that you are actually building a universe for Tara. Visualize Mount Meru, the continents and all the precious things. Sit facing East and say:

"I give praise and honour to Tara, Goddess of Compassion."

Chant: *"May all beings always have happiness, and the causes of happiness. May they all be free from suffering, and the causes of suffering."*

Tara, Goddess of Compassion

Bow, touching your forehead to the floor and say "*I bow to you, holy Tara, and present to You every type of offering, actual, and mentally transformed. I build a universe, and offer it to You.*"

Pick up the plate and Chant "*Om Vajra Bhumi Ah Hung*" "*I prepare a great and powerful ground of precious gold.*" Put a handful of grain on plate and rub it with wrist, Widdershins three times to purify, deosil three times to bestow blessings.

Chant "*Om Vajra Rekke Ah Hung*" "*At the outermost limit the chain of iron mountains surrounds Mount Meru, King of Mountains, and essence of protection.*" Place largest ring on the plate, visualizing it as a chain of mountains. Place a pile of grain in the centre of the cloth, visualizing it as Mount Meru.

"*In the East is the continent Purva-Videha*"
Place a pile of grain in the East, just inside ring.

"*In the South is the continent Jambudvipa*"
Place pile of grain in the South.

"*In the West is the continent Apara-Godaniya*"
Place pile of grain in the West.

"*In the North is the continent Uttarakuru*"
Place pile of grain in the North.

Each of the continents contains a special object

"*In the East the treasure mountain*"
Add more grain to East.

"*In the South the wish-granting tree*"
Add more grain to the South.

"*In the West the sacred wish-granting cow*"
Add more grain to the West.

"In the North the ever renewing, uncultivated crops"
Add more grain to the North.

"A second ring of mountains is placed within the first"
Place the second ring on the plate, within the piles of grain.

Eight more special things are placed within these mountains.

"The precious wheel"
Place pile of grain in the East, inside inner ring.

"The precious jewel"
Place pile of grain in the South, inside inner ring.

"The precious Queen"
Place pile of grain in the West, inside inner ring.

"The precious minister"
Place pile of grain in the North, inside inner ring.

"The precious elephant"
Place pile of grain in the South-East, inside inner ring.

"The precious horse"
Place pile of grain in the South-West, inside inner ring.

"The precious general"
Place pile of grain in the North-West, inside inner ring.

"The vase of great treasures"
Place pile of grain in the North-East, inside inner ring.

Eight offering Goddesses add their blessings to this universe.

"The Goddess of Grace"
Add grain to the East.

"The Goddess of Garlands"
Add grain to the South.

"The Goddess of Song"
Add grain to the West.

"The Goddess of Dance"
Add grain to the North.

"The Goddess of Flowers"
Add grain to the Southeast.

"The Goddess of Incense"
Add grain to the Southwest.

"The Goddess of Light"
Add grain to the Northwest.

"The Goddess of Perfume"
Add grain to the Northeast.

A third ring of mountains is placed in the universe, place the smallest ring in the centre.

"The sun is placed in the East"
Place pile of grain inside small circle, to the East.

"The moon is placed in the West"
Place pile of grain inside gold circle, to the West.

"And in the centre I place all possessions precious to Gods and humans"
Place offerings in the centre ring of the mandala - grain, beads, feathers, crystals, flowers, etc, including your precious thing.

"This magnificent and glorious collection, lacking in nothing, I offer to You Tara. For the welfare of all beings accept these offerings with compassion, and thus may I and the whole earth receive blessings. By the virtue of offering to You this mandala, built on a base resplendent with flowers and incense, adorned with mountains and the four continents, as well as the sun and the moon, may all beings share in its good effects."

Chant: "*Om Tare Tuttare Ture Svaha*"

Continue this chant, visualizing the Goddess Tara in front of you, sitting with her left leg drawn up, her right leg extended, ready to get up and help all beings. Her left hand is held up in a wish-bestowing gesture, her right hand rests on her knee, in the earth- touching gesture. As you continue the chant, see a thread of gold light coming from her left hand to you, with drops of divine nectar travelling along it to you. Then see another Tara come out of the central image, with each recitation of the mantra, with the final Tara entering your body, such that you become one with Her. Rest in the feeling of oneness for as long as it lasts.

Part Two

Religion and

Ritual

Chapter Twenty-three

The Goddess and the God

"I am all that is and was and ever shall be, no mortal man hath ever Me unveiled."

Such are the words of Isis in Ancient Egypt. It is very difficult to describe the Goddess and the God to people, as we all relate to deity in our own unique way. It is perhaps easier to describe our experiences of the Goddess and God, although again we are constrained by the restrictions of language, which are often inadequate to describe direct mystical experience or experience of the divine. We are of the belief that all Goddesses are aspects of One Goddess, and all Gods are aspects of One God, and that the Two are One. As we exist as male and female it helps us to interact with deity by perceiving it in personified forms in a framework formed around gender i.e. as Goddess and God.

Below are included the Charge of The Goddess used by witches, and a Charge of The God. Reading and meditating on these may give insights into the Goddess and God and help you develop clearly your own concepts and perceptions of them. We have also included excerpts from essays written by a few of our trainees to show how different people experience and perceive the Goddess and God in very different ways.

The Charge of the Goddess

"Listen to the words of the Great Mother, who of old was known amongst men as Artemis, Astarte, Bride, Melusine, Diana, Aradia, Isis, Ceridwen

and by many other names."

"Whenever you have need of anything, once in the month, and better it be when the Moon is full, then shall you assemble in some secret place and adore the spirit of Me, Who am Queen of all Witcheries. There shall you assemble, you who are fain to learn all sorcery, but have not yet won its deepest secrets; to these will I teach things that are yet unknown. And you shall be free from slavery; and as a sign that you be really free, you shall be naked in your rites; and you shall dance, sing, feast, make music and love, all in My praise. For Mine is the ecstasy of the spirit, and Mine also is joy on Earth; for My law is love unto all beings. Keep pure your highest ideal; strive ever towards it; let naught stop you or turn you aside. For Mine is the secret door which opens upon the Land of Youth, and Mine is the cup of the wine of life, and the Cauldron of Ceridwen, which is the Holy Grail of immortality. I am the gracious Goddess, who gives the gift of joy unto the heart of man. Upon Earth, I give the knowledge of the spirit eternal; and beyond death, I give peace and freedom, and reunion with those who have gone before. Nor do I demand sacrifice; for behold, I am the Mother of all living, and My love is poured out upon the Earth."

"Hear you the words of the Star Goddess, She in the dust of Whose feet are the hosts of heaven, and Whose body encircles the universe."

"I Who am the beauty of the green Earth, and the white Moon amongst the stars, and the mystery of the waters, and the desire of the heart of man, call unto thy soul. Arise, and come unto Me. For I am the soul of nature, Who gives life to the universe. From Me all things proceed, and unto Me all things must return; and before My face, beloved of Gods and of men, let thine innermost divine self be enfolded in the rapture of the infinite. Let My worship be within the heart that rejoiceth; for behold, all acts of love and pleasure are My rituals. And therefore let there be beauty and strength, power and compassion, honour and humility, mirth and reverence within you. And thou who thinkest to seek for Me, know thy seeking and yearning shall avail thee not unless thou knowest the mystery; that if that which thou seekest thou findest not within thee, thou wilt never find it without thee. For behold, I have been with thee from the beginning, and I am that which is attained at the end of desire."

Doreen Valiente

A Charge of the God

"Hear My words and dance My dance of Life, sing My song of joyous existence and chant My dirge of death and transformation.

For I am Pan, Herne, Dionysus, Osiris, Gwyn-Ap-Nudd, Zeus, Shiva, Cernunnos and all the faces of the God, and I am all and nothing in the arms of My love. I am the phallus of life and the seed planted in the depths of death to nurture and comfort with my growth, dying and reborn through the seasons of the Mother.

I am the horns of power on the brows of the Wise. Through veils and shadows I hunt and I guard: Lord of the Wild Hunt and Keeper of the Silent Peace. See My face all around you and know the joys of orgasm and death, transformed and reborn in the cauldron of dreams.

My rites are of lust and joy and ecstasy. Let the psyche be rendered and let the universe be destroyed at the climax of your rites, that they may be reformed in love and laughter.

Be strong, joyous, passionate, tender, wise and humble, and you will grow in spirit. Stand with me on the Earth and look about you. You are a child of all about you, and you must nurture each other, that I may grow in you, and whisper my song through you down the winds of the changing seasons."

David Rankine

"What do the God and the Goddess mean to me? I think they have always been a part of my life. From my earliest childhood memories I remember the Goddess ever- present in my dreams, her appearance often different, but however She appeared I always knew it was Her. I didn't know who She was then and at that early age I never really thought of Her as anything divine, She seemed so real, so natural, She was just a part of my life. It was not until much later when I tried to find out who She was, as I knew I would recognise Her and I knew She was real, that I knew Her as the Goddess.

The God too has always been there, even as a young child I was aware of His guiding hand in times of darkness. Of course at that young age I was not aware of Him as the God. My first vision of the God was very much as a father figure and perhaps ironically I saw him as Aslan. I still believe today, as C.S. Lewis did, that the Chronicles of Narnia were not an analogy for the story of Christ but something much deeper, and I've always thought there was something in the fact that much of the books came to Lewis in dreams and visions. Aslan is Lord of the Beasts, slain only to rise again bringing spring with His rebirth, dancing the wild dance, leading the Wild Hunt. It might be dressed in Christianity, but that's not surprising when you consider when and by whom the books were written.

My main interest has always been with European and mainly Celtic mythology, and so I think it is natural that I usually envisage the Goddess in one of Her many Celtic aspects as Danu, Macha, Arianrhod, Rhiannon, Brighid, Ceridwen and the multitude of other Celtic Goddesses so often in the triple form of Maiden, Mother and Crone. However the Goddess in the aspect of Athena, or to give Her another of Her many names Minerva, has for me been very important both as Goddess of Wisdom and a guardian as Goddess of War. I think though ultimately the Goddess is important to me in all aspects whether as Isis, Kali, Freya or any of Her multitude of forms She takes, and each aspect has an important role.

From my childhood view of the God as a father figure I now more than ever see Him as the Horned God, Celtic, wise yet wild and chaotic. A transition from Herne to the Lord of Misrule, Leader of the Wild Hunt, Loki, Robin Goodfellow, Coyote, flicking from the paternal Oberon to the chaos of Puck. I very much see a dual God, on one side the regal solar deity, Lugh, Apollo, Odin All Father. On the other side is the wild animal God of Pan and Loki. For me it seems logical for the God and Goddess to exist in numerous guises, each one there to fill a particular role, but each part of the whole like fingers on a hand. A look at mythologies from global cultures will show similarities popping up time after time; the spear of Lugh, Gungnir the spear of Odin, the Lance of Longinus. It is perhaps no surprise that both the God and Goddess so often appear in triplicate perhaps mirroring the Id, Ego, and Superego of our own personalities.

To me an important thing about both the Goddess and the God is their accessability. They are not some distant concept that you grovel before and are simply told about. They are more real than anything else, They are your friends, your family. To quote Alan Grant "sometimes the Goddess is your mother and will hold you, sometimes She is your sister and will befriend you, and sometimes She is your lover and will stick you in your back". The God and Goddess encompass everything, both the light and the dark; They are there to comfort you when you need it, but also quite happy to give you a good kick in the teeth when you need that as well. They are unpredictable and wild, but at the same time caring and nurturing, just as the world that surrounds us not only feeds and nurtures us but is also full of dangers and perils. They are approachable, ever present, a living part of the universe embodied in the world around us, not a concept on a dusty book on a forgotten shelf. To me the Goddess and God are an integral part of my life, they give me hope and courage and as the embodiment of the universe, as both life and death, the God and Goddess are present in all that surrounds us. Perhaps the most important thing is that with the God and the Goddess I know I will never truly be alone."

Chris

"I have learned to use the God inside me to find courage to carry on in the wake of diversity, to be forthright and responsible. But on finding these hidden sides, these qualities that have been stifled, we must learn to keep an equilibrium between the two aspects; a healthy balance which cannot be measured as no two people are the same, and therefore must find their own unique recipe for success. I cannot be independent to the extreme of excluding others from my life, but at the same time I must be true to what I feel, without suppressing emotions. To evolve we must experience all aspects in life and develop the ability to learn, either from the positions we put ourselves in or from what we perceive. Throughout my life I have never believed in a religion, it all sounded too contrived and unbelievable for my liking. But now I can appreciate the concept of the Goddess and God in relation to nature and the cycle of being, birth, growth and death. The Goddess is all, encompassing all, even the God. All I do in a sense reflects Her. The fruit I collect and eat is supplied by Her for Her in me and all Her other creations. She is bird, insect, plant, even the soil. Her energy is everywhere, penetrating and generating. Her lunar cycles and seasons that contribute towards the year are perpetual, but in those seasons is another shorter cycle of existence, that of the God. The continual cycle of life and death which He represents. Nothing is static, life necessitates death and death enables life. The God is eternally regenerated; He is the dormant winter seed which swells and splits its testa as the spring sunshine warms the soil, as the summer comes it stretches its new shoot through the soil upwards to grow and mature and finally reach its full potential to reproduce and bear a seed before it inevitably dies, leaving the seed to carry on its cycle of life.

As the seasons move on and change so does my image of the Goddess and the God. In the spring time, when the days grow warmer and new life starts to emerge I imagine the Goddess as a maiden and the God as Pan, both fresh and new. Pan wild, exciting and unleashed, and the maiden, Kore, more slowly and purposefully conducting Herself. By the summer solstice Pan has become more settled and is seated next to the Goddess who is now the Great Mother, the Queen of Summer seated next to the Sun King. Then as autumn comes the Goddess becomes the Crone and the God is killed, banished to the Underworld over winter, becoming Comforter of Souls, waiting to be reborn with the coming year.

The two aspects of the God and Goddess which I feel the most affinity for are the unleashed, wild and exciting image of Pan and all the anticipation he brings for the coming year, and the Goddess image of the Nymph or Mother, no longer naive but in full bloom at Her best."

Angie

"The Goddess is everything. She is the Great Mother of All. We are all born of Her though She, Herself, is unborn. She never dies. Between the worlds She is eternally creating. She gives birth to the world afresh at the end of each cycle of time, at Yule, when She gives birth to the God, Her Son, Her Lover, Her Consort. The seasonal festivals mark the passing year which They enact with Their own lives, bringing Their energies into the sacred circle so they may be communed with by those who seek Them. The Goddess is nameless, yet She has many names. She is known by all people. From the ancients to modern, in all the different religions and belief systems. She, in Her phases is Maid, Mother and Crone, is the birthbringer, the death taker and the rebirth giver of all. The complete circle, continuous.

She is the earth, the moon and the stars, waters. She is everything, Mother

Earth. She is the land for it is Her body. Through respect for Her I give respect to myself. To draw upon the power and strength of Her different aspects, I can strengthen my own self, enhance my life. Through the celebration of Her everchanging aspects, seasonal and lunar, I learn to celebrate the changes within my own body and self, for after all I am of Her creation. She is of me and I am of Her.

The God, Her Son, Consort and Lover, too is known by different names, yet also nameless. The Horned One, Pan, Cernunnos, Herne, The Wild One, the Piper, Lord of Animals, the Mischievous One. The God is the life force, the male aspect of all nature. He is sexual, earthy, passionate and wise. The Sun King, the Green Man. There is one God, though two aspects, the Lord of Day and Night, the Eagle and the Serpent, the Oak and Holly Kings, the Younger God and the Older. Through the Goddess He is born, dies and yet is reborn again. He is forceful yet gentle, the passion and the desire.

I personally feel more drawn to the Goddess than the God. For in Her I can identify with myself. To Her maiden self, to Artemis, to Diana, Her lunar self. She is wild, free and untamed. She is independent, the Virgin in control, She dances with the animals, She is their leader. She represents the gateway to the fairyfolk, the little people. She is newness, she brings beginnings like the Spring after the Winter. She is forever learning, experiencing new things. She is in control of what She wants. Artemis the Guardian of women, the Lady of the Hunt. She is freedom to show us how to rediscover feminine power, Mother of none, yet Mother of all."

Frances

"I relate to the Goddess and God through my music. Every day before I play, I meditate, clear my head and decide what I need and want to work on; every day I feel totally inspired to work once I have meditated. It is the God that inspires me, fills me with desire to hear that sound I make that fills the room with an unexplainable passion. It is for this I play with passion and He offers me the release of anger, the direct channel, always present, unmoving yet flexible. He takes my anger, bitterness and pain and returns music.

It is the Goddess, the Lady, that gives me the patience to work on specifics, scales, studies; the frustrating aspect of music that is so essential, yet so irritating when I want to do it now, not have to work on it. She keeps me calm as I try so desperately to perfect technique, rewards me when I succeed.

I play for them. He gives me the courage I need to release and directly channel my energy in music. She aids my patience and clams me at times, when in the past all I felt was the desire to slingshot my dearest viola through the nearest window.

Sometimes they dance when I play, I dance with them sometimes, other times they sit and listen, not always together but never alone. They are never displeased or disappointed with me."

Annyra-Leigh

Chapter Twenty-four

The Old Ones

Who or what are the Old Ones? You may not be familiar with the term, and the Old Ones deserve your attention as much as the elements or the Goddess and the God. We use the term Old Ones collectively to describe the spirits which govern the motion of the universe, the order of the stars and planets, as well as the spirits to be found in our environment around us, such as genius loci ("spirit of the place"), guardians of sacred sites, dryads, hamadryads, nymphs, fairies, etc. The Old Ones are also sometimes called the Timeless Ones, which gives an indication of their nature as personified forces of nature and of the universe. As with the Goddess and God, understanding of the Old Ones and how they affect your life and how best to interact with them comes with practice and experience. Try going to different sites, such as woodlands, lakes, mountains, seashore, stone circles, etc, and invoking Them and meditating afterwards. Try to contact them using the exercise in chapter 12 for contacting guardian spirits.

Invocation of the Old Ones

Hail Old Ones, Ancient Ones of Time and Space
You Who were before the first breath and will be after the last ember
Spirits Who dwell in the void of spirit between the worlds and the stars
Who govern the motions of the stars and the planets
Hail indwelling spirits of tree and rock and lake
Hail dryads, nymphs and fairies, guardians of sacred sites
I greet You all and invite You to join me now in this circle
Add your power to this rite and infuse me with your energy and wisdom

In the name of love I bid You Hail and Welcome

Chapter Twenty-five

Devotion

This chapter is an intense devotion to a deity of your choice. Serious contemplation and meditation should go into your choice of which deity to work with. The techniques given have been adapted from Aleister Crowley's Liber Astarte technique. The Liber Astarte technique should not be undertaken during periods of extreme stress in your own life, it is extremely demanding in time and energy, and may provoke jealousy from people with demands on your time. It is good if you can arrange it so the practice finishes at a time when you are not working so you can end with an intense finish. Do not feel you have to rush into this practice, it should be performed at an appropriate time when you wish to form a strong link with a deity.

Techniques of uniting oneself with a particular Deity by devotion

1] Considerations - the choice of a particular Deity should suit your own highest nature. However this method is not so suitable for austere deities like Saturn, or intellectual deities like Thoth. For any deities which partake in any way of love it is an ideal technique.

2] Prime Method - you should consider that although Osiris and Christ are aspects of one energy, the former is worshipped with Egyptian rites and the latter with Christian rites. There should, however, be one symbol declaring the transcendence of such limitations, and with regard to the Deity there should be one affirmation of her/his identity both with all other similar deities of other religions, and with the Supreme of whom all are partial reflections.

3] Chief Place of Devotion - is the Heart of the Devotee, to be represented symbolically by a shrine in a room or spot s/he holds dear, protected from the profane.

4] The Image of the Deity - should be present at the shrine, it being a reminder during meditation, and also because a certain power enters and inhabits it from the Deity by virtue of the rituals performed. The image should be the most beautiful and perfect you can obtain, if you can paint or carve the image, this is even better. For Deities with whose nature no Image is compatible, such as Brahman, let them be worshipped in an empty shrine.

5] Concerning the Shrine - it should be furnished with ornaments appropriate to the Deity. For example, ivy and pine-cones and grapes and wine for Bacchus. Talismans with the appropriate signs, planets, elements, etc, may also be used to adorn the shrine. You should take time to research the background to the Deity and meditate on the subject as much as possible to gain insight into what is appropriate for the shrine.

6] Concerning Rituals - the Devotee should prepare an Invocation of the particular Deity, which should consist of seven parts:- First, an Imprecation, as a Student to her Teacher, in awe. Second, an Oath, as a Vassal to a Liege, in fealty. Third, a Memorial, as a Child to Parent, in dependence. Fourth, an Orison, as a Priestess unto her Goddess, in adoration. Fifth, a Colloquy, as of Sister to Sibling, in confidence. Sixth, a Conjuration, as a Friend to Friend, in comradeship. Seventh, a Madrigal, as to a Lover, in passion.

7] Further Concerning the Ritual - the Invocation is the prime part of an ordered ceremony. You should keep the shrine area clean and garnish the place, sprinkling it with water or wine as appropriate to the Deity, and consecrating it with oil and ritual as seems most appropriate. This should be done with intensity and attention to minute detail.

8] Concerning the Period of Devotion - a fixed period should be set for the worship, on a cycle of nine; the minimum should be nine weeks, and the maximum sixty-three (nine x seven) years. The ritual should be performed between one and three times a day. You may assign set hours for the rituals, or perform the rituals as the spirit moves you, there is no set way. You may choose to break your sleep-pattern by performing the ritual during the night, this has the effect of stimulating the dream-contact with the Deity and strengthening the devotion.

9] Concerning the Ritual Techniques and Tools - they should be appropriate to the nature of the Deity. The Cup is the most appropriate tool, and the Sword or Dagger should not be used unless specific to the Deity. A coloured robe appropriate to the Deity should be worn, white may be worn as the colour of devotion if no colour can be found most appropriate. The incense should be appropriate to the nature of the Deity, such as Dittany for Persephone, Mastic for Mercury, etc. Libations should also be made with the appropriate liquids. Techniques such as singing, playing music, dancing, may be included in the ritual if appropriate. A mantra may be used with the Deity, reciting the mantra in the original language of the Deity is to be recommended (e.g. Greek for Dionysus, Chinese for Kwan-Yin, etc).

10] Way of Life - you should adapt your lifestyle to suit the nature of the Deity, so it is in harmony with and pleasing to, the Deity. During the period of the practise the Devotee should become more inflamed with love of the Deity through devotion in everyday activities, such as dedication of food and drink, or of any activities performed, to the honour and love and grace of the Deity (this may be done silently). In this way love of the Deity will be enkindled in your heart like a flame, which grows and consumes you with its passion, your heart becoming the shrine and your body the temple. A piece of appropriate jewellery may be worn during the period of the working, to serve as a focus for your energy during silent invocations and whilst transmuting energy in the love of the Deity.

11] Resistance - after a time you may encounter all manners of resistance to your practise. Temptations to break the practise, pressure from others and yourself (through inertia, laziness, etc), psychosomatic health disorders, and more may attempt to turn you away from your practise. Remember, there is no such thing as coincidence - these are tests to your devotion, do not give in to them or you destroy the value of your works and devotion.

12] Dryness - (usually) after resistance has been encountered and overcome, periods of dryness are common, where you cannot seem to feel the connection with the Deity, and your love and devotion seems to have dried up. This is a further test and can seem like hell, in extreme cases it may lead to a dark night of the soul. Do not give in to despair, persevere, and the love of the Deity will remanifest stronger and brighter than before, like a mighty flame burning away all dross and base feelings.

13] Ending - the Devotee may wish to end the practise with a few days retreat or a special ceremony. At the end of the specified period you should stop the practise and cover or dismantle the shrine, continuing life in normal fashion and busying yourself with other tasks. This is to avoid obsession and the love of the Deity turning into jealous love or manifesting as overzealous attempts at conversion. Remember all Deities are true and valid emanations of the Supreme One, and do not allow yourself to become so obsessed with one aspect that you denigrate others, for this is not true love of Deity.

Revised and Adapted from *Liber Astarte vel Berylli sub figura* CLXXV Appendix VII, pp460-471, *Magick* by Aleister Crowley.

Chapter Twenty-six

The Sabbats

The Sabbats are seasonal festivals which mark the turning of the year and the cycles of nature. Most western pagans celebrate eight sabbats; the Summer and Winter Solstices, the Spring and Autumn Equinoxes and the quarter days or fire festivals - Samhain, Imbolc, Beltaine and Lammas or Lughnasadh. A solitary ritual is given here for each of these sabbats, to help you tune in to the cycles of nature as they exist within you as well as without. It should be remembered, however, that the energies at different times of the year are different depending on where you are. If you are living in the southern hemisphere, for example, the Winter Solstice (December 21st) will not be celebrated as the death of the Old Sun and the rebirth of the Sun God. This will instead take place on the Summer Solstice. It is important to try to learn what you can about the myths, legends, beliefs and festivals of the land you live in, to enable you to tune in to the natural energies as perceived by the inhabitants of the land through time. The information and rituals given here are suitable for those living in Britain and Western Europe, and should be adapted as necessary if you live in another part of the world.

Samhain - 31st October

Samhain, or Halloween, is the death festival, marking the descent of Winter. The leaves are falling from the trees in drifts, and life is drawn away from the surface of the earth, and descends deep into the earth. Life is now in the roots and bulbs of plants which rest over the Winter. The Horned God who was Lord of Life and the Wild Greenwood has now truly taken His throne as Lord of the Underworld, the dread Lord of Shadows,

Out of the spirals, out of the mist,
out of the House of Death,
the Horned One rises

the comforter of souls. The earth prepares for sleep and draws energy inwards. This is a time for introspection, as we too draw our energy within and prepare for the Winter. The Earth is becoming cold, and barren, and we see Her as the Cailleach, the Crone, the Wise One. She is the Dark Mother who devours the God that She may give birth to Him again. Her womb is also the tomb, and the Underworld, and the Horned God thus resides within Her womb over the Winter months.

Samhain is a time of transformation and inner work. It is also a sombre time of remembrance, when we remember and honour those who have died. The veil is thinnest between the worlds and we call on the spirits of the dead and invite them to feast with us on this, the feast of death. We call upon our ancestors and contact the ancient wisdom. It is a time of endings, but also a time of beginnings, as Samhain is a Celtic New Year's Eve festival. Thus we give up the past and look to the future. It is the end of one cycle and the beginning of another. Samhain is a good time for banishings, and for sorting out unfinished business. At Samhain we look back and take stock of the past year and contemplate what we have learned. Samhain is also the time to face our shadow, the dark side of ourselves.

We find no wild flowers blooming, yet the colours of nature are rich and warm. Magick mushrooms grow to help us explore other realms, to make the veil thinner still. Samhain is also a harvest festival, but a harvest of flesh. The livestock would be killed at this time that there be meat throughout the bleak Winter. The wind blows, Jack Frost makes patterns on our windows and the mists rise. It is no wonder this season is one of mystery.

Ritual for Samhain

Decorate the circle with fir cones, ferns and seasonal vegetation. Pumpkins may be hollowed out to make spirit lanterns. On the alter place an apple, and a black and a red candle, and a chalice of cider, red wine or mead. Myrrh is an appropriate incense. Cast the circle in your preferred way. Invoke the elements asking the East for insight and clarity of inner vision, the South for knowledge of the Life/Death force, the West for understanding and the key to the unconscious, and the North for the stillness of mind needed for inner work. Invoke the Goddess as the Old

One, the Cailleach. Invoke the God as Dread Lord of Shadows.

Say: *Out of the spirals, out of the mist*
         Out of the House of Death, the Horned One rises
         Out of sleep, out of stone, out of the womb
         The Horned One rises
         He cometh to lead the Hunt, He cometh to lead the Dance,
         He cometh to hold the hand till Winter passes

Light the black candle, the candle of death. Meditate on the Dark Goddess and let Her devour you. All becomes darkness as you are consumed by Her. You find yourself spinning and falling until you land in a strange and dark realm. Here, you must face your fears, and all that you cannot accept within yourself. All that you have pushed aside or repressed, the things you don't like, or didn't even know were there. These you must face. You hear a laugh echoing throughout this strange realm, and a cloaked figure emerges from the darkness. He is silent, but points. Where He points other figures and scenes appear. These are scenes from your own life, or connected with you or your inner life in some way. Scenes appear and fade, each showing you something of yourself. Watch these and learn from them. When the scenes have stopped appearing, rest in the company of the Lord of Death, for He is also the comforter, the giver of peace and rest.

Chant softly: *Hekate, Ceridwen, Dark Mother take me in*
                  Hekate, Ceridwen, let me be reborn

and feel yourself emerging once more, refreshed and renewed with new insight, light the red candle, the candle of life. If you have a cauldron you may wish to write down things you wish to get rid of in your life on paper, and burn the paper in the cauldron, thus banishing those things from your life as you go forward into the new year.

Leave behind all hindrances to your growth. Cut the apple in half, revealing the pentagram of seeds within. The apple is the fruit of life and death. Contemplate this as you eat half the apple, leave the other half of the apple as an offering. Bless the wine and make a toast to the coming year. Thank the Goddess, God and Elements and close the circle.

The Winter Solstice:
Yule - 21st December

Yule is the time we celebrate the return of the waxing sun. Light and life can be seen to be returning and conquering death. Yule is a turning point, a point of change, where the tides of the year turn and begin to flow in the opposite direction. It is the darkest time of the year, the time of the longest night, but there is the promise of the return of light. We encourage the sun to rise and to grow in power, and we remember the seasons of plenty. Magickally we bring back the season of plenty, and we feast on rich foods and drinks. The fir tree represents life amidst death, it is evergreen, representing everlasting life, and lasting friendship. Holly and Mistletoe bear berries at this time, symbolizing fertility. Mistletoe berries are white, representing the semen of the Horned God, the Holly berries are blood red, symbolizing both the menstrual blood of the Goddess and the sacrifice of the God.

Evergreen trees also represent youth and freshness, and are symbols of the promise of spring. A yule custom, still practised at Christmas is to dress an evergreen tree, and make offerings. We honour the spirit of the tree, and what it represents. It is sad that a custom of honouring the living tree has been replaced by the meaningless decoration of ghastly plastic or tinsel trees, or the cutting down of thousands of living trees so that people can have them in their living rooms for a couple of weeks, and then dump them, causing environmental damage. It is far better to honour a living tree, outdoors. The tree may be decorated with appropriate offerings, fruit, decorated pine cones, jewellery, symbols of the sun, symbols of fertility, birds, animals, etc.

At yule we say goodbye to the dying sun, and wait through the long, cold night for the sun's rebirth. The night belongs to the Goddess, and is a night of waiting, through her pregnancy, for the Child of Promise. In the morning we greet the new sun and celebrate the waxing year. The rising sun brings the promise of the spring and the gifts that will bring. It is still a long time before the sun will be strong, but we hope and we trust. The sun is now the Child of Promise, the young hero God. It is a time of making wishes and hopes for the coming year, and of setting resolutions. From the

darkness comes light.

Rituals for Yule

Two rituals are given here, one for the evening before the longest night, which should be performed as close to sunset as possible. The other for sunrise following the longest night. The night in between may be spent in vigil, meditating, but don't feel you have to do this, as the demands of modern life may make this extremely difficult.

The altar should be decorated with holly, mistletoe, pine, fir cones, fruit and symbols of plenty. Have a chalice of mead or wine and some food - fruit, nuts, chocolates, cake biscuits or any rich food. It is good to perform the rituals outdoors, preferably on a hill, from where sunset and sunrise can be seen clearly, but also where there are some evergreen trees. If this is not possible, it may be performed indoors, the evening ritual in a room with a west facing window, and the morning ritual in a room with an east facing window, so that the sun rise may be seen. If indoors, you may wish to have a small evergreen tree growing in a pot, as the tree to be decorated. This can be the traditional Xmas tree (Norway Spruce), but we prefer to have a native tree, such as Yew, the tree of life in death and death in life, Silver Fir, tree of foresight, or Scots Pine, tree of vitality, uprightness and strength of character. But other trees, such as Cedar, tree of strength, nobility, and associated with the sun, or Juniper, used for warding off bad spirits, protection and confidence may also be used.

Evening Ritual

Cast a circle in the usual way, or visualize a sphere of love and protection around you. Invoke the elements, asking for new beginnings, and a good spring in the east, for vitality and the return of life force in the south, for love and understanding of the seasons in the west, and for strength, resolution, and a good material foundation in the north.

Light a gold candle, or a fire outdoors, to represent the sun, saying *"May the golden light of the sun ever warm me and nourish me, even now He has reached his weakest point. With light and with joy shall I call him back to birth"*.

Invoke the God as the Sun King, come to the end of his reign, and ready to be sacrificed that he may be reborn and renewed. Invoke also the Dark Lord who rules the dark half of the year, and remember Him as the comforter. Contemplate the following charge of the God:

> *"I am the dying God, I face my death tonight*
> *I am the God reborn, the Bringer of the Light*
> *This is the hour of sacrifice, I go now to my tomb*
> *The place of darkness and of rest, which is the Mother's womb*
> *Sacrifice with Me in love tonight, and as darkness turns to day*
> *I will step once more into the light and guide you on your way."*

Invoke the Goddess, as the Great Mother, who gives birth to the sun, and as the fiery goddess of the sun itself, but also as the barren and icy Goddess of the winter earth. Contemplate the following charge of the Goddess:

"I am the Primordial Darkness, from which all emerges, and to which all must return. I am the full pregnant moon, and the moon's eclipse. Offer to me slips of yew - the tree of death and rebirth. I am called by many names, Nuit, Nox, Arianrhod, Ceridwen, Aradia. Mine is the long winter night, the night of waiting, the pregnant pause. Have patience. In the bleak winter night I give my promise of rebirth. Come to me in love, as willing sacrifice, that ye may be reborn, just as the sun God dies this night, and rests within my womb, for His longest night of rest. Be sure that I, as Goddess of the Dawn will give birth to Him again. But now, be patient and trust. Make ye your sacrifices in perfect love and perfect trust."

Dance slowly in a circle round the tree, chanting *"To die and be reborn, the wheel is turning, what shall I lose to the night?"* then shout out the name of something you want to lose, (eg. fear, poverty, bad luck, etc.). Repeat this, still circling, until you have run out of things to be rid of. Let these things be lost in the darkness. Be prepared for the dark waiting time, but encourage the return of the light by making resolutions, of what you will do in the coming year. For each resolution light a small candle from the gold solar candle or fire, and place it on the tree. Place offerings on the tree as well, giving a blessing to the tree, to nature and to the earth in general.

Bless the mead and the food, and feast, concentrating on the return of

richness to the earth.
Thank the Goddess and God and the Elements and close the circle.

Sunrise Ritual

Cast the circle as usual, calling upon the elements for their blessings on the coming year. This ritual should be started about 15 minutes before sunrise. Facing east, invoke:

> *"Queen of the Moon, Queen of the Sun*
> *Queen of the Heavens, Queen of the Stars*
> *Queen of the Waters, Queen of the Earth,*
> *Bring to us the Child of Promise!*
> *It is the Great Mother who giveth birth to Him,*
> *It is the Lord of Life who is born again*
> *Darkness and tears are set aside when the sun shall come up early.*
> *Golden Sun of the Mountains, Illumine the land.*
> *Light up the world, illumine the seas and the rivers.*
> *Sorrows be laid, joy to the world!*
> *Blessed Be the Great Goddess without beginning, without end*
> *Everlasting to eternity, Io Evohe*
> *Blessed Be."*

After a few moments of silence, contemplating these words, begin to drum or clap, and chant: "*Holy shining sunlight, radiant, radiant Brother, come to us*" until the sun appears over the horizon, then let out a cheer, and dance with the chant "*We are at one with the infinite sun, forever and ever and ever*"

If it is too cloudy to see the sun rise, try to get an impression of where on the horizon the energy of the sun is coming from, and at what point it is rising. Sometimes there is a narrow strip of cloud just on the horizon, and you may have to wait for the sun to rise above this.

Bless some mead, and make a toast to the sun.

Thank the Goddess, God and Elements and close the circle.

Imbolc - 1st February

The Festival of Imbolc or Bride, is celebrated around 2nd February by Pagans, and by Christians who call it Candlemas. Imbolc is Irish-Gaelic, translated variously as "in the belly" and "ewe's milk", and represents the quickening of Light and Life. The first stirrings of the coming of Spring can be seen, as the first flowers (snowdrops and winter aconite) begin to appear. Seeds which have lain dormant within the Earth over the cold Winter months begin to stir with life, as yet unseen.

At Imbolc we celebrate the Waking Light of the soul. Our spirits begin to quicken as we anticipate the rebirth of Nature. In Wicca it is the traditional time for initiation. Now is the time for the banishing of Winter and the welcoming of Spring. We welcome the Goddess Who is renewed, reborn as the Flower Maiden. She has passed through Her phase as the Hag, Crone or Wise One, and is a Maiden again.

Bride or Brigid is a three-fold Celtic Goddess who has been christianized into St. Brigid, whose day is celebrated on 1st February. In Ireland, St. Brigid's cross is made of rushes and straw, and goes back to pre- Christian times, representing the Sun Wheel or Fire Wheel. It may also be linked to an ancient ceremony connected with the preparation of the grain for sowing in the Spring. It was believed that the Spirit of the Grain, or the Goddess Herself, resided in the last grain harvested, and the last grain from the Harvest Festival was ritually brought into the house at Imbolc, blessed and planted as the first seed of the next harvest. The grain may also be made into a female figure, the Brideog (little Brighde) and dressed. Bride's bed is made, and She is welcomed in.

The Goddess is seen in Her three aspects at Imbolc, as the new-born Flower Maiden; the Mother, or bride of fertility, awaiting the fertilizing Sun God, and the Dark Crone of the dark half of the year. The sun is growing in strength, the Child of Promise, re-born at Yule, is now the Conquering Child. What was born at the Solstice begins to manifest, and this is the time for individuation, as we each light our own light, and set ourselves tasks and challenges. We nurture and kindle our resolutions and begin to look outwards again, do outer activity, although first we look deep

within to discover what potential lies there waiting to be fulfilled. Through the weeks ahead the days grow gradually longer, but we are still in the dark half of the year (until Beltaine) and this is the time to develop non-physical skills, such as psychometry, clairvoyance and precognition. The Oak King and Holly king have equal power now, but the Oak King is starting to gain ascendancy, while the Holly King's power wanes.

Those who do not belong to a Coven, or Pagan group, may wish to celebrate Imbolc alone. Below is an idea for a solitary Imbolc ritual which may be adapted as appropriate.

Ritual for Imbolc

If indoors set up an altar decorated with early flowers:- snowdrops, or winter aconite, and new shoots. Newly sown or recently sprouted seeds in a pot may also be placed on the altar. Have a supply of candles as well. If outdoors, choose a site where new shoots and early flowers can be found.

Ground and centre yourself. Feel your connection with the Earth.

Visualize a sphere of protection around yourself, which may be in the form of a bubble. Feel safe within your sphere. Call upon the guardians of the four directions, the powers of Air, Fire, Water and Earth, asking for their help and guidance. Air, to bring self- knowledge and inspiration, fire to strengthen your spirit and will, and to bring illumination. Water, to bring understanding and depth, earth to wake the qualities you desire to manifest. Call upon the Goddess as Maiden, Mother and Wise One and ask that you may understand Her mysteries. Call upon the God, as Lord of Life and Death.

Feel the increasing power of the Sun, warming the Earth and making all stir to life. Be aware also of the rotted leaves and plant and animal remains which fertilise the Earth allowing new life to grow. Think about the old and unhelpful parts of yourself which you wish to get rid of, and think how they can be transformed into useful material for growth. All those things which you cast away at Samhain and at Yule to allow rebirth to occur. How can they now be used and balanced and help you to grow, brought back in a new form? Re-integrate what you cast aside, as inappropriate or excessive at the time, in a more balanced form. (For example, you may have needed to deal with anger, and cast it away at Samhain, because it was inappropriate or excessive. But anger can also be a positive emotion, giving used the impetus to change. Thus if we do not re-integrate our anger, we will not grow).

Look deep within and see what is stirring within you, waiting to grow, if only it is given the nurturing it requires. Ask for the Love of the Goddess and the Light of the God to help you grow, and set yourself a task or tasks, and/or new skills or talents to develop. These may be physical, practical, social, mental, emotional or psychic skills. For each resolution, light a candle. (Do not set yourself impossible tasks, but make sure each task is achievable, and that you do achieve it). Finally, plant a seed and ask the Goddess and God for something that you would like to grow in your life, saying:

"As this seed grows, so will .... grow."

Be sure now that Spring is on its way, and that the process of growth and new life has well and truly started.

Chant circling with a drum:

> *Thus we banish Winter*
> *Thus we welcome Spring*
> *Say farewell to what is dead*
> *And greet each living thing*
> *Thus we banish Winter*
> *Thus we welcome Spring*

Bless some wine or mil and honey, and some cake or bread. If outdoors, pour a libation and leave some cake or bread as an offering to be eaten by wild birds, etc. If indoors, leave a little to be placed outdoors later. As you eat and drink, be aware of the Life all around you.

Thank the Goddess and God, and the Elements, and draw the sphere back into yourself.

Eostre: The Spring Equinox - 21st March

This festival is named after the Anglo-Saxon Goddess Eostre or Eastre, also known in Old German as Ostara. Little is known about this Goddess, except that her festival was celebrated at the Spring Equinox, and became Easter, and that She was a Goddess of fertility, and was connected with hares and eggs. She may have been a Goddess of the Dawn, as was the proto Germanic Austron, who was also connected with the Equinox. She may also be connected with the Greek Eos and the Roman Aurora, both Dawn Goddesses, and with the Babylonian Ishtar and Phoenician Astarte, both love Goddesses. The Anglo-Saxon lunar month, which became April, was called Eastermonath.

The equinox is a time both of fertility and new life, and of balance and harmony. Light and dark are here in balance, but the light is growing stronger. It is a time of birth, and of manifestation. Daffodils, tulips and crocuses are all in full bloom, blossom appears on trees and catkins can be found on the hazel and willow. Rites are best performed at dawn or dusk, (but better at Dawn) that time between light and dark.

The days grow lighter and the earth grows warmer. As at Imbolc, seeds may be blessed and planted. Seeds of wisdom, understanding, and magickal skills may also be planted. Eggs may be used for the creation of talismans, or ritually eaten. The egg is a symbol of rebirth, and its yolk represents the sun, its white, the White Goddess. Egg production in hens is stimulated when the bird's retina is stimulated by more than 12 hours of light, thus more eggs are produced after the equinox. This is a time both of growth and of balance, and we may work on balancing ourselves and the subtle energies within us, such as our chakras, the inner masculine and feminine qualities, the light and dark aspects, etc.

The equinox is also the time of Persephone's return from the underworld, to re-unite with Her mother Demeter, making the earth green again. This is the time of spring's return, the joyful time, the seed time, when life bursts forth from the earth and the chains of winter are broken. It is a time of balance when all the elements within must be brought into new harmony. The Prince of the Sun reaches out His hand, and the Kore, the maiden, returns from the dark underworld. Where they dance, wild flowers appear,

THE FIRST NOTE OF THE DAY IS STRUCK

sorrow turns to joy, and scarcity turns to abundance.

Ritual for Eostre

If indoors, the altar should be decked with spring flowers and symbols of balance and new life. If outdoors, find a place where there are flowers, blossom or catkins. Have a pot of earth, or a seed tray, and some seeds for which the planting time is march or april. You may also like to have a chalice containing fruit or blossom wine, and some bread or cake, or eggs.

Ground and centre yourself. Cast a circle in your usual way. Invoke the elements, breathing each one in and asking for them to be balanced within you, and meditate a while on the balancing of the elements before invoking the Goddess and God.

Invoke the Goddess as Eostre, Eos, Aurora, Rhiannon, and feel the love and abundance She brings. Invoke the God as Bellenos, the warming and fertilizing Sun God, as Lugh, Balder, Mabon, the Lord of Light, and feel His power.

Contemplate the Goddess's power to change and transform the earth, and to change you. Chant:

> *She changes everything She touches*
> *And everything She touches changes*
> *Change us, Touch us*
> *Touch us, Change us*

The Goddess comes in many forms, sometimes in animal form, and has sacred animals and helpers. The hare is one such animal, which is particularly venerated at this time. Call upon the hare, the sacred animal of Eostre. Visualize the hare coming to you, until it sits in front of you. Think about all the things in your life you wish to get rid of, such as poverty, ill-health, etc. and give them to the hare, with this rune:

> *Hare spirit, swift as lightning*
> *These afflictions need affrighting*
> *Lady bright and Lord of might*
> *Send them from me, give them flight*
> *Now they do reside in you*

Run, run, hare spirit, till fall of dew

This will not harm the hare, for the hare can take them and carry them off for you, and so purify them. Visualize the hare running away with all that you have given it. You may also wish to add to the power of this spell by drawing a hare on a slip of paper, and writing on it, the afflictions which you wish to be rid of. Burn it in a candle flame, repeating the above chant. Meditate upon the swiftness and grace of the hare, and let your soul take flight. Imagine yourself transformed into a hare, and run free over hills and meadows. Feel the thrill of the wild spirit. When you are ready, come back to your body, and thank the hare spirit. If you are outdoors, and see a real hare at Eostre, this is particularly auspicious.

Meditate again on the balancing of the elements within yourself, and on the balancing of light and dark. As the sun is growing stronger and the days are growing longer, open yourself up to the sun and the light. This is a time when outer activity should be increasing, and you will be feeling more active. Think about what you want to increase, and what you want to grow in your life. What projects or actions do you want to get done? For each thing that you want to grow, bless and plant a seed, saying "*As this seed grows, so may ... grow*". (If outdoors, in a wild place, do not plant seeds that do not already belong there, as you can upset the natural balance of the place. Plant them in a pot or seed tray, and take them home.)

Ask the Goddess and God to help you in your work, and to watch over the seeds. Bless the wine and food, leave some as an offering and consume the rest. Thank the Goddess and God, and thank and dismiss the elements. Close the circle.

Beltaine - 1st May

"This is the time when sweet desire weds wild delight. The Maiden of Spring and the Lord of the Waxing Year meet in the greening fields and rejoice together under the warm Sun. The shaft of life is twined in the spiral web and all of nature is renewed. We meet in the time of flowering, to dance the dance of Life"

- Starhawk, The Spiral Dance

Beltaine (also spelled Bealteinne, Bealtaine and various other ways) is the beginning of the Celtic Summer, the light season of the year. Like Samhain, it is a time when the veil is thin between the worlds, a time to communicate with spirits, particularly at this time nature spirits.

In Irish Gaelic, Bealtaine is the name of the month of May. In Scottish Gaelic Bealtuinn means May Day. The word originally meant "Bel Fire", and Beltane is associated with the Celtic God Bel, also known as Balor or Belenus. Bel is a God of Light and Fire and has been equated with the Greek Apollo, and associated with the Sun, although He is not specifically a Sun God.

Fires were traditionally built at Beltane, and people would jump over the fire. Young, unmarried people would leap the bonfire and wish for a husband or wife, young women would leap it to ensure their fertility and couples leap it to strengthen a bond. Cattle were driven through the ashes or between two Beltane fires to ensure a good milk yield.

The maypole, still used in Mayday festivities, represents both the phallus and the Goddess. It is also the World Tree connecting the three Worlds, its root in the Underworld, its branches in the Heavens. The shaman`s spirit may travel between the realms via the World Tree, and the phallus is also connected with life, love and death. For those who believe in reincarnation, the spirit re- enters a physical body after death and prior to rebirth via the phallus. Orgasm also is known as "le petit mort". The phallus and the World Tree may be seen as two aspects of the God in His relationship to the Goddess in His cycle of birth, death and rebirth.

The May Queen is still elected in many village May Day festivals, although the May King is largely left out these days (apart from in Pagan circles). The May King is the Green Man, and was often covered entirely with leaves. The mating of the Green Man with the Goddess as Queen of May was a magickal act necessary for the fertility of the Earth. Beltane is a time of fertility and is also an excellent time for Handfastings, the couple enacting the Heiros-gamos, or sacred marriage. The Great Rite may be performed, the couple channelling the Goddess and God, achieving unity with Deity, and ensuring that the Handfasting has a truly magickal start.

But what can the solitary pagan do to celebrate Beltane, and attune to the energies of the season? Remember the words of the Goddess "All acts of love and pleasure are my rituals", and this is particularly appropriate at Beltane. Beltane is a time of merry-making and love, all in the name of the Goddess. The Hawthorn tree (also called the May tree) blossoms at this time, and we are in the Hawthorn month. The blossoms can be gathered, and a delicious wine made from them, to be drunk the following Beltane. Celebrate Beltane by taking pleasure in life and enjoying the gifts of the Goddess. Meditate on the abundance and fecundity of Nature, take time to communicate with nature, with trees, and with nature spirits.

Another old Beltane practice was the making of a "Tallow Maid" which was a log with two branches like "Arms" which would be covered with candles and decorated with ribbons. Women would also weave locks of their hair onto it. A fire would be built, representing the God of Light and fire (or Sun God) and the Tallow Maid would be placed on it, representing the union of Goddess and God. This is a type of symbolic Great Rite, and the solitary pagan may wish to include some kind of symbolic union of Goddess and God as part of a Beltane ritual. Below is an idea for a solitary Beltane ritual, which may be adapted, added to or changed as appropriate.

Ritual for Beltaine

Decorate your altar (whether outdoors or indoors) with May blossom (Hawthorn), May flowers and young oak leaves. Ground and centre yourself, feeling your connection with the Earth. Cast a circle in whichever way you are used to, or visualize a sphere of protection around yourself in the form of a bubble.

Call upon the elements of the four directions, asking them to bring you their qualities. Call upon the Goddess as the fertile Queen of May and ask for Her blessings of love and joy. Call upon the God as the Green Man, God of the Wild Woods, and ask for his blessings of vigour and strength.

Be aware of the life and fertility around you. The readiness of all life to create more life, the vibrant flowers blooming, open, calling ready to be fertilised, the animals courting and mating. Contemplate the ever spiralling dance of life, the dance of the Goddess and God. You may wish to dance and chant an appropriate chant. Feel the life force surging within you. The seeds planted within at Imbolc and the Spring Equinox are bursting with life, blooming, ready, fertile. Honour the life force within you and all around. The Lady and Lord dance within you as well as without, and their union will bring fruitfulness. Meditate on the God and Goddess within, and on the masculine and feminine aspects within yourself. How balanced are they, and how well do they communicate with each other? Feel the flow of energy between them. If your masculine side is weak, let the feminine nourish it, if the feminine side is weak, let the masculine empower it.

Contemplate the creative energy that will be produced by the masculine and feminine within when balanced and united. Think of what you will do with that creative power and visualize your inner Goddess and God dancing together and uniting. On an outer level, symbolically enact this union by consecrating a chalice of wine with a wand or athame, saying:

"As the cup is to the Goddess, so the athame/wand is to the God, and conjoined they bring blessedness and creation. Lady and Lord, Bless this wine. All life is your own, your union, your dance. I thank you for blessings and abundance, for life and love, for joy and growth. Join with me, drink with me, feast with me."

Pour a libation on the earth if outdoors, and then drink the wine, communing with the Goddess and God, and all of nature. Food may be consecrated and consumed, leaving a little as an offering, to be eaten by wild birds and animals, or to return to the Earth. If you have a fire (a candle in a cauldron will suffice) you may want to end by jumping the fire, making a wish as you do so.

Thank the Goddess and God, and the elements, and open the circle.

Litha: Summer Solstice - 21st June

At the Summer Solstice the sun is at its highest and brightest and the day is at its longest. The Lord of Light has fought the powers of darkness, and is triumphant, ensuring fertility in the land. But in so doing, He sows the seeds of His own death. The Wheel turns and the Dark God (the Holly King) begins to wax in power as the Light God (Oak King) wanes. The Goddess shows Her Death-in-Life aspect, the Earth is fertile, and all is in bloom, the Goddess reaches out to the fertilizing Sun God at the height of His powers. At the same time She presides over the death of the God. The Goddess dances Her dance of Life and Death, the Sun God loves Her, and dies of His love. The Summer Solstice is a time of fulfilment of love. Flowers are in bloom everywhere, i.e. in sexual maturity, ready for pollination, fertilization, yet once fertilized they die, that the seeds and fruits may develop. At the same time, summer fruits appear, for a short but delicious season.

June was considered by some to be the luckiest month to be married in, and is the time of the mead moon, or honey moon. A tradition (which should be revived!) was for newly weds to drink mead daily for a month after their wedding, hence the post wedding holiday being named the honeymoon. Although the days begin to grow shorter after the Summer Solstice, the time of greatest abundance is still to come. The promises of the Goddess and God are still to be fulfilled. This is a time of beauty, love, strength, energy, rejoicing in the warmth of the sun, and the promise of the fruitfulness to come. It seems a carefree time, yet in the knowledge of life, is the knowledge of death, and beauty is but transitory. We celebrate life, and the triumph of light, but acknowledge death, and the power of the Dark Lord which now begins to grow stronger.

At this time of year, our physical energy is generally at its peak, and we are active and strong. Games involving a show of strength, such as tug of war, wrestling, etc. are appropriate here, and are often staged at summer fayres. This can be considered a remnant of pagan customs involving the battle between the light and dark Gods.

Ritual for Litha

Have on your altar, summer flowers and fruits - a display of the beauty and abundance of the season, and the promise of more fruitfulness to come. It is all the better if the ritual can be performed outdoors, in a place where flowers are blooming. The presence of bees and butterflies will make it all the better. Have also a chalice of mead, or if this is not available, a mixture of milk and honey, which is a traditional drink symbolizing abundance, and also a traditional offering to nature spirits.

Create your circle in your usual way, and call upon the elements. In the East, ask for the gentle summer breeze, which refreshes and awakens the spirit and mind. In the South ask for the radiant energy of the sun and the passion of the season. In the West, ask for the love, joy and beauty of the season. In the North ask for the fruitfulness of the season, and for wisdom and understanding.

Call upon the Goddess as the Great Queen, the abundant Mother, the beautiful One with many faces, She who rules both Life and Death, Whose beauty men would die for, Whose love is both cruel and kind. Light a red and a green candle for the two aspects and meditate on both - the Mother who nurtures and gives us everything, and the dark spider Goddess, who devours Her mate immediately after the consummation of their love, that new life may be nourished and grow within Her. Both are necessary and beautiful.

Call upon the God, as Lord of Light, the powerful, radiant Sun God who illumines the land, illumines our spirits, illumines our hearts and minds. Feel the energy He gives, the courage, the determination and inner strength. Feel powerful and alive. Call also on His other side, His alter-ego, the Lord of Darkness, the Dread Lord of Shadows, also known as the Comforter. Light a gold and a black candle and meditate on both aspects - the splendour of the Lord of Light, who illumines all, and dazzles us with His radiance, and the Lord of Shadows, who provides rest and comfort, yet is feared because we cannot see in the dark, and are afraid of what we cannot see. We must learn to see with the inner eye, with the Dark Lord's help, and for this we need to escape the glaring light of the sun. Even when the sun is at its height, the Dark Lord waits in the shadows cast by the sun.

Both are necessary and beautiful.

This is a time of showing strength and skill. Offer to the God and Goddess a skill you have. You may have a piece of artwork or craft which you have prepared at an earlier time, or a symbol of the work you do, or you may wish to carve a wand, write a poem, embroider something etc. as part of the ritual, and offer it to the Goddess and God. With the offering of the skill, ask for their blessings, that you may grow in skill. Remember always after this, that your work in that area is dedicated to the Goddess and God and you will surely grow in skill. It is appropriate also, to sing and dance, or to play an instrument, and offer your joy to the Gods.

Now feast your senses on the abundance of the season. Smell the flowers and the fruit, take in the beauty of the vibrant colours, hear the birdsong around you. Even in a city you will hear birds singing if you listen. Feel the textures of petals, of the grass beneath you if you are outdoors, of moss, of the fruit on your altar, and of rock, stone and wood.

Consecrate the mead, (or milk and honey) asking for the blessings of the Goddess and God on it, and drink, tasting the richness and sweetness of the honey - and remembering the sting of the bee! Bless, and eat the fruit, remembering, that the flower must wither and die, so that the fruit may grow, and that the fruit must decay so that the seed may grow (although now the fruit dies to nourish you!).

Pour a libation, and leave some fruit, and the flowers as an offering to the spirits of the place. Thank the Goddess and God. Thank and dismiss the elements, and open the circle.

Lughnasadh - 1st August

Lughnasadh or Lammas is celebrated on August eve or August 1st and is the festival of the first of the harvest. Lammas is the Anglo-Saxon name for the festival, meaning Loaf mass. Lughnasadh is the festival of Lugh, a Celtic God of Light and Fire and God of crafts and skills. His Welsh form is Llew Law Gyffes, and in the Mabinogion story of Blodeuwidd and Llew, the theme of Llew as the sacrificed God can be seen (we need of course to consider the pre-Christian origins of the story). Gronw can be seen as the Dark God of the Waning year, and Llew as the Bright Lord of the Waxing year, Blodeuwidd represents the Goddess in Her Flower Maiden aspect.

Lammas or Lughnasadh then has the theme of the sacrificed God of the harvest, but he is sacrificed and transformed, rather than descending into the underworld to become Lord of Death, which comes later in the year. Lammas is a time of the fullness of Life, and a celebration of the bountiful earth. It is a time of the sacrificial mating, of Goddess and God, where the Corn King, given life by the Goddess and tasting of Her love is sacrificed and transformed into bread and ale which feeds us. The main themes of Lammas may therefore be seen as, thanksgiving to the Goddess for Her bountiful harvest, stating our hopes for what we wish to harvest (for Lammas is the very beginning of the harvest), sacrifice, transformation, and a sharing of the energy of the Corn King.

Ritual for Lammas

Set up an altar with a sheaf of wheat or barley, bread, and ale. A quiet place outdoors is always preferable.

Cast your circle or visualize a sphere of love and protection around yourself. Feel the energy of the earth and ground and centre yourself. Invoke the elements at the quarters asking for the fresh breeze of inspiration and clarity in the east, the fire of transformation in the South, the waters of Life and love in the West, and the abundance of the earth in the North.

Invoke the Goddess as the Bountiful Lady, Habundia, Cerridwen, Demeter,

Kore, with Her cornucopia or horn of plenty pouring forth the fruits of life. Imagine Her with sheaves of wheat in Her arms bringing all to fruition. She is the Maiden, the Kore, the potential in us waiting to be harvested. She is the Mother of all Life, all fruits of the Earth are fruits of Her womb, and She is the Crone, the Reaper who cuts the corn, and transforms it in Her cauldron of Change. State what you hope to harvest this year.

Invoke the God as Lugh, God of Light and Fire, and as the Corn King. Feel the Sun on your body and contemplate the healing and nourishing power of the Sun, how it has warmed and nourished the Earth and the crops, and how the Sun god has made the earth fertile. He has reached His highest point at the Solstice and his power has begun to wane, yet still He is strong, still he warms the Earth and enlivens the crops. The spirit of the Sun is embodied in the crops, the Corn King is the God on Earth. Visualize fields of ripe corn and the spirit of the God dancing in the corn fields.

Sing, play or contemplate the Ballad of John Barleycorn, perhaps dancing or acting out parts of the story. Then, think about what you want to change or transform in yourself or your life.

What habits will you change, what sacrifice will you make? Contemplate this and make a statement, a pledge to the Goddess. Bless the bread and ale, and know that this is the body and spirit of the Corn King, filled with the power of the Sun and Life. Pour a libation to the earth, giving back to the Mother some of what She has given out, and then drink the rest of the ale, drinking in the energy of the God, and eat the bread, eating of the life that ever dies and is reborn. Leave a little bread as an offering.

Feel the power of transformation, be enlivened by the power of the God, and feel the Love of the Goddess. You may wish to dance, feast, etc. Thank the God for His sacrifice and His energy. Thank the Goddess for Her bounty. Thank the elements and close the circle.

The Ballad of John Barleycorn

There were three men came from the west
Their fortune for to try,
And they have sworn a solemn oath,
John Barleycorn should die.

They have laid him in three furrows deep,
Laid clods upon his head,
And they have sworn a solemn vow,
John Barleycorn was dead.

They let him lie for a very long time,
Till the rain from heaven did fall,
Then little Sir John sprang up his head,
And He did amaze them all.

They let him stand till Midsummer day,
Till he looked both pale and wan,
Then little Sir John he grew a long beard,
And so became a man.

They have hired men with scythes so sharp,
To cut him off at knee,
They rolled and they tied him round the waist,
And they served him barbarously.

They have hired men with the crab tree sticks,
To cut him skin from bone,
And the Miller has served him worse than that,
For he's ground him between two stones.

They've wheeled him here and they've wheeled him there,
They've wheeled him to a barn,
And they have served him worse than that,
They've bunged him in a vat.

They have worked their will on John Barleycorn,
But he lived to tell the tale,
For they poured him out of an old brown jug,
And they called him Barley Ale.

The Autumnal Equinox - 21st September

The two equinoxes are times of equilibrium. Day and night are equal and the tide of the year flows steadily, but whilst the Spring Equinox manifests the equilibrium before action, the Autumnal Equinox represents the repose after action, the time to take satisfaction in the work of the summer and reap its benefits. The Autumnal Equinox is celebrated on 21st September, and is the second harvest festival, both grain and fruit having been gathered in. We celebrate the abundance of the earth, and make wine from the excess fruit, to preserve the richness of the fruits of the earth to give us joy throughout the year.

This is the time of the Vine. The God, who was Lord of the Greenwood, in the summer and the Corn King at Lughnasadh now dances his last dance upon the earth, as Dionysus, God of wine, music and dance, before making his descent to the underworld to take up his role as Dread Lord of Shadows. The Lord of Light, the Sun King, his power waning, exists briefly in balance with the Dark Lord before giving way to the growing power of darkness, but the power of the sun is encapsulated in the grape and the fruits of the earth. The wine will remind us of his power throughout the year.

The leaves falling from the trees and rotting into the earth are a reflection of the Horned God's journey from the Greenwood to the underworld, deep into the womb of the mother, where He will reside until He begins to emerge with the new green shoots in the spring. The Autumnal Equinox marks the completion of the harvest, and thanksgiving, with the emphasis on the future return of that abundance. The Eleusinian mysteries took place at this time, during which the initiate was said to have been shown a single ear of grain with the words "*In silence is the seed of wisdom gained*".

The themes then of the Autumnal Equinox are the completion of the harvest, the balance of light and dark, and of male and female, and an acknowledgement of the waning power of the sun and the waxing power of the Dark Lord.

Ritual for the Autumnal Equinox

Decorate your altar with sheaves of corn and fruits of the season. It is best to go out and harvest the wild fruit yourself. Blackberries, sloes, elderberries, etc. can be placed around the altar, or perform your ritual where these things are growing. Have a chalice of wine on the altar. Wine made from last years fruit harvest is particularly good for the purpose, as we then have both the unchanged fruit, and the wine as symbol of transformation. Have also a black and a white candle.

Ground and centre yourself. Visualize a sphere of love and protection around yourself. Invoke the four elements, asking for them to be balanced within you, and upon the earth. Spend some time in meditation upon the balancing of the elements within your own psyche.

Call upon the Goddess as bountiful mother, thanking Her for the abundance which She has given us. Remember that from Her all things proceed, and to Her all things must return. Meditate on the abundance of the season, and on the falling leaves and decaying vegetation. Meditate on the return to the earth, the return to the Mother of all things. She is both the bright abundant mother, and the dark sterile mother, who presides over death, in order to transform and bring rebirth. She is both Earth Goddess and Cosmic Goddess, and just as vegetation on the earth must die and decay so that new life may emerge, so in the macrocosm must planets and stars eventually die, so that creation may take place. All is flux and change. Meditate on this constant change, on the impermanence of all things, except the Goddess Herself. Chant:

> *She changes everything She touches*
> *And everything She touches changes*
>
> *There is a woman who weaves the night sky*
> *See how She spins, see Her fingers fly*
> *She weaves within us, beginning to end*
> *Our grandmother, sister and friend*
> *She is the needle, we are the thread*
> *She is the weaver, we are the web*

She changes everything She touches
And everything She touches changes
Change is, touch is
Touch us, change us
We are changers everything we touch can change

Each seed She deeply buries
She weaves the web of seasons
Her sacred darkness carries
She loves beyond all reason

She changes everything She touches...etc.

Call upon the God as the Lord of Dance, Dionysus, Pan, Cernunnos. Dance with Him in joy, with the chant

Dionysus, growing vine
Transformation, flowing wine
Energy, ecstasy
Dionysus dance with me
Bring out my creativity
Dionysus live in me

Feel the joy of the season, and the abundance. Feel the carefree nature of the time of abundance, and revel in it for a while. When tired of this, remember that there is a more serious task in hand, that of descent and facing darkness. Call on the God again, but this time as Lord of the Underworld, Dread Lord of Shadows, and ask for His help in facing your own shadow in the season to come. For now simply acknowledge its presence, accepting the light and dark within yourself.

Light the white and the black candles, and contemplate the opposites of order and chaos. There is a time for wild abandonment and joy, and there is a time for restraint and control, but neither of these exists entirely alone. On the spiritual path, each must be tempered with the other, although one may be stronger at any one time. Ask the Goddess and God for the wisdom to distinguish what is necessary in all situations, to let go, or to stay in control.

Take an ear of corn from the altar, and say

"Behold the mystery, in silence is the seed of wisdom gained"

Contemplate this for a while. Consecrate the wine and the fruit, asking that some of the fruit may be blessed and transformed to create wine to sustain you throughout the year. Drink and feast.

Thank the Goddess and God and the elements and close the circle.

After the ritual begin the process of making wine from the fruit, ready or next years Autumnal equinox. A libation of wine should be poured in honour of the trees from which the fruit came, if possible.

Chapter Twenty-seven

The Esbats

"Esbat" is the name given by modern witches to the lunar rituals, generally performed on the Full Moon. Whereas the Sabbats are mainly celebratory rituals, where any magickal work done is inner work or simple earth healing, the Esbats are the rituals where spellcraft is practised. The moon rules the tides, our unconscious minds, and is said to rule the flow of magick. It is also the Prime symbol of the Goddess in modern Wicca. In working esbats we tune in to the cycles of the moon, and use its energy to work magick. Although most covens perform their workings mainly at full moons, esbats performed during other phases of the moon are also valid, and depending on the desired results, can in some cases be more appropriate.

The new moon is a time of new beginnings, and is a good time to perform spells for initiating new projects or attaining new things, and it symbolizes the maiden aspect of the Goddess. Magick generally works best if spells are performed often, rather than just as one offs, and beginning a series of workings at the new moon and culminating at the full moon can achieve a quick and positive result. The full moon is the time of the Mother, when the moon is said to be at the height of her power, and there is plenty of magickal energy to be used, a time of creativity. The waning moon is a time for cleansing and banishing, and attuning oneself with the Dark Goddess, the Crone or Wise One. It is also a good time to perform binding spells, to bind the power of others so that they cannot harm you. The Dark Moon is used for works of wrath and retribution (cursing), and introspection. It is connected, again with the Crone or Hag Goddess.

Spell and ritual construction has been explained in chapter 17, so you can design your own esbats following those rules, and the rules above.

Generally, a solitary Esbat would involve, in order, purifying, casting the circle, invocation of the Elements, invocation of the Goddess, God and Old Ones, meditation on the phase of the moon, raising of energy, spellcraft, consecration of cakes and wine, feasting, thanking and saying goodbye to the Old Ones, God and Goddess, dismissing the Elements and closing the circle. Spellcraft may consist of candle magick (see chapter 17), talismanic magick (see chapter 19), herbal charms (see chapter 13), knot magick, creating a poppet, or a number of other techniques.

For knot magick, you will require a length of cord in an appropriate colour for the working. Knots are tied in the cord whilst you state your intent. Generally three knots are tied, and the intent is stated in three different ways, whilst visualizing the desired result. It is good to visualize the result having been achieved fully when you tie the last knot. Afterwards, put the cord away, on your pentacle, or wrapped in silk, until your next working, or until the result has been achieved, when you will untie it. Unlike poppets, and candle magick, the same cord can be used again in another spell. The cords are magickal tools and it is good to have a set of them in different colours for different types of working.

For poppet magick you will need to make an image of the person you wish to have an effect on (e.g. healing), and try to make it look as much like them as possible. If possible, include some object links in its construction, such as hair or fingernail clippings. The poppet may be made out of cloth, wax, clay, wood, or other materials. If cloth, it may be stuffed with appropriate herbs. The poppet should then be blessed and named, visualizing it as the person it represents, and knowing that it will act as a sort of double, such that what you do to the poppet will be done to the person. It can then be bathed in healing water, bound with cord, its conscience pricked with a needle, etc.

Apart from working generally with the phases of the moon, we can also work with the larger cycle of the seasons in our lunar rituals, and there are various versions of the lunar calendar, many based on the celtic tree alphabet or Ogham. A number of books have appeared in recent years on the subject of the Tree Calender, and all are slightly different, and it can be very confusing. The version given here is the one we use, but it should be stressed that there is no overall right way, and other versions are equally valid.

The year is split into thirteen lunar months, plus a short, three day month which lasts from the day before, to the day after the winter solstice. The three days of the Winter Solstice are sacred to the Yew Tree, the tree of death and rebirth, great age and the renewed spirit. The first lunar month begins immediately after the yew "month", and the first full moon after the solstice is the birch tree esbat. The birch is a tree of purity, cleansing, insight and new beginnings. The second lunar month begins with the next new moon, and the Esbat will be the Rowan Tree Esbat. For more details about the attributes of the trees see chapter 13. Here follows a list of the lunar months:

1] Birch
2] Rowan
3] Ash
4] Alder
5] Willow
6] May Tree (Hawthorn)
7] Oak
8] Holly
9] Hazel (and Apple)
10] Apple (or Vine)
11] Vine (or Ivy)
12] Ivy (or Reed)
13] Elder
14] Yew 3 day "month".

The thirteenth month will often not be a full month, and sometimes there will be no full moon during it. It is okay to call on the powers of more than one tree in a particular month, or to call on one tree for two months running. There are no hard and fast rules as to which trees fit exactly with which lunar months. There are just broad periods of the year when you may find that the influence of a particular tree is stronger. The various forms of the tree calendar can help us to tune into these times, but one should not be rigid about them. It is a framework from which to explore, and you can work your esbats according to the energies present. For example, use the Rowan Tree Esbat for spells of magickal protection.

Other influences which can be used for your Esbats are planetary influences and astrology. Planetary influences may be as simple as performing a Martial ritual in March (March is ruled by Mars), or on a day of the week ruled by the planet (Tuesday for Mars). Or you may go into detailed analysis of planetary hours and astrological charts. As different planets have different cycles, often taking years, it is good to "go through the moon" to your chosen planet. I.e. work your planetary spell within an Esbat, asking for the blessings of the moon, and working with the lunar phases as above.

Chapter Twenty-eight

Working in a Group

There comes a time for most people, when they feel the need to make contact with, and perhaps work rituals with, other like minded people. You may already have friends who share your interests, in which case you might organize a simple ritual, such as a sabbat celebration which they can take part in. Many people prefer to work on their own, following a solitary magickal and mystical path, but wish to celebrate the religious side of the path with other people.

All religions have a social side - Churches have various different clubs and societies associated with them, and the Christian festivals are times of parties and celebration. Paganism is no exception, and the Sabbat rituals are often followed by feasting and merry- making. An advantage of paganism, is because we recognize all Goddesses and Gods, from all cultures, we can generally find a feast day whenever we want one! We would recommend *"Juno Covella - A Perpetual Calender of the Fellowship of Isis"* available from the Fellowship of Isis for finding which dates are associated with which Goddesses. There are also various pagan calendars available which have information about festival dates. However, most western pagans concentrate on celebrating the eight sabbats described in chapter 25.

If you decide that you want to organize some open rituals yourself, you might want to open it up to other people than just friends. You can make contact with people through organizations such as the Pagan Federation, Pagan Link and the Guild of Pagans, in Britain, the Fellowship of Isis (worldwide), the Church of All Worlds in America, and various other organizations. There are also many pagan magazines available, some of which have contact sections.

If you do decide to organise open rituals yourself, how do you go about it? When constructing a ritual, the first thing you consider is the Intent - why are you doing this ritual and who or what will benefit. The second thing to consider is the Environment - are you going to be working outdoors, at a sacred site, in a temple, a church hall?

A ritual should always be in sympathy with its environment. In the case of working outdoors this means going to the site first and attuning to the site, meditating there, contacting the site guardians and making sure the site is the right place to do your ritual, not just "a stone circle because I fancy doing my ritual at one". If working indoors you may have considerations of partner, other people in the house, neighbours, etc - these are also part of your environment and should not be forgotten about.

Now the serious Planning can begin - ask yourself how many people will be in the ritual, and what are their relative levels of experience of the techniques you intend to use to raise energy. Open rituals usually have a percentage (often large) of participants with little or no magickal training (and let us not forget this is true of a lot of pagans) so in these cases the rituals need to be kept simple - techniques like drumming, dancing, chanting, pathworking, ritual drama (enactment of myths and legends with experienced practitioners), etc. Remember open rituals should look visually impressive, so use of regalia, robes, jewellery, etc, all help (and be sure people know who is using which magickal tools, etc). Open rituals should have a large element of participation for all - ritual drama is all well and good, but works better if the audience are taking part in activities themselves as well, to feel part of the ritual and opening the channels to their unconscious where knowledge and insight can be stored and energy released.

Having planned the ritual and got the people together, the Format of the ritual should be explained to everybody - what techniques are going to be used, what visualisations should be done, what chants are going to be used (with rehearsals if required, to ensure the energy will flow well), and of course what the Intention of the ritual is. During the ritual the other consideration you should be mindful of is Efficiency. Many pagan rituals we have been to have been unfortunately full of faffing around and dispersing the energy raised, simply because little details have not been worked out beforehand. If the details have been worked out beforehand and everybody knows what they are supposed to do in the ritual, it will work, and work well, which is of course what to aim for when doing group rituals.

After a ritual there should always be a Grounding - feasting is a very good way, but if there is any excess energy left at the end of the ritual it should be directed to some useful purpose, like earth healing (and again people should know beforehand what to do in this instance). If you are running the ritual you should ensure that all participants are grounded and in a fit state to depart afterwards, as it may happen that some people are affected by the energies of the ritual, and be knocked off balance. In such instances some counselling may be required. It must be emphasised that if you run a ritual with other people in, you are in a position of power (power with rather than power over) and are responsible for their wellbeing, and they should leave feeling earthed and with that warm afterglow.

You might also want to make contact with established Pagan or magickal groups, and these can be found in all cities and most towns if you look hard enough. The organizations mentioned previously can be of help in finding them. Many universities have student pagan societies, which are often open to non-students, so check out your local students union if you live in a university town. There are many different types of magickal groups, pagan groups and covens, and it is important to find a group that is right for you. Even within the same tradition, practices and standards vary considerably.

Within witchcraft there are many traditions, but each coven is autonomous. Most covens operate a degree system of some kind, either a two degree, or a three degree system. Covens are closed groups, (although some covens may run open sabbat rituals at times) and the people within them become very close. Joining a coven is much like becoming part of a family, and a great deal of commitment is required. Pagan groups on the other hand, are generally looser collections of people who get together to perform sabbat rituals and perhaps eco-magick and earth healing rites. They may also organize social occasions, discussion groups, workshops and trips to sacred sites, but they are generally non initiatory groups. There are some pagan groups who call themselves covens, but we consider covens to be something quite different, and to anyone who has been initiated into a coven, the differences will generally be quite apparent, although there are of course variations.

There are also variations within covens that use a degree system as to what the degrees mean, and what standards are required for a person to be elevated to a certain degree. With some groups it seems to be merely a case of time - i.e. the person has an initiation a year! In most groups, however, the highest degree is often not taken for several years, and some people never take it at all. The following is the degree system as we see it, with the standards which we require for initiation and elevation in our own coven.

Degrees

Non-initiated Pagans

People who have a feel for paganism, but do not wish to be actively involved, or cannot commit themselves at present. The "Laity". They may attend open Sabbat gatherings run by covens or pagan societies. They might also attend the odd workshop. They might wish to perform a simple self-blessing ritual for themselves.

0o Probationer's Initiation

These are people who have decided that they want to take the plunge and join a coven, and have been accepted by the coven as trainees. The probationary initiation marks a turning point, and a deeper commitment to the Craft is required. A task or quest is set for the initiation as a sign of commitment, and certain basic vows are made. The time between probationary initiation and first degree is taken up with learning the basics of meditation, work with nature spirits, healing, alternative medicine, therapy, etc.

The probationer should also learn all they can about the cycles of nature and the Sabbats, and they are expected to attend all coven sabbat rituals and pre first degree training sessions. It is also a time for getting to know members of the coven before joining fully. The individual is expected to do a certain amount of solitary study.

1o Craft Initiation

The person is accepted into the coven as a witch, with a ritual which involves a symbolic death and rebirth, and a new name is taken. The new witch continues to learn about the subjects above, but also learns about Craft magickal and ritual techniques, and group energy. Each individual brings something unique into the group, which they can share with others. After 1^0, the person should begin to think about what s/he can offer in terms of sharing knowledge and teaching others, and should take an active part in the running of training sessions for probationers (under supervision). S/He should start to think about specialising in a specific area (if they have not already) e.g. healing, tarot, astrology, herbalism, runes, therapy, voice work, body work, music, crafting ritual objects, etc. The person should study her chosen specialism on her own, but may bring her knowledge back to the group. She should also start designing and leading rituals (sabbats at first, then later, when approaching 2^0, esbats), and practising casting the circle, etc.

First degree initiation will take place when the individual feels ready, and the coven is willing to accept her. If a person feels a significant shift in her life, and wants to mark it with initiation, but the coven do not feel that she would work well with that particular group, she may be referred on to another group.

Prior to the initiation, the candidate spends the day fasting and purifying. They should have an athame, which will be consecrated in the initiation ritual, and cords and a blank book to become their Book of Shadows. After the initiation they will be given the Books of Shadows to copy from, and instructed in techniques of magick.

2o Second Degree Initiation - Coming Into Power

Personal Development Level - This marks a change in the person's life where they are really coming into their own power, and experiencing themselves in a new way. They should also be developing the ability to facilitate the empowering of others. The 2^0 initiation should involve working with power and using the tools of the art. The candidate should make herself a power object, such as a wand, knife, drum, rattle, piece of jewellery, etc. The ritual should involve a "facing of death" that we may learn from it, and has a different emphasis to the 1^0 death and rebirth ritual. The ritual also involves a willing of power into the individual - empowerment by magickal method.

The 2^0 witch should also be working with channelling God/Goddess forms, and should work with male/female energies for a deeper understanding of polarity in preparation for third degree. They should also be working with other polarities, such as light and dark, anima and animus, yin and yang, etc, and should begin to face their shadow sides. The 2^0 initiation is preceded by a night spent alone in the wilds, meditating.

Practical Level - The person should be fully competent in designing and leading spells and rituals, and in running training sessions, before taking 2^0. 2^0 is an initiation which confers High Priest/ess status, and the 2^0 witch may hive to form their own coven, under the supervision of their parent coven. It is not recommended that people hive immediately on taking 2^0, however. In general they should wait at least a year before hiving. When a couple, or individual, hives, the parent coven will not get involved in training the newly hived HP/HPS' trainees, but will meet with the HP/HPS on a regular basis to give supervision and guidance. This avoidance of contact between the new coven's trainees and the parent coven HP and HPS is known as voiding the coven, and it is necessary in order to avoid undermining the authority of the new HP and HPS in their new coven. Many, however, will prefer to stay in their parent coven, as coven elders, rather than hiving to form their own coven.

3^0 Sacred Marriage - Ritual of Taking Responsibility

Personal Development Level - The individual should have a thorough understanding of polarity, and should be able to channel the God/dess effectively, and to see their own partner as the God/dess. This person becomes aware of her own divinity upon this earth, and sees the inherent divinity of others. This does not mean that one does not recognise ones own faults, but rather that we accept ourselves with our faults, and give ourselves unconditional love and respect. Unconditional respect for others, and love for the world will follow. This does not mean a suppression of supposedly "negative" emotions, but rather, full and vibrant contact with the emotions, and the ability to channel them in the most positive way. Suppression of the emotions equals suppression of energy. With the flow of the emotions, power flows. The third degree witch should have the capability to facilitate the empowerment of others.

Practical Level - 3^0 means that one is a fully independent HP or HPS, capable of running a coven without supervision. One must be skilled in counselling, training people in the Craft, leading rituals, and have knowledge of group process. 3^0 is more a ritual of acknowledgement than initiation, and should only be taken when one has proved oneself capable of running a coven independently. Witches may hive at 2^0, run a new coven under supervision of their initiating HPS and HP, and when they reach the point that they are fully capable of running the group without supervision, take 3^0 as an acknowledgement of this.

The Great Rite and 3^0

In most covens, 3^0 initiation includes the Great Rite in one form or another. This may be taken in "actual" form, or in "token" or symbolic form, depending on the relationship between initiator and initiate. In actual form, the Great Rite is a ritual of Sacred Sex, in token form it is a ritual of gender. In either case, it is a symbol for the balancing of opposites within one's own psyche. There are a minority of groups who insist that the Great Rite is always performed in actuality, and a few who even say that it is more spiritual to do it with someone who is not one's partner, but even in actuality the Great Rite is only a symbol, and there is nothing spiritual about attachment to the symbol itself. This is not to say that the Great Rite in actuality may not be a profound experience - it can be when there is love there between those taking it, but if the initiate and initiator are not lovers, then there are other, more appropriate methods of achieving a mystical state. Our own view, which we believe is shared by most witches, is that the Great Rite should only be performed in actuality between people who are already in a sexual relationship. Janet and Stewart Farrar present a well thought out case for this in "*The Witches Way*" and in "*Eight Sabbats for Witches*", but we would add further considerations.

Firstly, to perform it in actuality with someone who is not one's usual partner can destroy the brother-sister relationships within the coven, and if the people concerned have other partners, it is likely to destroy their respective relationships. We believe that the bond between lovers is sacred and pleasing to the Gods, and doing anything that may damage the bond is not. Also, sex magick takes practice, and knowing each other's minds and bodies. To perform a ritual such as 3^0 sexually with someone one has never had sex with before, is not likely to lead to a profound experience, but there will be more concern with the "technical" side of the sex act itself. It is far better to do with someone who you are relaxed with, and where there is love, trust, desire and passion.

We feel that the idea that 3^0 is only real if the Great Rite is taken in actuality is a very dangerous one, as young, impressionable people can be made to feel that they have to have sex with their initiators, and then they have to suffer the consequences afterwards. We have also known people to deceive their partners, telling them they are taking it in token, but really having a sexual initiation, and personally we cannot accept these 3^0 s as valid, as the act of deception shows a lack of readiness for 3^0 , and is not exactly spiritual. The idea that it has to be actual misses the point and shows a lack of understanding of the deeper mysteries.

The idea of "Tantra" is often used as an excuse for sexual rituals, but it should be remembered, that although Tantra employs sexual symbolism (much as the Great Rite in token does) most forms of Tantra are not sexual. There are also a few covens who use sexual initiations for first degree, and who practice sexual magick in all rituals, expecting everyone to take part.

When you make contact with a group find out what their attitudes on such matters are, and do not be pushed into doing anything that you don't want to do, or that doesn't feel right to you, in the name of the Craft. It is better to continue working alone than to join a dodgy group. Also, don't be afraid to ask questions. Most groups will appreciate questions, because it shows that you are thinking things through. If a group discourages questions, or gives unsatisfactory answers, then go no further with the group. Being accepted into a coven is a two-way process. The coven are judging you and deciding whether or not to accept you, but you are also deciding whether or not you want to join the coven.

Changes following the third degree may also be marked with initiations, though we see no need for further degrees. There may also be additional rites of initiation between degrees, when people come to a point of change in their lives, and want to mark it with a ritual, but are not yet ready for their next degree. There may also be rites of initiation that a whole coven may take together, such as planetary initiations, initiations of different God-forms, etc.

It is also good for men to learn to channel the Goddess, and women to channel the God, for further balancing of energies. All initiations are preceded by a period of purification, fasting, and meditation. Normally the candidate fasts for 24 hours before the initiation ritual, and tries to achieve a contemplative, meditative and reflective state of mind throughout this time. She will spend some time in proper meditation before the ritual - usually about half an hour to an hour meditating on death and rebirth before first degree, and several hours meditating in the wilds before second degree. The initiator may also fast with the candidate.

It should also be noted that not everyone will go through all the degrees. Some people will be happy to stay at first degree, and not go any further than this. It is quite common for people to remain at 2^0, and not go any further - after all not everyone wants to run their own coven. No pressure should be put on people to go through the degrees, although continued personal development should be stressed. As a metaphor, the degrees may be likened to academic qualifications, with 1^0 being like a BA or Bsc. This is a qualification in subject, enables one to practice at a certain level, which can be built on with experience, but one won't get a job as a university lecturer with it! 2^0 may be seen as being like an MA or Msc. It is a higher qualification, and you may also get some work at the university teaching undergraduates. 3^0 would be more like a doctorate. with which you have proved yourself with a piece of original research, and can take up a lectureship post. How far people go, which degree they stop at, depends partly on interest, partly on capability. It is important that people are aware of their capabilities and limitations, and that degrees are taken at the right time, when the right level has been reached. However, the standards vary considerably from coven to coven. The standards listed are those that we apply.

Appendix 1

The Consecration of the Temple

The ritual given here is a simple ritual for consecrating a place that has been set aside as a temple. You may add to it or change it as you feel appropriate. You will need the following equipment:

Salt and water in small bowls, with a spare empty third bowl

Chalice of wine

Pentacle or plate with cake/bread or other appropriate food

Candles - green, yellow, red, blue and purple (or black)
Censer and incense or joss sticks

Anointing oil

Athame (optional)

Broom (optional)

All of this equipment should be on your altar in the north (or east if that is your preference) apart from the other three elemental candles which should be in the appropriate quarters, with the purple or black candle for spirit in the middle of the room, and the broom (if used) being in the north by the altar (if this is the altar location).

Before the ritual ensure the room you intend to consecrate as your temple is clean, and have a ritual purificatory bath.

Consecration Ritual

Perform the Lesser Banishing Ritual of the Pentagram (or other banishing) to clear away any unwanted influences or residues of occupation that may linger in the room. You may also wish to sweep the room with a broom (widdershins as you are clearing the space first).

Light the candles, starting with the air candle (the east being the place of new beginnings), then light the fire candle from the air candle, the water candle from the fire candle, and the earth candle from the water candle. Light the incense or joss. Consecrate the salt and water as described previously in chapter 16, using the third bowl to mix them in, and being sure to leave some of the salt and water in their respective bowls. Walk around the room sprinkling the consecrated salt water until you have returned full circle to the altar. Cast the circle as described in chapter 17.

Go to the east and inscribe the invoking pentagram of air in yellow, see the elemental landscape of air through the pentagon in the centre of the pentagram. Invite the sylphs to dwell in your temple, feeling the rush of the winds through the pentagram into your temple as you say:

"Powers of Air, I call on you and invite you to dwell within this temple. Share your qualities and powers with me, that I may learn from them. In the name of love I bid you hail and welcome."

Offer the incense to the elementals of air, saying:

"With sweet smelling incense I consecrate this temple with the powers of air. May the powers of air dwell within this sacred space, and may I ever learn and practice the qualities of air, knowledge, discrimination and communication."

Walk deosil around the temple until you are back in the east, leave the censer or joss there with the air candle and move deosil to the south.

Inscribe the invoking pentagram of fire in red, see the elemental landscape of fire through the pentagon in the centre of the pentagram. Invite the salamanders to dwell in your temple, feeling the heat of fire rushing into the room through the pentagram as you say:

"Powers of Fire, I call on you and invite you to dwell within this temple. Share your qualities and powers with me, that I may learn from them. In the name of love I bid you hail and welcome."

Offer the red fire candle to the elementals of fire, saying:

"With fire bright and true I consecrate this temple with the powers of fire. May the powers of fire dwell within this sacred space, and may I ever will and practice the qualities of fire, determination, passion and courage."

Walk deosil around the temple until you are back in the south, return the candle to its position, and return to the altar to collect the bowl of water then move deosil to the west.

In the west inscribe the invoking pentagram of water in blue, see the elemental landscape of water through the centre of the pentagram. Invite the sylphs to dwell in your temple, feeling the cool dampness of water flowing into the room through the pentagram as you say:

"Powers of Water, I call on you and invite you to dwell within this temple. Share your qualities and powers with me, that I may learn from them. In the name of love I bid you hail and welcome."

Offer the bowl of water to the elementals of water, saying:

"With the waters of life I consecrate this temple with the powers of water. May the powers of water dwell within this sacred space, and may I ever feel and practice the qualities of water, love, compassion and expression of the emotions."

Walk deosil around the temple until you are back in the west and place the bowl with the west candle. Then move to the north.

Inscribe an invoking pentagram of earth in green, see the elemental landscape of earth through the centre of the pentagram. Invite the gnomes to dwell in your temple, feeling the solidity and strength of earth permeating the room, rising from the ground below (or around if you are in a cellar) as you say:

"Powers of Earth, I call to you and invite you to dwell within this temple. Share your qualities and powers with me, that I may learn from them. In the name of love I bid you hail and welcome."

Offer the bowl of salt to the elementals of earth, saying:

"With the salt of purity I consecrate this temple with the powers of earth. May the powers of earth dwell within this sacred space, and may I ever be and practice the qualities of earth, patience, steadfastness and firmness."

Walk deosil around the temple until you are back in the north and replace the salt on the altar.

Now invoke the Goddess and the God in the names you feel the strongest connections with (or not using names if you prefer) and the Old Ones, and ask for their blessings on your temple and that they will dwell in your temple and inspire you.

Now anoint the spirit candle with the oil (as you do this concentrate on the Goddess and the God), starting at the middle of the candle and moving up the candle, then moving from the centre to the bottom of the candle, and then a flowing stroke from the bottom of the candle to the top and then back to the bottom again saying:

"From above to below Flows the pattern of perfection
From desire to manifestation Flows the pattern of magick
From within to without Flows the pattern of my will"

Light the candle as you reach the last line (ideally so the flame takes as you say "my will"), then offer the purple or black candle to the skies, visualising the room filling with a brilliant white light as you say:

"With the eternal flame of spirit I consecrate this temple with the powers of spirit. May the powers of spirit dwell within this sacred space, and may I ever practice my will and be true to myself, the Goddess and the God, and the Old Ones in all I do."

Bless the wine and cakes with a simple blessing, channelling energy into them as you say something like:

"In the mighty and holy names of the Goddess and the God I bless and purify this wine (or cake). May it be fit sacrament for their rites."

Feast and write up your experiences.

When you close the circle, in this instance you do not need to dismiss the Goddess, God, Old Ones or Elements as you have just invited them to dwell in your temple, and this would be rather bad manners! Say farewell and thank them when you leave the temple. Remember though in subsequent rituals you would invite and then say goodbye to them, it is their spirit rather than their presence you are focusing in your temple, to act as a beacon to which they will be drawn for subsequent works.

You may wish to add other qualities for the elements when consecrating the temple. The pentagrams may be inscribed with your athame or with your preferred hand.

Deconsecration

Circumstances (such as moving house or an addition to the family) may require you to temporarily give up your temple space, and with this in mind we present a deconsecration ritual, which can be used to focus the energies you have gathered into your temple, and store them to be released into your new temple.

You will need five elementally coloured candles (as well as the candles you normally use) and a piece of black silk and a white cord.

Deconsecration Ritual

Have the candles placed unlit at the appropriate quarters, with the spirit candle in the middle of the room.

Cast the circle as normal. Invoke the elements, Goddess, God and Old Ones.

Starting in the north, light the north candle and move round the circle widdershins lighting each of the candles in turn, until you reach the spirit candle. Let the five candles burn for a few minutes, and see them absorbing the appropriate elemental or deity energies. Bring the elemental candles into the centre with the spirit candle, then tie the candles together (still lit) saying:

"I bind the power of this temple into these candles."

Let them burn for a few minutes, and then put all the candles out, and wrap them in the silk and store them for use in the next consecration ritual.

Close the circle as you would normally. Then perform the lesser banishing ritual of the pentagram (or other banishing).

Appendix 2

The Lesser Rituals of the Pentagram

The Pentagram rituals are one of the most basic foundations of western magick, and have been worked very effectively by a lot of people over a long time period, gaining a natural "flow" when worked and having a lot of inherent energy from regular and repeated use. Even if you are not comfortable with the idea of using Hebrew, it is worth learning these rituals and being proficient in them - they are a good example of the combination of voicework, visualisation, telesmatic imagery and body work. Once the ritual is known and fluent, you can always experiment with using for example, Celtic deities instead of the Hebrew Divine Names on the Quarters, or the rulers of the Elements on the quarters instead of the Archangels. With proficiency you will then always have a good banishing/invoking ritual "under your belt" that can be used at any time or place.

1 The Qabalistic Cross

Face east and see yourself growing and rising up to the heavens with your feet firmly on the earth, growing until the earth is a globe supporting your feet. See a sphere of blinding whiteness above but not touching your head. Trace with your preferred hand (with first two fingers straight and other two fingers folded with thumb folded onto them) a line of energy down to your third eye, touch the third eye with your hand and vibrate:

ATOH (Ah-toh)

This means `thou art`, as you say it use willed imagination such that what you say echoes throughout the universe.

Move the hand down along your body and touch about $1^{1}/_{2}$" below the sternum. As you do this see the energy continue down through the body until it reaches your feet on the earth. When you have done this vibrate:

MALKUTH (Mal-kut)

This means `the kingdom`, again the phrase echoes through the universe.

Touch the right shoulder with your hand and feeling a reservoir of energy activating on the right side, vibrate:

VE-GEBURAH (Ve-geh-vur-ah)

This means `and the power`, as before the name echoes throughout the universe.

Now move your hand across the body tracing a line of energy and touch the left shoulder, again feeling a reservoir of energy activating, this time on the left side, vibrate:

VE-GEDULAH (Ve-geh-du-lah)

This means `and the glory` the name echoes throughout the whole universe as before.

Crossing arms across breast (posture of Osiris slain) vibrate:

LE-OLAHM, AMEN (Le-oh-lahm, amen)

This means `to the ages, amen`, as you say it see the cross now formed within your body vibrate with the words and hear them echoing throughout the universe, as before.

2 Setting the Circle and Inscribing the Pentagrams

Facing east inscribe a pentagram in front of you starting with your hand at a position corresponding to your left hip and moving up to the top point of the pentagram (which is approximately level with the top of your head), then continue on to complete pentagram. As you inscribe pentagram see it forming in the air in front of you. With the pentagram flaming in front of you stab it`s centre and intone:

YHVH (Yah-weh)

This divine name is the creative word of divinity.

Then from the east with your hand extended out in front of you, turn to the south, see a circle of flame starting to be formed around you as you turn to the south. Now facing south inscribe a pentagram in front of you in the manner described above except that as you strike centre of pentagram, intone:

ADNI (Ah-doh-nye)

This means Lord, we see this divine name as referring to the higher self.

Now from the south turn to the west, again with hand outstretched, and see the circle of flame continuing to be formed. In the west inscribe another pentagram as previously described, intoning:

AHIH (Eh-heh-yay)

The first emanation 'I am that I am'

Turning to the north still with your hand outstretched, seeing the circle of flame continuing to be formed. In the north inscribe another pentagram in the same manner and intone:

AGLA (Ah-glah)

An abbreviation of 'Ateh Gebor Le-olahm Amen' - `unto thee O Lord the glory`, referring to the higher self.

Now finish inscribing the circle of flame by turning to the east with hand outstretched and finishing at your starting point.

3 Calling the Archangels

Facing east with arms outstretched to either side, say:

"Before me RAPHAEL,"

As you intone the Archangel's name visualise him before you outside the circle - at least 8ft tall, his face too bright to see. He wears a yellow robe, and there are flashes of purple about his form, he holds a sword and the air element enters the circle from the east.

Still facing east say:

"Behind me GABRIEL,"

This time as you intone the Archangel's name visualise him behind you outside the circle, again at least 8ft tall, his face blindingly bright. Gabriel wears a blue robe and holds aloft a chalice, around his form there are flashes of orange. From behind you in the west the element of water enters the circle.

Still facing east say:

"On my right hand MICHAEL,"

As you intone the Archangel's name visualise him to the right of you outside the circle with the same towering height, same blinding visage as the others, his robe is bright red and there are flashes of green around him as he holds a wand. From the right of you in the south the element of fire enters the circle.

Continuing to face east say:

"On my left hand AURIEL,"

Intoning the Archangels name visualise him to the left of you outside the circle towering and bright like his brothers, his robe of citrine, olive, russet and a small amount of black. He holds the a pentacle and from the north to your left the element of earth enters the circle.

Now say:

"For about me flames the pentagram, and in the column shines the six-rayed star."

As you say this see the four pentagrams that you inscribed around you and yourself in a column of brilliance with a hexagram shining above your head and below your feet.

4 The Qabalistic Cross

Repeat Section 1.

Note: There are two differences between the lesser banishing of the pentagram and the lesser invoking of the pentagram, detailed below.

In section 3 when banishing the pentagram is inscribed starting from a point in front of you corresponding to the position of the left hip and moving up to the topmost point and then continuing on to complete the pentagram. For invoking the pentagram is begun from a point in front of you at the level of your forehead, then moving down to the point corresponding to the position of your left hip and then continuing on to complete the pentagram. Alternatively the invoking or banishing elemental pentagrams may be used on each appropriate quarter.

In section 4 when each elemental energy enters the circle, for the banishing it should pass through you take away any 'staleness' of that element in you. For the invoking as each element enters the circle it should fill you with its force.

Appendix 3

Bibliography

A.H.E.H.'O., Frater *Angelic Images*, The Sorcerors Apprentice Press, 1984

Avalon, Arthur *The Serpent Power*, Dover, 1974

Aziz, Peter *Shamanic Healing*, Points Press, 1994

Bayer, Stephan *The Cult of Tara*, University of California Press, 1978

Butler, W.E. *The Magician, His Training & Work*, Aquarian, 1972

Campanelli, Pauline *Wheel of the Year: Living the Magical Life*, Llewellyn Publications, 1989

Cleary, Thomas (trans) *The Book of Balance and Harmony*, Rider, 1989

Clough, Nigel R *How to Make and Use Magic Mirrors*, Aquarian Press, 1977

Cooper, J.C. *An Illustrated Encyclopedia of Traditional Symbols*, Thames & Hudson, 1978

Crowley, Aleister *Magick,* Guild Publishing Ltd, 1986

Crowley, Vivianne *Wicca: The Old Religion in the New Age*, Aquarian, 1989

Culpeper, Nicholas *Culpeper's Complete Herbal*, Omega Books, 1985

Cunningham, Scott *Cunningham's Encyclopedia of Magical Herbs*, Llewellyn Publications, 1989

Cunningham, Scott *Magical Aromatherapy,* Llewellyn Publications, 1992

Cunningham, Scott *Magical Herbalism*, Llewellyn Publications, 1985

de Bray, Lys *Midsummer Silver*, J M Dent & Sons Ltd, 1980

Deren, Maya *The Voodoo Gods*, Paladin, 1975 (originally published as The Divine Horsemen)

Devereux, Paul *Flying Shamans and the Mystery Lines*, Kindred Spirit magazine, Volume 7 No.2, Summer 1992

Durdin-Robertson, Lawrence *Juno Covella - Perpetual Calendar of the Fellowship of Isis*, Cesara Publications, 1982

Eliade, Mircea *Shamanism: Archaic Techniques of Ecstasy,*

Farrar, Janet & Stewart *Eight Sabbats For Witches*, Robert Hale, 1985

Farrar, Janet & Stewart *The Witches' Way*, Robert Hale, 1984

Fontana, Dr David *The Meditators Handbook*, Element Books, 1992

Fortune, Dion *Moon Magic*, Weiser, 1985

Gordon, L *The Language of Flowers*, Grange Books, 1993

Goswami, Shyam Sundar *Layayoga: An Advanced Method of Concentration,*
　　　　Routledge & Kegan Paul, 1980
Hoffmann, David *The Holistic Herbal,* Element Books, 1986
Iyengar, B.K.S. *Light On Yoga*, George Allen & Unwin Ltd, 1964
Johari, Haresh *Tools For Tantra*, Destiny Books 1986
Judith, Anodea *Wheels of Life*, Llewellyn Publications, 1987
Jung, C.G. *Man and His Symbols*, Aldus, 1979
Keleman, Stanley *Emotional Anatomy*, Center Press, 1985
King, Francis & Skinner, Stephen *Techniques of High Magic*, Sphere Books Ltd,
　　　　1981
Kourimski, Dr J. *The Illustrated Encyclopedia of Minerals and Rocks*, Select
　　　　Editions, 1992
Lust, John *The Herb Book*, Bantam Book, 1974
Miller, R.A. *The Magical and Ritual Use of Aphrodisiacs*, Destiny Books 1985
Miller, R.A. *The Magical and Ritual Use of Herbs,* Destiny Books 1983
Nahmad, C *Earth Magic*, Rider, 1993
Radha, Swami Sivananda *Mantras: Words of Power*, Timeless Books, 1994
Rainbird, Ariadne *Imbolc, Spring Equinox, Beltane, Summer Solstice, Lughnasadh,*
　　　　Autumnal Equinox, Samhain, Yule articles in *Dragon's Brew* magazine,
　　　　no.'s 11-18, 1993-1994
Rankine, David *Meditation, Talking Stick* magazine, no. 9, 1992
Rankine, David *Power and Panic in Pagan Paradise, Dragons Brew* magazine,
　　　　no. 11, 1993
Rankine, David *The 6P Principle, Talking Stick* magazine, no.'s 3 & 4, 1991
Rankine, David *Treesong, Aisling* magazine, 1995
Schultes, Richard & Hofmann, Albert *Plants of the Gods,* Hutchinson & Co Ltd,
　　　　1980
Starhawk *The Spiral Dance*, Harper San Francisco, 1989
Webster, Robert *Gemmologists' Compendium*, N.A.G. Press, 1979
Zalewski, C.L. *Herbs in Magic and Alchemy,* Prism Press, 1990

FREE DETAILED CATALOGUE

A detailed illustrated catalogue is available on request, SAE or International Postal Coupon appreciated. Titles are available direct from Capall Bann, post free in the UK (cheque or PO with order) or from good bookshops and specialist outlets. Titles currently available include:

Animals, Mind Body Spirit & Folklore
Angels and Goddesses - Celtic Christianity & Paganism by Michael Howard
Arthur - The Legend Unveiled by C Johnson & E Lung
Auguries and Omens - The Magical Lore of Birds by Yvonne Aburrow
Book of the Veil The by Peter Paddon
Caer Sidhe - Celtic Astrology and Astronomy by Michael Bayley
Call of the Horned Piper by Nigel Jackson
Cats' Company by Ann Walker
Celtic Lore & Druidic Ritual by Rhiannon Ryall
Compleat Vampyre - The Vampyre Shaman: Werewolves & Witchery by Nigel Jackson
Crystal Clear - A Guide to Quartz Crystal by Jennifer Dent
Earth Dance - A Year of Pagan Rituals by Jan Brodie
Earth Harmony - Places of Power, Holiness and Healing by Nigel Pennick
Earth Magic by Margaret McArthur
Enchanted Forest - The Magical Lore of Trees by Yvonne Aburrow
Familiars - Animal Powers of Britain by Anna Franklin
Healing Homes by Jennifer Dent
Herbcraft - Shamanic & Ritual Use of Herbs by Susan Lavender & Anna Franklin
In Search of Herne the Hunter by Eric Fitch
Inner Space Workbook - Developing Counselling & Magical Skills Through the Tarot
Kecks, Keddles & Kesh by Michael Bayley
Living Tarot by Ann Walker
Magical Incenses and Perfumes by Jan Brodie
Magical Lore of Cats by Marion Davies
Magical Lore of Herbs by Marion Davies
Masks of Misrule - The Horned God & His Cult in Europe by Nigel Jackson
Mysteries of the Runes by Michael Howard
Oracle of Geomancy by Nigel Pennick
Patchwork of Magic by Julia Day
Pathworking - A Practical Book of Guided Meditations by Pete Jennings
Pickingill Papers - The Origins of Gardnerian Wicca by Michael Howard
Psychic Animals by Dennis Bardens
Psychic Self Defence - Real Solutions by Jan Brodie
Runic Astrology by Nigel Pennick
Sacred Animals by Gordon MacLellan
Sacred Grove - The Mysteries of the Forest by Yvonne Aburrow
Sacred Geometry   by Nigel Pennick
Sacred Lore of Horses The by Marion Davies
Sacred Ring - Pagan Origins British Folk Festivals & Customs by Michael Howard
Seasonal Magic - Diary of a Village Witch by Paddy Slade
Secret Places of the Goddess by Philip Heselton
Talking to the Earth by Gordon Maclellan
Taming the Wolf - Full Moon Meditations by Steve Hounsome
The Goddess Year by Nigel Pennick & Helen Field
West Country Wicca by Rhiannon Ryall
Witches of Oz The by Matthew & Julia Phillips

Capall Bann is owned and run by people actively involved in many of the areas in which we publish. Our list is expanding rapidly so do contact us for details on the latest releases.

Capall Bann Publishing, Freshfields, Chieveley, Berks, RG20 8TF